CURRENT CONFUSION

CURRENT CONFUSION

Kitty Grey

Walker and Company
New York

Copyright © 1989 by Kitty Grey

All rights reserved. No part of this book may be reproduced or transmitted in any form or by any means, electronic or mechanical, including photocopying, recording, or by any information storage and retrieval system, without permission in writing from the Publisher.

All the characters and events portrayed in this story are fictitious.

First published in the United States of America in 1989 by Walker Publishing Company, Inc.

Published simultaneously in Canada by Thomas Allen & Son Canada, Limited, Markham, Ontario.

Library of Congress Cataloging-in-Publication Data

Grey, Kitty, 1961–
Current confusion.

I. Title.
PS3557.R482C8   1989   813'54   89-5343
ISBN 0-8027-1060-3

Printed in the United States of America

10 9 8 7 6 5 4 3 2 1

To a lady from Spondon

=1=

CASSANDRA BROWN STEPPED back so that the visitors might have a better view of the 4-D accelerator, then she heard the sound of an explosion, and suddenly the familiar gleaming clutter of machines, equipment, and computer terminals had vanished, along with her colleagues and the visitors. There was a strong, unfamiliar smell of ozone.

It took her a moment to realize that she was still in the lab. Without the electric lights the room seemed darker and smaller, the stone walls dank; but there was no mistaking the irregular shape of the room. The offensive orange antistatic carpet was gone, too, and she could see the brass memorial tablets that she'd been told were set in the floor. The iron staircase, which had crouched over the older stone stairs like a cage, had also disappeared, and the original stairs looked larger without it. She could see deep worn places in the middle of each tread.

At the far end of the room stood a tall, blond man, quaintly dressed in tight dun-colour trousers and a brown jacket. He was rubbing a pair of tiny gold-rimmed spectacles on a rag, and looked, Cassandra thought, like a refugee from the set of a BBC production of *Pride and Prejudice*.

Cassandra stepped forward. "What happened? Did something blow up?"

"Electric discharge." The man pointed toward a number of bottles lined up on a table and a collection of wires which were strung in such a way that they passed out the high window.

"Leyden jars?"

"How did you know? Are you omniscient, madam?" Although he spoke quietly, he sounded puzzled.

Cassandra marched straight up to him. She was confused, and rather frightened, but she wasn't about to let him know. "I'm a physicist, and I don't know everything. For a start, I'd like to know what is going on."

"I imagine you are an *houri*, and an hallucination."

"I beg your pardon!" Cassandra wondered if this was one of those dreams where you start by thinking you are living through an ordinary day, and then everything goes haywire.

"Madam, I crave yours." The man bowed. "An *houri* is a sort of angel in the mythology of Arabia."

"I know that."

She didn't think that baggy pink sweat pants and a long white lab coat looked very like a harem costume, but apparently he did; nor did she think "angel" was a very accurate word to describe the sort of creature who would provide Islamic warriors with their eternal reward.

They stood about twelve inches apart, regarding each other intently until the man spoke. "I collect you are neither an angel nor an apparition?"

"I'm real, if that's what you mean. Are you?"

"Yes. I am Harry Font, or did you know—" The rest of his sentence was cut off by the boom of another discharge. "Forgive me." He separated two wires by pulling on a twist of cloth tied to one of them.

"Why don't you use wooden tongs?"

"Wood is a conductor of the electric spark, madam."

"Of course, the voltage is too high."

"Voltage? Do you mean signor Volta?"

Suddenly Cassandra was afraid she knew what had happened. From the day it was formed, her work team had split into two factions. There were the Jokers, organized by Will Hollister, and the Sobersides. As team leader, Cassandra found herself *de facto* leader of the outraged Sobers, who expected her to "do something" about Will. Since none of the pranks could ever actually be traced to Will, there was little Cassandra could do. This time the Jokers had outdone themselves.

"I'm still in Font House, aren't I?" she asked.

"We call it Font Hall, madam, but yes, you are here. You look a little pale; would you care to sit down?"

He drew a ladder-back chair from one of the tables and placed it near her. He held himself a little stiffly, as if he wasn't sure what to expect from her next.

The man watched her carefully as she sat down. "I first surmised that I was suffering from an hallucination. Now it seems more reasonable that you are dressed for a masquerade, though the reason for wearing such a costume at three in the afternoon escapes me. Did you let yourself into the house and wander into the workroom while I was distracted by the discharge?"

"No."

"Are you certain? I was somewhat dazzled. I haven't experienced anything quite like it. Indeed, I'm not certain what caused it. Or perhaps you entered through a secret passage?" He seemed less surprised now, his voice was almost teasing. "My sister-in-law tells me they are all the rage in novels."

Cassandra knew from experience that Will delighted in one of three reactions from his victims—rage, panic, or a moment's silence followed by a detailed explanation of how the joke had been carried out. It was the last defence which had earned Cassandra and her fellow Sobers their name. So she ignored the man and his chatter—beyond noting that she didn't recognize him, which meant he was most likely a friend of Will's—and studied the room. Suddenly she jumped to her feet, then knelt down to examine the floor.

"Some of the equipment was bolted to the floor and I don't see any scars."

"Scars, madam?"

"Somebody must have found a way to move everything, mirrors or something. . . ." She spoke very slowly. "I'm sorry, this time Will is going to have to tell me how he did it. I suppose everyone was in on it. Those visitors—hey, you're that Font guy with a wig. How ever did you get the director to let you in? I thought that rumour about your claiming to be the rightful owner of Font House was pretty fishy, and Dr. Jenkins would never cooperate with Will on a joke."

"No one let me in. I *am* the owner, and I live here, madam. I am trying to ascertain how you came into the house. It is possible—"

Cassandra, oblivious to the excitement in his voice, barely aware that he was speaking, in fact, had climbed onto the table to look out the window. Her face went white, then flushed, and she felt hot and weak, as though she had just climbed a dozen flights of stairs.

It would be beyond even Will's talent to produce the scene she saw in the yard. Where fifteen minutes ago she had parked her car on a paved parking lot, a girl of about fifteen or sixteen, dressed in a long yellow skirt hiked up halfway to her knees and with some sort of overskirt bundled up round her hips, was taking stockings and old-fashioned shirts—the sort that were pulled on over the head—off a clothesline. The pegs she used were the clumsy sort, made from split twigs that Cassandra had always imagined Victorian gypsies selling.

A terrier puppy chased a chicken along the far wall, until the unhappy bird, with a supreme effort, fluttered the couple of feet to the top of the stone block in the middle of the muddy yard. Cassandra realized that it was a mounting block, and swallowed. A wide field, dotted with leafless trees, stretched from the low stone wall which surrounded the yard to the narrow lane beyond. In the middle of the lane stood a horse and cart, and a man, dressed in a blue smock and a tall hat, was doing something to one of the horse's hooves.

It wasn't a movie set. This was no isolated reenactment edged by cameras and sound vans. Nor was it a picture projected on a screen to trick her. It was frighteningly real. Where she had expected to see modern buildings and a four-lane highway, she saw another age.

She let the man help her down from the table. "It isn't spring anymore, is it? It's almost winter outside," she said. It was easier to worry about a gap of a few months than one of centuries. He urged her to sit down again, but she leaned against the wall: the stone felt familiar.

"Today is the sixth day of November."

"What do you know about the nature of time?" she asked, striving to keep her voice calm.

"The ancients maintained one could draw an analogy between the flow of a river and that of time."

He knows, she thought. Could he have brought me here? And if he did, is it really sometime in the past or the future made to look like the past or right now—I mean, right when I left, but somewhere else. . . . Get a grip on yourself. Talk to him.

"And like a river it flows in only one direction."

"Yes," he agreed.

"Couldn't a person float on top of it, in a boat or something."

"Do you mean that a craft of some sort might float on the stream of time?"

"Yes, and carry people in it."

"But surely the boat would move at the same rate as the current. . . ."

"Only if you were just sitting in it. If you had some sort of oars . . ."

"Are you suggesting you propelled yourself here from ancient Arabia?" The disbelief in his voice was obvious. He'd been humouring her. "Why do you have this obsession with Arabia? I'm suggesting, as you put it, that I was propelled backwards from England's future."

She started towards him, and he jumped back. "I can-prove it, too." From the deep pockets of her lab coat she pulled ballpoint pens, the hole-punched edges of computer paper, two telephone-message memos, and several coins. She grabbed his hand and forced the coins into it.

"See, the dates, 1979, 1981 . . . and that queen is Elizabeth the Second."

"My dear madam, these aren't British coins. We don't mint coins with the words, 'fifty pence' on them."

"They've gone decimal, about twenty years ago. Now a pound has '100 P.' But I suppose I could have had these made. I can't tell you what's going to happen in the immediate future—what *you'd* call the immediate future—because I don't know history well enough. I mean, if it were July 1, 1776, I could tell you that they were about to sign the Declaration of Independence. But then, since it was something people were expecting to happen, I could have just guessed, and so it isn't a very good proof. It would only work in America, anyway, because it must take weeks before you know what's going on there."

She paused for breath, then asked, "What year is it anyway?"

"It is 1815, madam." His voice was very dry.

"How can I convince you? I know. Could you imagine a machine, a tool, that could do mathematical calculations? Not a slide rule or a machine that you could use to add and subtract like an abacus. Could you see someone building one that could fit in the palm of your hand and do complex calculations quicker than you could?"

"No, I really can't, but why don't you tell me about it as we walk upstairs." He spoke very slowly as he handed the coins back to her. "My housekeeper will find you something good to eat, and then you can tell us where you live and—"

"Then if I showed you one, you'd believe me?"

Cassandra fought panic. He obviously thought she was insane, and was humouring her. She wanted to scream 'It's true!' but she knew that this would only serve to convince him further that she was mad.

"In the absence of a better hypothesis, yes. But wouldn't you like to come upstairs, where you'd be more comfortable?"

"Here, it's a calculator."

He moved closer and took her arm, urging her towards the narrow stone stairs. "Why, what a smart memorandum book!"

Cassandra flipped it open, hoping that this man, who seemed to be a primitive scientist, would be more open-minded than his successors. She'd seen enough people in her own time bury evidence that contradicted their pet theory to expect him to try to destroy the calculator and have her locked up in the local insane asylum. She recalled descriptions of Bedlam she'd read in history books and knew that she'd never leave such a place sane—or alive. Willing a calmness she did not feel into her voice, she said, "Don't stand in the light, it's solar-powered."

Harry Font took it and ran his fingers over the buttons.

Cassandra turned him so that the light from the window fell across the solar panel, and a string of numbers appeared. "Press the clear, that button. Now the one, down there, plus sign, yes, and the three, and the equals."

"Good Lord, it says four."

"Try something more difficult. No, you have to press them in the right order. 'C' will clear the screen—when you want to try a new calculation." Harry tried several complicated sums, some division, played with the percentages, and worked out a few compound-interest problems, checking the answers with his slide rule.

"I believe that this machine came from a society more advanced than ours. And I am willing to believe, for now at least, that it came from the future." Gone was the skepticism of a moment before. He sounded completely entranced by the possibilities her presence suggested. "Can you imagine intercourse with those to come?"

Cassandra wondered if *he* had gone mad.

"To be able to talk to the great men of another age, to see the advancement of rational man! I can hardly believe this. Please, sit down, I have so many questions. I scarce know where to begin. My own interests are philosophical, but for the sake of my fellows, I should question you about politics. Oh, I assume you are the first visitor. Will there be others, have you come to guide us?"

"Be quiet," Cassandra snapped. "And stop asking me to sit down. I didn't come to guide you. In fact, I didn't mean to come here at all. I don't know what happened, or how I'm going to get back."

Harry bowed. "My apologies, madam."

He seemed ready to launch into another long speech, so Cassandra quickly cut him off by asking. "Were you trying to do something with time travel?"

"I was not. Do you mean . . . why, I wonder if it could have something to do with my apparatus?"

"With ours, more likely. Oh, stop looking at the calculator. I really am here, God help me."

"You may rely on me completely, madam, although I'm not certain what I can do. You wish to return to your home?"

"Of course."

Cassandra remembered the let's-pretend games she'd played as a child—let's pretend we're on a wagon train going west, let's pretend we're knights of the Round Table, even let's pretend we've gone back in time to the revolution and are going to tell George Washington to sneak across the Delaware and attack the Hessians. The imagined, and somewhat anachronistic, fear that they could be burned as witches if anyone in 1776 learnt that they were from the future was nothing compared to the real fear that something beyond her control had just happened and stranded her in the past.

Harry Font jammed his hands into his pockets. "Well, what do we know?"

Cassandra laughed, then stopped. Surely she was on the verge of hysteria. "I know your name, but you don't know mine. I'm Cassandra Brown."

"Miss Brown, or Mrs. Brown?"

"Dr. Brown," she corrected automatically.

"I beg your pardon?"

"I have my Ph.D.—doctor of philosophy—in particle physics from M.I.T.—a university in Boston, in America."

"A lady with a degree? And I am not sure I understand what you mean by particle physics."

Cassandra chose to answer his first question. She didn't think she was capable of explaining atomic theory to someone who undoubtedly thought that Newton was the last word in physics, at least not until she'd had a little while to recover from the shock. "It is very common where, I mean, *when* I come from," she said. "I'll tell you about atomic particles later."

He nodded, thoughtful. "And you are from one of the United States. I thought I detected something odd in your speech."

"I expect you thought it was the tone of madness. Look, if you don't mind, I think I should stand where I was before. My colleagues might realize what's happened and find a way to get me back. I guess it has something to do with the 4-D accelerator. It was the only thing running and we're trying to get electrons to jump through time with it. That's what the 4-D stands for, you know."

"I have no wish to detain you, Miss Brown," he said.

Cassandra went to the far end of the room.

Harry again put his hand into his pocket. "If I may summarize—"

"You give lectures, don't you," Cassandra interrupted.

"Yes, Miss Brown, I do. But right now I am trying to help you. I gather you were with other scientists, conducting an experiment. Were you performing a new procedure or trying to obtain results to confirm an earlier one?"

"As far as I know, it was just a standard run, although I suppose something might have been miscalibrated."

"We shall assume that there was nothing out of the ordinary. Is it not possible, then, that some action at this end of time—and I am now assuming time to be a long rope with one end attached in 1815 and one end in your year—what year would that be?"

"Do you mean you think your"—Cassandra gestured vaguely at the primitive equipment—" whatever had some effect?"

"It seems reasonable. Indeed, it is probably the sole agent. How could the future, which has not yet happened, have an effect on the present?"

"But as far as I'm concerned, it—your present—is the past. In fact this has already happened."

"I wonder, could you by some action here change the course of your own time. Imagine you prevent the marriage of your parents. Therefore, you never exist. But if you never exist, you cannot prevent the marriage. A paradox."

"Perhaps I'd create two futures—one in which I exist, and one in which I don't. I bet you can guess which one I'd want to be in."

Cassandra wondered how she could be so calm and so excited at the same time. Perhaps Harry's collected enthusiasm had rubbed off on her.

"A moment's reflection will show you the fallacy in that, Miss Brown. If time were split in such a fashion, some people would have to exist in both times, and this is impossible. What would happen to their souls? A soul cannot be sundered. But consider once again the possibility of your having changed your own time—"

"It's called the Conservation of Reality."

"I beg your pardon?" he said stiffly.

Cassandra assumed he objected not to the interruption, but to her choice of words. "Let's say you're right about it being impossible for more than one possible world to exist, that it's not possible for time to be split. That means whatever happens is real, right? Also, since it's possible—really possible—to travel along time, then everything really happens concurrently. You could go from here to my time, or last week, and at the same time, someone from last week could go to your first birthday. Since it is impossible to change anything, whatever I or anyone else does that might change what we'll call the relative future, will somehow be corrected."

"You do not accept the doctrine of free will, Miss Brown."

Cassandra suppressed an urge to scream. This Harry Font wasn't stupid, he just saw the world in a different way. And she was less than two hundred years in the past. What if she'd gone back a thousand years, or ten thousand years?

There was a loud knock. "My lord, my lord," a girl's voice called.

"What is it, Martha? Don't come down."

"Mrs. Font has come, sir."

"I shall be up directly. I didn't hear the carriage."

"Thank you, my lord."

He shoved the calculator into his pocket and ran his hand through his curly hair. "I can't keep her waiting, she'll come looking for me. And she mustn't see you. Are you sure you couldn't send yourself away and then come back here?"

"I can't even manage the first."

"Then please would you stay here, and as soon as we've dined I'll be back. The servants won't come down here, so you should be safe enough. Just don't connect the wires, because Mrs. Font will ask me to make the banging noise stop, and she may well come down with me. The place frightens her a little, and she likes to come down as she finds it gothick."

"I don't see what else I can do but wait here."

"Thank you, so sorry, please excuse me—and *do* sit down. I'm afraid there's nothing to read." He ran up the stairs and Cassandra heard what had to be bolts being shot home.

Of course Cassandra's first action was to climb the steps herself and try the door. It was locked. After muttering a few choice words about Harry Font, the situation in general, and Will, just in case he'd pulled this off by drugging her or, an even more infuriating thought, by inventing a time machine and trying it out on her, she carefully explored the lab.

The room, she knew, had once been the crypt of a castle chapel. According to the rather gushing pamphlet which some historical organization had left in the receptionist's office, one of the early owners—the fourth or fifth baron if she remembered rightly—had been a younger son who'd taken monastic vows. When his four brothers were all killed in battle, his dying father had ordered retainers to drag the surviving son from the monastery by brute force, and had compelled the erstwhile monk to marry one of his cousins. Cassandra thought that both procedures were of dubious legality. Nonetheless, he had inherited his father's estates and title, begotten a son, and devoted the remainder of his life to building an immense chapel with an even larger crypt.

At some point near the beginning of the Industrial Revolution, the family had died out, and there had been no more Barons Font. The Crown had taken over the estate, which, Cassandra gathered, was the usual course of events. Since then, Font Hall had housed various institutions, most recently the Center for Subtemporal Displacement Studies. Now that she thought about it, the name did sound rather like a place for studying time travel, but in fact it was concerned solely with the movement of subatomic particles.

Cassandra had joined the Center six months ago, the ink on her Ph.D. barely dry, ready to set the world on end by proving that when electrons move about the nucleus of an atom, they "jump" instantaneously, and are thus travelling in Einstein's fourth dimension—time.

As she looked about the room, it did not take Cassandra long to decide that she was either in an exact copy of the room the way it had been before the Center took it over, or in that very room itself. Not only were the scars gone where the heavy equipment had been bolted down, but there was no sign that the metal staircase had ever been installed. Even the rust marks where it was attached to the wall were gone. When the equipment had been moved in, a large part of the wall around the door had been torn down and rebuilt with new stone. But a small, heavy oak door, with iron hinges formed like dragon's heads, was set in what seemed to be the original doorway.

Cassandra wondered which was more unlikely, that she'd moved through time or that she'd been tricked into thinking that. She could imagine a replica of the room being built somewhere, but she didn't believe that a drug existed which could knock her out instantly and restore her to consciousness without any other effect. Nor did she think she'd been hypnotised. Once, in college, she'd let someone hypnotise her, and she remembered experiencing a calmness that was far from the way she felt now.

There was also no possible motive for someone to fool her that way. Her work had no possible military applications—or at least it hadn't before this most unexpected turn of events—and even if it had, it seemed very unlikely that the KGB, or anyone else, would take such trouble.

Harry Font had not purposefully brought her here. Of that she was certain. He seemed as confused as she. Was he one of the barons? Martha, whoever she was, had called him my lord. Cassandra had never taken enough interest in such things to know how one addressed a baron. Perhaps he was the last baron, and the family had died out because she, Cassandra, had come from the future and done something to end the line—though she could not think of what, short of killing him or taking him back with her.

She turned her attention to the objects on the table. She recognized most of them although they were new, not the museum pieces she was used to seeing. Harry, it seemed, was trying to establish a relationship between electricity and magnetism. There were several sheets of paper, which Cassandra read without a qualm of conscience, feeling rather like Catherine in *Northanger Abbey*, a young woman trapped in a gothick house. Had *Northanger Abbey* even been written in 1815?

What Cassandra read was more interesting than a laundry list. It seemed to be a copy of sections of scientific notes that Harry had made on a visit to Italy and on his own experiments with electricity and magnetism. When Cassandra arrived, he'd been charging his Leyden jars, primitive batteries, planning to discharge them later and calibrate the amount of what he called "electric essence" in each jar. The wire, which passed through the window, was part of a mile-long piece that Harry had strung on poles to attract electricity from the atmosphere.

Two unlabeled jars stood side by side. One held the charge Harry had captured just after she'd arrived. He'd mentioned that he'd been distracted by a discharge a moment before—an unusual one. Had it been concurrent with her arrival, and did the second jar hold it?

Cassandra swallowed. She thought she had the answer. If, as she'd assumed when she designed her experiments, in the instant when the electron made the quantum leap from one shell of an atom to another it spent an infinitesimal amount of time in a place where other electrons, also in mid-leap, congregated, then perhaps, the electron that started the leap around one atom, ended it around a different one. Harry Font's wire might have attracted electrons from her time and somehow have pulled the electrons in her body, not to mention the rest of her body, and her clothes, with them into 1815.

But why her? She'd been standing apart from the others, between the 4-D accelerator and the wall, and she was standing on one of the brass plaques when she arrived. She looked out of the window again. Yes, the wire was strung along the wall there, so the space she'd occupied had been bounded on one side (and in one year) by the 4-D accelerator, and on the other (and in another) by the wire. If Harry's current was strong enough to overcome the resistance of wood, an anti-stat carpet and a bit of brass would be nothing.

She had no proof, but she did have a theory worth investigating. For a moment she was elated by the thought of a possible proof of her theory about subtemporal displacement, and a whole new effect—time travel—the Brown effect! But the proof had put her in an awful situation. Even if she could analyse what had happened, with no other tools than her pocket calculator, which was now in someone else's pocket, and whatever primitive help Harry Font could provide, was there any hope she could reproduce the effect in reverse?

She'd need to be able to re-create the conditions exactly. There were paper labels fastened around the necks of the bottles with scraps of silk. Cassandra used one of her ballpoint pens to write on them. On the back of Harry's notes she drew maps of the room at the instant she left it, in the present and the instant she'd arrived in the past. Then she started to write down everything she recalled about the experiment she'd been running.

Cassandra soon forgot where and when she was. The problem might have been a hypothetical exercise for all the emotion it elicited. She had taught herself years ago to bury worry in work, a technique that had helped her earn a Ph.D. just before her twenty-fourth birthday.

Consequently, she did not hear the door opening.

2

" 'IT IS A TRUTH universally acknowledged that a man is in search of a wife,' " Anna Font misquoted triumphantly. "That is a wise observation, and the fact that you are twenty-seven, and a baron, and your fortune, as your cousin Tom is fond of remarking, close to Tick River, although he says it about himself, for he would never make such a personal remark about another, does not make it less true."

"Hum, yes," replied Harry.

In the last hour he had quickly changed into his best coat, greeted Anna, apologized for being occupied when she arrived, and sat down to eat in as much state as Font Hall could provide. Yet he had no memory of doing so. He had listened to Anna's recital of the doings of various Fonts with feigned interest. She was a Font by marriage, but had the zeal of a convert when it came to keeping abreast of the family's news.

She would leave soon. He always made sure that she passed beyond the dangerous outskirts of the city before dark. It was ridiculous, really, the way she insisted on making these monthly pilgrimages to the childhood home of her husband. Never before had he begrudged her presence, but now he wanted only to return to his laboratory and Miss Brown—if she were not a figment of his imagination.

Although the meal was nearly finished, they remained in the dining room. Once the weather grew cold enough to demand a fire, those at Font Hall stopped following the fashion that demanded the final sweet course must be eaten in the parlour. Anna apparently felt it was time to broach a serious topic.

"I don't like to mention it, because it does seem a little indelicate, but your father and grandfather had difficulty in producing sons—they were both quite old . . ." Anna did not finish her sentence.

"So they were."

Could Miss Brown be real? Many of the fantastic things she had told him suggested that she was. They seemed too farfetched for him to have imagined. She had said that she was a doctor of philosophy. Could he have thought of something so bizarre as a woman with a university education?

"Indeed, I don't think one could imagine anything more foolish than the fact that you haven't married," said Anna with a little laugh.

Harry, who was thinking of something quite different, and equally foolish, replied, "Oh yes, I could."

Anna dropped her spoon in a dish of custard and groped for a handkerchief. "I do wish you would take me seriously. My little Edmund is fated to become a tyrant."

Harry had always been fond of his little sister-in-law. Just now, with her blue eyes full of tears and her generous lips on the verge of a pout, she looked like a child. Of course, she had been absurdly young—not quite seventeen—when she'd married his brother Edmund, father of the little Edmund for whom she predicted tyranthood. She was still two months short of her twenty-first birthday.

"Come now, my dear," Harry tried to reassure her, "the little lad's three years old, not yet a despot."

"When your cousin Charles was five, he strode around the estate on his pony saying, 'When *this* is mine . . .' He threatened to sack every servant he spoke to. I know it's true, because Aunt Seppie told me!"

"But you will bring up my nephew in a far more sensible

way. Remember, when Cousin Charles was born, my father's first wife had already been pronounced barren. Charles was regarded as the heir apparent, not the heir presumptive."

"Too presumptive by half," remarked Anna. She put her handkerchief away and looked straight at Harry. "If your own father's sad tale does not convince you to marry, I do not know what will."

Harry's gaze shifted from Anna's face to the portrait of his parents which hung in the place of honour above the mantel. His father, white-haired, ramrod straight for all his fifty years, stood next to his new bride, a thin but cheerful-looking woman some ten years younger than he. When her marriage made her Lady Font, she had been a widow, a childless widow. Who would have believed that after six years of marriage this couple, almost beyond their middle years, would have produced not one, but two children? Harry's father had often joked that he should have followed the example set by the patriarchs and named the sons of his old age Isaac and Benjamin.

"I hardly think our situations are similar." Harry smiled so that Anna would not feel his words were meant as a rebuke, and let his thoughts return to Miss Brown.

His initial assumption, that she was an *houri*, was, he now admitted, foolish in the extreme, although he had been very much taken aback when she appeared before him in his laboratory. Her attire, a long white coat and loose pink trowsers, taken with that long braid of reddish brown hair, had certainly called to mind descriptions he had read in books on pagan religions. But her complexion was fair and her eyes were green, and that seemed wrong. Surely a creature of Arabian mythology would not have European characteristics? He pulled himself up sharply. He'd been over this ground before, while eating a course of prunes and venison, and it had not proved a profitable line of thought.

"But the situations are very much the same," Anna

insisted. "Your father, like you, was the elder son. Your cousin Charles is the son of a younger brother, as is my little Edmund. In both generations, the heir is childless. When the younger brother dies"—Anna's voice shook—"he leaves a son, who is looked upon as the heir. Then, in your father's case, a son is born to the baron, leaving the sometime heir embittered and miserable."

Harry was silent, recalling the time, some twenty years earlier, when his father, who was aware that the only way to keep gossip from a boy's ears was to keep the boy from society and servants, decided to make sure that he heard the sordid story from him first. At the appropriate time the old baron took it upon himself to tell his sons that on the day of Harry's birth, Charles had questioned the paternity of the child and, for his impudence, had been banished from his uncle's home. After thirty-four years, Charles had been confident in his position as heir and must have hoped, at the very least, that the baroness would have the courtesy to be delivered of a daughter.

Anna, using the kindest terms and a gossamer tissue of veiled reference, continued the story.

Harry listened with half an ear. He knew the tale well. As he'd grown older, other, less kindly sources had added various details to his father's account. Some were shocking, such as the exact, coarse language in which Charles had chosen to express his opinion of his young cousin's descent.

Yet there were other anecdotes which Harry had to admit he found amusing, but it wouldn't do to tell Anna of them. He suspected that she would be distressed to hear that Charles' son, Arthur, who was eleven at the time, had fallen into a fit of temper, kicking his heels and crying, "But you *promised* I'd be Lord Font! You *promised*!" Indeed, Anna might well use that story for ammunition in her campaign to see him to the altar.

All trace of tears was gone from Anna's voice, and Harry turned again to his more pressing, secret predicament—the woman who had suddenly appeared in his laboratory. Once he was certain she wasn't an *houri*, he had, understandably, taken her for a lunatic. But there was no hospital nearby from which she could have escaped. Even if there were one, he doubted that an institution would let a patient dress in so eccentric a manner. Her shoes, he recalled, were clumsy canvas slippers. Not at all, now he came to think of it, the sort of thing he expected a maiden from a heathen paradise to wear.

He ran his mind over the families living in the neighbourhood. He did not mingle with them a great deal. As a bachelor living alone, he found it difficult to return hospitality. Still, he was certain the rumour of a madwoman hidden away by one of them would have reached him. Perhaps he should have sent for the doctor after all. He would know if there were any lunatics in the neighbourhood.

And if she were not a lunatic, was she real? Surely if the woman, and the peculiar conversation they had held, were a hallucination, simply leaving the room wouldn't have ended it. Rather he would still be caught in the fancy, imagining that she was sitting at the table with them. Perhaps he should have brought her upstairs with him. If Anna or one of the servants could see her, it would prove that she was real.

Anna must have asked him a question, for she looked at him intently until he said, "Why, yes."

Apparently that was the right answer, for she nodded and delicately mentioned that Charles had been very spoiled, then quickly added that it had not been the fault of his uncle. She could not bring herself to imply that her beloved Edmund's father had been at fault. Nonetheless, Harry knew that his father had always been too indulgent with his nephew. There had been a generous allowance, the repeated clearing of debts, the promise of seeing to Arthur's education, which had been kept even after Charles' spectacular fall from grace.

At the time the late Lord Font had not seemed so very

foolish to spend freely. Mrs. Charles Font, the former Miss Verity Ponddabble, had expectations of a sizable fortune from her father, who had done rather well in the weaving and dyeing of red woolen cloth. Lord Font had naturally assumed that this inheritance, which would, after all, be her husband's, would one day be put to the estate.

Harry's attention wandered again. Could Miss Brown be a ghost? Now where had that disconcerting thought come from? If she were an unquiet spirit haunting the place of her death, she must have come from the past, not the future. Since the only Font to go on a crusade had been a Knight Templar, he could hardly have brought back an Arabian bride. But he could have brought back a mistress, which might be why no mention was ever made of her. She would have been born a heathen, and might not have converted, or if she had, it might not have been a sincere conversion. If she'd been interred in the crypt, denied the funeral rites of her own religion, she might well have come to haunt the Font family.

Meanwhile, Anna digressed to a bit of gossip one of her aunts by marriage must have told her, for the incident had taken place before she was born. With Edmund's birth, a mere six months after the first anniversary of Harry's natal day, it was clear that there were not just one, but *two* healthy infants between Charles and the coveted title. His father-in-law, the soul of exactness, stated that his blunt had been for a barony, and nothing else. He made it known that he was changing his will in favor of a niece, who immediately thereafter attracted the attention of a marquis. An unfortunate piece of doggerel then appeared in the popular press:

> He thought, with blunt, a barony,
> Yet one was not procured.
> And so, with haste, a codicil:
> A marchioness appeared.

Charles had expressed himself much more clearly. To anyone who cared to listen, and to a great many who did not, he declared that in addition to all the other ills done to him, old Lord Font had lost him a fortune.

But, Harry decided—his thoughts still adrift—the woman couldn't be a ghost. It was too farfetched—not that her claim to be from the future was any more reasonable. The only possible explanation was that she had to be mad. Yet she had sounded rational. Frightened, on the edge of panic, but intelligent and rational. And she had shown him her mathematical machine. He had held it, used it.

"Harry, Brother Harry, are you attending to me?"

"I beg your pardon?"

"I was saying that the only difference between little Edmund's situation and that of Charles is that my son is still too young to be aware of the circumstance. I have taken, and I will continue to take, the greatest pains to ensure that he does not know, but sooner or later he will find out. And sooner or later you will marry. You will find a woman you love, and marry her. And if it is later, and there are sons . . ."

"But I can't marry her until I find her, can I?" Harry said carelessly.

He had to stop speculating and apply rigorous thinking to the problem of the strange woman in the laboratory. Since it is unreasonable for her to be there, assume she is *not* really there. . . ."

"It would be a great deal easier for you to find her if you weren't buried on the estate."

"Yes."

He could be insane. *He* could be imagining that there was a woman from the future in his laboratory. It would be consistent, then, that once he left the room he no longer saw her, because, in his mad imaginings, she was still downstairs. He could also have just as easily imagined her wondrous machine.

"You must come to London for Christmas, for the Little

Season. You know that I do not entertain, but something can be arranged. Come before November is out, and stay through the new year. I vow there are not so many maidens in town now as there were in the Season—I mean"—she blushed—"fewer people come to town now, but I have always maintained that those young ladies who do not marry before the end of their first Season are superior to those who do. They have the virtue of patience, and are often retiring and gentle creatures, too."

Harry wrenched his mind from the distressing possibility that he was a lunatic and gave some attention to the second part of Anna's speech. "Knowing you, Anna, and your own history, I cannot endorse your theory."

If he were mad, thank heaven that Anna had fallen in love with Edmund and not him. Better, surely, to be a young widow than leg-shackled to a raving fool. And if his children were to be touched by this insanity, too . . .

"Why is it, Harry, that you are able to flirt quite beautifully with me, yet are often tongue-tied in the presence of a girl."

Harry amazed himself by replying with the utmost calm, as if he had not just diagnosed his own madness, "Because your beauty is exceeded only by your graciousness," and wondered if this detachment was a symptom.

Anna smiled, her reward for his compliment. "Silly, I am a staid old matron with a son—a son I plan to do right by."

Harry could feel the hard corner of the calculating machine press into his leg. He had shoved it into his pocket as he ran upstairs. The machine had seemed such a miracle, and now he knew it was nothing but a symptom of his madness. He could ease it out of his pocket under the table. Yet what would it prove? It could be anything, a piece of string even, and he'd just imagined that it was a box which could do mathematics. Anna was still talking. He heard the words with a desperate clarity—a counterpoint of sanity.

"You know I will be able to see him comfortably into a

profession. I hope he will be a clergyman, but I will be content as long as it is not the navy or the army. Since Edmund was able to purchase the house with his prize money and his portion of your father's estate, I have not yet touched the main part of my own money—the part which produces the interest. I understand it is called the capital. Mama lets me do as I wish, you know, and anyway, I shall be of age soon. There is no need for you to remain unmarried to assure little Edmund of the estate."

That was an old song with Anna, and Harry could make his response by rote. "I assure you, I would not so martyr myself or little Edmund. The estate's income is so mortgaged that my grandchildren will be lucky to see a ha'penny from it."

"That is something else I'll never understand," said Anna, rising from her chair. "My Edmund told me often that your poor grandfather lost funds in the South Sea Bubble, but surely the men to whom he owed money are dead now."

Harry stood, too, simply letting the familiar conversation continue. "Yes, dear, but my grandfather discharged his debts—and found dowries for eight daughters—by selling everything which wasn't entailed and borrowing against the estate's future income. Let us assume that in one year each acre—" His hand went to his pocket and touched the calculating machine, or what he fancied was the machine, while his mind filled with unpleasant visions of keepers and straitjackets. And after all of Anna's efforts, her son would inherit his title and land.

"Thank you," said Anna, misunderstanding his sudden silence. "You should not stray from the subject. I will have to leave soon, for Mama will not want Edmund underfoot while she is dressing, and I do not like him to be alone in the nursery with no one but Hester to watch him. I want your solemn promise that you will remember to pry yourself away from your experiments occasionally. You will come to visit me in the Little Season, and I shall find you a bride." Anna put out a pleading hand to Harry.

She always wore white. When her young husband died before they had been married a year, she'd declared her intention of remaining in mourning for the rest of her life. Once her child had been born, however, her mother-in-law had persuaded her that it would be too disheartening for little Edmund to see his mama always in black, and she had moved to half-mourning. She was vain enough to know that grey made her brown hair seem dull, and that lavender and mauve turned the color in her pink cheeks florid, but not vain enough to realize just how well white became her.

Now, as she stood at the door of the great, half-empty room which the Font's had used as their dining parlour since the time of Queen Elizabeth, with the light from the solar behind her, and her face half-eager, half-hopeful, Harry was lost. He was struggling to convince himself of his own sanity, he had no idea what she had just asked him, yet he took her hand in his, and raised it to his lips.

"Dear sister, I am, as always, yours to command."

"Then you shall come, the week after next!"

Anna's groom was summoned from the kitchen, and Harry bid her good-bye.

"I cannot tell you how grateful I am that you have agreed to my plan, Brother Harry. Our little Edmund is the sweetest angel, and it is your duty as his uncle to save him from unpleasantness," she said as Harry shut her carriage door.

As soon as he was back indoors, Harry pulled the machine from his pocket. When he opened it, the dark panel where the numbers had appeared remained grey. Miss Brown had said that one had to stand in the light to use it. The corridor, he assumed, was too dark.

The machine seemed very real to him. He had seen it work. He had spoken to the woman. Did a madman know that he was insane? Did not the very fact that he doubted his reason prove that it was sound?

Both the machine and the woman were real. Why was it more attractive to believe he was mad than to acknowledge that a woman could move through time, instantly, backwardly, instead of plodding hour by hour, heartbeat by heartbeat, as all men did until their allotted portion was measured out. She was a miracle. A miracle entrusted to him.

= 3 =

"Miss Brown. Miss Brown!"

"What?" Cassandra nearly jumped out of her skin. Harry stood next to her, a look of exasperation on his face. She wondered how many times he'd had to call her name. "Sorry. It's hard to get my attention when I'm concentrating. Here, look at this. See, that's dt. The x, y, and z axes are the dimensions of this room, t, of course is time. I'm almost sure the space carved out of the 3-D universe was rotated around the t-axis. Don't you think that makes sense?"

"I won't pretend I understand *that*." His tone of voice suggested that he doubted that she understood it either. "I do wish, Miss Brown, that you had thought to ask my leave before amusing yourself by scribbling on my papers."

"Scribbling! I'm halfway to solving everything. And you locked me in. I could hardly ask your permission or for something to write on under the circumstances. I think locking me up was both unnecessary *and* unkind." There was nothing, Cassandra had found, like meeting an attack with a diversion.

"I always lock the door. Not that anyone would come down without my permission, or go through my things—but for the sake of safety. Someone might have remarked on it if I hadn't." His voice became warmer. "Actually, I didn't even think about it. I was so excited, I simply acted from habit. I do apologize. And just now, when I scolded you, I was so relieved that I hadn't gone mad and *fancied* that you were here, I rather forgot myself."

"Yes, well, I suppose I shouldn't have messed about with your things. But there wasn't anything else to write on." He had apologized for locking her in, but he still could have done it on purpose. She wasn't about to admit she'd snooped. "I think I know what happened, or at least, what we need to do to find out what happened."

"I would be glad to help you, Miss Brown. I am something of a natural philosopher myself."

Cassandra's immediate thought was that he'd be no help at all, since she obviously knew a great deal more than he. She wondered if his offer was meant to imply that he didn't think a woman was capable of solving any sort of problem. Well, if nothing else, he could check her calculations, and it would not be wise to offend her host by suggesting that he was ignorant.

"Thank you. It may be rather hard to explain, because you haven't realized the atom is divisible yet. I do hope you understand calculus, because I'm going to need all the help I can get with the equations."

It took only a few minutes for Cassandra to realize that these things were going to be very hard to explain. As she'd noticed before, Harry wasn't stupid, but he was the product of a different age, one which, from Cassandra's point of view, lacked two centuries of scientific knowledge.

"This is going to take me some time to understand," he said regretfully. "Am I right in assuming that you haven't worked it all out yourself?"

"I think I know what happened, but it could take me weeks to know how, and even longer to know why."

The light had begun to fade. A church clock struck four. Cassandra realized that it could well be the clock on the tower of the old church near a cluster of chic shops called The Leighs about five minutes' walk from the Center. At least, it was surrounded by boutiques in her time. Now, St. Anne's Church probably stood in a tiny village.

Harry, who'd been pacing, stopped and put his hands into his pockets, a familiar gesture. "We might conjecture that when you do return, it will be at exactly the time when you left, so that they won't have a chance to notice your absence and act upon it," he suggested comfortingly. "I would like to try an experiment myself, reversing the current in the wire."

He matched actions to words, but the only result was a *boom*.

"Harry," Cassandra said. He looked startled at her use of his first name, and she remembered the formality of address used by Jane Austen in her novels. "Mr. Font."

"Lord Font, actually, Miss Brown, but pray don't concern yourself with that, if you regard titles with the same repugnance as many of your countrymen do."

Cassandra assumed he was making a joke—and wondered if now was the time to remind him that she preferred to be called Dr. Brown. She shrugged. There were more important things to deal with at the moment.

"Look, it's going to take weeks before I'll know if the effect that caused the time travel can be reversed. Maybe we should decide what we'll do if I am stuck here for a while." Or for ever, she added silently.

"I can't hide you in my laboratory for very long, that is certain. Sooner or later you'll have to come out. While you *might* return home at any moment, it seems more likely that you will remain here for some time. Indeed, it will be difficult to hide you anywhere in the house. I would have to bring you food, and Mrs. Drinkwater would notice that. Yet claiming you are a visitor from the future will only lead to Bedlam for us both."

"I really am sorry. I didn't mean to get you into this mess."

"I am happy to be of assistance."

"I do appreciate it."

Silence followed this exchange of platitudes, then Lord

Font said, "I think we must first find suitable clothes for you. Excuse me."

This time, to Cassandra's relief, he did not lock the door after him. She began to tremble as she gathered her notes together, determined to keep them with her. She really was here, in the year 1815. It seemed obvious that Harry Font was one of the Fonts who'd built Font House, or Hall, or whatever it was called.

Earlier that morning—or perhaps she should say that day, since it had been afternoon when she arrived here, but only ten o'clock when she'd left—Dr. Jenkins, the director, had brought an American couple into the lab to observe. That had been unusual in itself, for visitors were not encouraged at the Center. Even odder was the story that Will, a tireless gatherer of scuttlebutt from members of the administration, had told her before the visitors arrived.

Will said that the Americans were Brad and Janet Font, and that Brad claimed he was the owner of the house. He said he was a lord and that Font House was part of the estate which went with the title. Both Will and Cassandra had been more concerned about the rumour that Brad Font supported nuclear disarmament and opposed all applications of nuclear energy. Of course, he was a crank, but the possibility, no matter how remote, that he might legally own Font House and would turn the Center out was of great interest to the Center's employees.

Cassandra had noticed a similarity between Harry Font and Brad Font. They had the same curly blond hair and deep blue eyes. They seemed to be the same age, late twenties, though Brad's hair was thinning, and Harry was taller and more muscular, as if he'd lived harder.

Harry Font returned quickly. "The servants are all either outside or busy in the kitchen. We can go up the front stairs and then to the attics."

"What about Mrs. Font?"

"She's left."

"Oh. What are you going to tell her, about me?"

"Nothing," Harry said blandly.

"Don't you think your wife ought to be told the truth?"

"Mrs. Font is my late brother's widow. If I had a wife, she would be Lady Font. Now, I think we had better not talk until we are upstairs."

Patronizing, thought Cassandra as she followed him. I'd planned on singing arias on every landing.

She recognized the upper part of the house. Very few changes had been made between this time and her present. The stairs from the lab led into an empty stone hall. In her day, it was partitioned into cubicles, each one a scientist's office. Behind her were the kitchens, which would one day house the Center's generators. Harry led her into a plastered passage, then into another, much smaller hall. The front door was at one end. A table, the only piece of furniture, stood next to it. There was a light patch on the wall where a picture or mirror had hung. The stairs were at the other end. "Built in the time of Queen Anne," Harry whispered.

"Hush!"

As in Cassandra's time, the warren of small rooms tucked under the rafters were crammed, but rather than the familiar file cabinets—storage from all the organizations which had used Font House—and the stacks of computer printouts and boxes of film which the Center produced, there were trunks, and old furniture, a pile of rusting pikes here, heaps of moth-eaten cloth there.

Harry went directly to some trunks. "Uncle Fortinbras' sea trunk. I think these are my geologic specimens from Derbyshire, yes."

"I'm going to have to pretend to be someone visiting you."

"Of course, you will be my cousin from the United States."

"Why a cousin? Won't that make it too complicated?"

"Because there is no one here to lend you countenance, save Mrs. Drinkwater, my housekeeper," he replied stiffly.

"Countenance?"

"Your reputation must be considered."

Cassandra repressed an urge to laugh. What a thing to worry about in the middle of this crisis! It was like polishing the brass on a sinking ship.

Harry opened another trunk. "Aunt Sophie's—no, she's always been very stout, and I believe these are ball gowns. She wore panniers, but you could easily alter one."

"Sorry, buddy, I don't know how to sew."

"Miss Brown, I don't know what conventions of speech are considered correct in your time, but here, when a lady addresses a gentleman she has only just met, it is customary for her to address him either by his name or as sir. I mention this only to spare you embarrassment later."

"Thanks, I mean, thank you, sir."

"Pray, think no more of it." He was searching another chest. "Would this fit you, madam?"

He held up a dress that a slender twelve-year-old might have crammed herself into.

"I fear not, sir. There, do I sound more, er, conventional?"

"Much more so." He smiled at her. "I do hope that you are not frightened. I shall do my best to see that no harm comes to you. As we are to be cousins, we might follow the custom of my family and address each other as such, if that is agreeable to you, Cousin Brown?"

"How exactly are we related, Cousin Font?"

"Let me consider. My father's father was the only survivor of his generation, but his father, my great-grandfather, had two brothers. They had five daughters between them, but my aunts would know of all of the daughters' children and grandchildren. Perhaps, if you don't object, I could discredit the memory of my great-grandfather by giving him a son from another connection, for while my aunt Seppie takes a great interest in the family, she might not know of an . . . illegitimate child. That son could have settled in the Americas, and you could be his grandchild. I am sorry that you are driven to lying, madam."

It was clear to Cassandra that he was uncomfortable with the idea of telling lies. She wondered if it was his character or simply another sign of the age in which he lived.

"Do I have to be a Font? Why not graft me onto your mother's family tree? Or do you have an aunt with genealogical interests on your mother's side, too?"

"That is an excellent notion. My mother's great-uncle fought to suppress the colonial rebellion, and afterwards bought himself land somewhere in the southern part of the country. You could be one of his granddaughters." He opened a trunk which contained several black dresses. He shook one out and Cassandra thought it would fit well enough. Harry left the attic so she could try it on.

Trying on the dress brought home once again the reality that she had stepped into another time. The garment had a round neck and long sleeves. The neck and high waist had drawstrings and the back buttoned. Cassandra wondered if it was one of those round gowns heroines wore in regency novels. It took her some time and struggle to manage the buttons, for the back was narrow and the sleeves very tight.

Harry, when he entered in response to her call, remarked, "A trifle short."

"Do I have it on back to front? There seems to be something wrong with the waist. There's too much material."

"Mrs. Font wore it during her confinement, but I think the gown fits you tolerably well, and I don't imagine we'll be able to do better."

Cassandra thought he had rather poor taste when it came to women's clothes, but since beggars can't be choosers she only asked, "What should I do with my own clothes?"

"Put them in the trunk, I think."

"What if your sister-in-law wants it?" Cassandra asked, folding her lab coat around her sweat pants. She left the pens and coins in the pocket, but kept her notes out.

"If Mrs. Font sends for it, I'll take them out. What *are* you wearing on your feet, Miss Brown?"

"High-tops. Shoes for basketball."

"What is basketball?"

"American netball."

He still looked confused.

"I'll explain later."

Harry found her a pair of old boots, which, once the toes were stuffed with papers, were fairly comfortable, and a heavy cloak.

"My mother wore this for gardening."

Aunt Sophie's trunk yielded three stockings, one yellow, one white, and one blue.

"Wear the white one with the yellow one," he suggested. "It's so old it looks yellow."

"But how will I keep them up?"

"Garters, madam, garters. However else?"

A further search of Mrs. Font's trunk provided gloves, a rather crushed bonnet, and a sickly-looking green velvet reticule. Cassandra pounced on the last and put her notes in it.

Under Harry's direction, she packed a small valise with other clothes from the trunk, then sent him outside again so she could change her underwear for some of Mrs. Font's overlarge plain linen drawers. She improvised garters with a couple of bits of ribbon. When, after several false starts she'd tied them tightly enough that the stockings didn't fall down, she felt as though she'd cut off the circulation in her legs.

When Harry joined her again, he said, with the air of a man who has foreseen the one flaw which will cause an entire empire to flounder, "Hairpins. We must find hairpins. You can't go out with your hair down your back."

After a futile search for hairpins, Cassandra wrapped her braid around the back of her head and secured it with a ribbon threaded through the braid and anchored to the hair close to her scalp. The bonnet had a high crown and a wide brim, covering her bundled-up hair and the wisps which had come loose from her braid, Cassandra having decided the dangers of Harry being seen as he carried a hairbrush up to the attic outweighed the benefit of sending him for one. The right glove had a tear in the palm.

"Carry it," Harry said when she showed it to him. He looked at her critically. "You don't look too disreputable, but it's a good thing it's nearly dark," he finally pronounced. "I think you had better be a widow, to account for the mourning."

"Didn't people—I mean, don't people wear mourning for other relatives. Or maybe I just like black."

"Yes, but your travelling alone will be less irregular. And it would be better if your husband were related to the family—that would account for your not knowing a great deal about us. "You'll need a wedding ring. . . ."

Cassandra hesitated a moment. She didn't like the idea, but had to admit it sounded safer. Slowly she took off the plain gold band she wore on her right ring finger. It had been her mother's. Cassandra, who had been fourteen when her parents were killed, had worn it first on her forefinger. It was a bit loose on her left hand, but she was fairly sure it wouldn't slip off.

"What did he do, this husband of mine?" she asked, trying to cheer herself up. "I think his name was Erasmus."

"What about Richard?"

"All right, Richard Brown."

"He was a ship chandler, I think."

"That won't do. I don't even know what that is."

"A man who sells naval stores, supplies for ships. Tar, ropes, sailors' slops. That is, their clothing," he added as she stared at him perplexed.

"But Mr. Font, I mean, cousin, we need to choose something I understand. It stands to reason that I'd know all about my husband's work."

"Not if he were well enough off that you didn't work in the shop. It is obvious you are a spinster, Cousin Brown, or you would know that most married ladies do not concern themselves with their husbands' affairs and we gentlemen prefer that."

Cassandra muttered something which sounded like "M.C.P." then added, "When in Rome . . . the late lamented Mr. Richard Brown was a ship chandler, and I never bothered my little head with his business. I just hope I can carry off the charade of having been married. I wouldn't want to seem too assertive."

"I have every confidence in you."

"Would you mind telling me how you're addressed? As your cousin, I ought to know. Should I refer to you in the third person as his grace?"

"I'm only a baron, not a duke, so I'm addressed as my lord. My ancestor, Henri La Font, was ennobled in 1067 by William the Conqueror. And he was the last notable Font. As you can see, the family was never honoured with a higher title. We have the distinction of being one of the oldest creations, and holding the lowest rank. But we must hurry, cousin. I'll let you out the side door, you must wait there, by the lane."

He pointed to the end of the long drive, just visible from the dormer window. "Then I'll take the curricle and meet you, but we shall pretend you came on the stage from London. No, if we wait half an hour more, we can pretend you came on the stage from Plymouth. Mrs. Drinkwater's nephew works at the Dove and Willow, where the London stage stops, and might remember not seeing you. I'd better tell Mrs. Drinkwater that Anna brought a letter telling me of your arrival."

And so Cassandra found herself waiting in a muddy lane while dusk became full dark, then driving for half an hour hidden under a blanket on the floor of the curricle (which made her feel ill), and finally driving back to the house, a considerable improvement, since this time she was allowed to sit on the seat.

All the while she wondered if she had gone mad. Lord Font drove the old horses and wondered, in the teeth of the evidence, the same about himself.

= 4 =

As THE CURRICLE clattered over the uneven flagstones in front of the house, a small boy ran out to hold the horses.

"Thank you, Job. Bring Mrs. Brown's bag in when you've finished with the horses. Mrs. Drinkwater will tell you where to put it." Harry turned to help Cassandra down.

She'd already started her descent and had put her foot on the step before noticing that her skirt was caught under her boot. She tried to step back into the carriage and managed to catch more of the material under her heel.

"I'm stuck," she hissed.

He put his hands around her waist and swung her down. "Pray, take my arm, the ground is somewhat uneven."

A short, angular woman, dressed in a black wool gown and a large white cap, a candlestick in her hand, stood by the open front door. She hastened forward. "Lord bless you, ma'am, for He has vouchsafed you over the seas and preserved you from monsters. And from savages, too, no doubt, for his lordship tells me you come from America. I was telling Drinkwater only now of them heathens what murdered your poor husband, God rest his soul, and ate him, too, I've no doubt. But my lord, you mustn't keep Mrs. Brown in the night air, for she's had a long journey."

She all but shooed Cassandra before her. "I am Mrs. Drinkwater, ma'am, and I make so bold as to welcome you to Font Hall, on behalf of the staff, though there's only Drinkwater and my niece Martha, though she's a clever girl, and Job what was taken from the parish house as a work of Christian charity. You shall sleep in her ladyship's room, for the mattress was turned only last week, and Martha's taken up a jug of hot water already, for there's only soup and cold meats and they can wait.

"Do take care for the loose step, ma'am. It was very kind of Mrs. Font not to tell me you were coming, I'm sure, for she did not mean to worry me over what to feed you, and the fire will have taken the chill off the room, yet with some notice I could have roasted a hen.

"Here you are, ma'am, her ladyship's room, always kept ready against a visit from Mrs. Font, though she's not spent the night here since little Mr. Edmund was born—no, I lie to you, for she did stay here five weeks after his birth, but since then not one night. Of course, Lady Font was with us then, but she and Mrs. Font both wanted Mr. Edmund's child born in the same bed as Mr. Edmund."

Mrs. Drinkwater lit a pair of candles which stood on the mantelpiece. There were plodding footsteps in the corridor, and Mrs. Drinkwater opened the door again. Job came in with the valise. Cassandra thought he was about ten until she saw the down on his face and realized he was an undersized teenager. His skin was pitted. He stared at her until Mrs. Drinkwater took the valise from him.

"Get along with you, my lad."

Job jerked his head and left.

"Now, ma'am, I would be pleased to put your things away, yet I have thought me that there is ham to be fried, and so I make so bold as to take my leave, and shall send Martha to you." She curtsied.

Cassandra, who had understood only every other word of Mrs. Drinkwater's speech, said, "Thank you," and as soon as the housekeeper was gone, she took off the cloak and bonnet and sat on the high bed shaking her head.

The room was comfortably furnished, but everything looked old and shabby. A table and two straight chairs stood in a corner. There was what seemed to be a cross between a dressing table and a washstand with a hole cut in the middle for a bowl, but it also had two shallow drawers and an adjustable mirror. There was a large, well-made cupboard. The carpet was worn and seemed to have been darned. The wallpaper was peeling and cracked. The design was vaguely Chinese. The bed was covered with a faded green cloth appliquéd with birds of paradise. The mattress sagged. Net to the bed stood a small cabinet, and Cassandra feared it held a chamber pot. The room had none of the elegance she associated with the British Regency.

"Be you ill, ma'am?"

Cassandra looked up to see the girl who'd been taking in the washing now standing in the doorway. "I'm fine, just tired. You must be Martha."

"Yes, ma'am. Do you wish to be changing of yourself. There be water in the jug." She opened the valise and shook out both the dresses. "Oh, these do need the iron, ma'am, and they don't look as if they'd fit you better than the one you be wearing."

"They aren't mine. I mean, someone gave them to me—after the flood swept everything away." Cassandra realized she was close to babbling. "Look, Martha, I really am tired. Do you think Mrs. Drinkwater could give me some soup to eat up here, and then I'll go to bed."

It was only eight o'clock, but she didn't want to test her role as Widow Brown any more than she had to. As soon as everyone was asleep, she'd get her real clothes and wait in the lab in the hope of being transported back to her own time.

Martha brought her a thick game soup and more candles for the table. She put away the few clothes while Cassandra ate. "Where are your caps, ma'am?"

"Caps?"

"Yes, ma'am, you've not got a one in this bag."

"Oh, yes, I—er—lost them." It seemed that the resourceful Harry Font had not thought of everything.

39

Martha shook her head and left, to return a few minutes later with a starched and frilled scrap of muslin and "Mrs. Drinkwater's compliments, ma'am."

Martha offered, a little awkwardly, to help her undress, but Cassandra asked her to leave. I've just dismissed a servant, she thought, and laughed wryly. She blew out the candles and lay on the bed to wait.

A few noises filtered upstairs. Although Cassandra tried to rest, her thoughts kept spinning. When the clock struck ten, she heard footsteps pass her door and saw the dim light of a candle go by. Harry Font going to bed, she guessed.

At eleven she got up and fumbled until she'd tied on the cap. She took the bag with her notes and left the room. There was very little light in the room, and less in the hallway. The floors creaked alarmingly, but Cassandra found her way to the attic. Forcing herself to move slowly, she found her clothes. She would change in the lab, she decided. It was possible that she'd be able to bluff her way out of trouble if someone saw her dressed as Mrs. Brown, but in her own clothes she'd not stand a chance.

The night was intolerably long. It was twenty minutes before midnight when she took her place exactly where she'd been standing when she'd "arrived." The next few minutes, until the clock struck midnight, felt like an hour. She remembered that Harry Font still had her calculator, and wondered what effect that might have on history.

At twelve-thirty her legs gave out, and she sat on the floor. At one point she thought she'd slept. She seemed to have missed hearing the clock strike four, but when it next chimed, she realized that she had just miscounted.

Sometimes she managed to get used to the idea of being in 1815. At other times it was as frightening as ever. And she was tormented by uncertainty.

What if Will and Dr. Jenkins and the others had tried to bring her home earlier, when she wasn't in the lab?

It was very cold, much colder than she'd expected, and

her teeth began to chatter. There was a glimmer of light coming through the east windows when Harry Font, dressed as he had been the day before and carrying a candlestick, came in.

"It's almost six, cousin. Mrs. Drinkwater will be in the kitchen soon," he said.

"How did you know I was here?"

"I went to your room. I meant to knock and ask you to join me downstairs, but when I saw the door open, I guessed where you'd gone."

"I thought I'd shut it."

"The catch is stiff. I do think you should change again. I'll wait for you upstairs."

There was, Cassandra supposed, nothing else to do.

Harry was waiting for her when she came downstairs, dressed again in the black gown. He took her modern clothes at once.

"I'll hide them again. Be so kind as to wait in the kitchen— I've lit the stove."

Cassandra was getting a little tired of constantly being told to wait.

The kitchen was a large room. The floor was covered with flagstones, the low ceiling stained with smoke and hung with hams and strings of onions. There was a large scrubbed table, benches, and a dresser covered with pans, tin, and pottery.

The stove was very like one she'd seen at a girl-scout camp. There was a box for the fire, although this one burned coal rather than wood, with a boiler for heating water on one side and an oven on the other. His lordship, one hand wrapped in a bit of rag, was trying to pour milk from a kettle into a bowl.

"I thought you could do with something warm." He managed to avoid scalding either himself or a cat which wound around his legs. "Do you think I should beat it?"

"The cat?"

"No, the posset, I put three eggs in it, and they seem to be congealing."

"Yes, beat it, by all means."

Harry worked in silence, adding first a knob of butter, then something that smelled like beer. "Here you are, cousin." With a flourish he poured the mess into a mug and set it before her.

"Thank you."

It tasted like a hot, alcoholic milkshake, with a rather raw aftertaste. The lumps of cooked egg were quite unpalatable. Harry poured himself some, then put the bowl on the floor for the cat, who took one sniff and jumped away onto the dresser.

"I hardly slept, and when I did, I dreamt of you. In fact, I was so certain the events of yesterday were a dream that I went to your room as soon as it was light to call to you through the door and make sure you were still here."

"Why didn't you come to see me last night—I mean, after you'd eaten your supper? I wanted to talk to you."

"Martha said you'd retired, and I rather thought your journey and the shock had tired you out. I did wait up, hoping you'd come back downstairs after you'd rested. I was trying to make sense of what you'd told me." Even though he was sitting, his hands slid toward his pockets. "How much of the experiment—the one in the future—did the men explain to you?"

"I don't know what you think I did there, but I had my own team, I reported only to Dr. Jenkins. In other words, I designed that experiment."

"I rather imagined you recorded the results, helped your father . . ."

Cassandra let him squirm a moment longer, then stopped frowning. "It's all right."

She'd have to remember that in his world, women couldn't vote, when a woman married, everything she owned became her husband's, the idea of a young, unmarried woman living alone was almost unheard of. It obviously hadn't occurred to Lord Font that she didn't live with her parents.

"You have to realize that things have changed," she told him. "Women can vote now—in Britain, as well as America."

"Which women are enfranchised? Those like you, with a degree?"

"Everyone can vote—men and women."

"You mean anyone—regardless of who or what they are? Anarchy?"

"No, democracy. You just let men who own a lot of property vote, yes?"

"Yes, those men who have an interest in seeing that the country is well governed are in the best position to choose Great Britain's statesmen. I find it almost impossible to imagine any benefits from mob rule."

"Well, I don't want to argue, but I'll just give you a few facts about the future. A lot of women, as many women as men, go to college. In fact, most people, at least half the population, go to college. And we have compulsory education, too. Most women work, not just inside the home."

"Most women work here, Cousin Brown, although they are generally domestic servants, or wives helping their husbands in their trade, or on the farm."

"In my time, they have the same sorts of jobs as men, physicians, and scientists, truck drivers—coachmen would be a good analogy, I guess. Women own property, and after they marry, they retain the right to their own property. We have more freedom. I don't want to shock you, but I live alone, without any guardian, and have since I was sixteen and went to college—and I'm not unusual. You have to think of me as a responsible adult who's just as able as any man. Otherwise, we're not going to get anywhere, and I'm going to need your help."

He was frowning now. "So *we* together are to discover how you got here, and how to return you? I'm not altogether sure that you wouldn't be better off staying here."

"If that is a joke, I find it in very poor taste, sir."

"Pax, pax, cousin. I assumed from the start that your age would be more advanced than ours in all things. Until you have had a chance to explain your world fully, I will reserve judgement."

"All right." One thing certainly wasn't different, Cassandra thought. She still heard that same sort of halfhearted apology, which was really just another sort of criticism. "I'm afraid it's going to be tough for you to let a woman teach you anything, but if we both try . . ."

Lord Font managed to smile. Whatever else had changed in the years between his era and that of Mrs. Brown, women hadn't lost that infuriating habit of offering a little insult in terms that a man couldn't object to without seeming completely unreasonable. Yet he was more than willing to forgive her. She was a treasure house of knowledge.

"Cousin Brown, don't feel you have to finish your posset, I expect the pigs will enjoy it." He caught sight of Martha standing by the door. "Come in."

Martha came in quietly, but gasped at the sight of the kettle. "Aunt will say you should have used a pot, my lord, but I'll give it a good scrub."

"Well, it doesn't seem to have come to any harm. I expect Mrs. Brown would like some hot water. I lit the fire."

"Why, so you did, my lord." She dipped out some barely warm water for Cassandra. "Shall I carry it upstairs, ma'am?"

"No, don't bother, I'll take it."

"Thank you very much, ma'am."

Cassandra took the jug and walked wearily through the passages and up the stair. The sound of her footsteps and the water sloshing in the jug seemed very loud, and very real.

Breakfast was served an hour later in the dining room. In the few weeks she had spent in modern London, Cassandra had grown used to the enormous breakfasts that the British ate, and had been told that in the old days the meal was even more substantial and varied. But at Font Hall the food, while plentiful, was simple. Harry carved her several slices of bacon from a boiled joint while she helped herself to a fried egg. Harry drank beer. Cassandra asked for and was given boiled water, although Martha seemed rather put out by the request.

Cassandra, despite her almost sleepless night, was anxious to get started, so as soon as Mrs. Drinkwater had cleared away the last of the breakfast dishes, the lessons began. By midmorning Harry had a good understanding of atomic theory. They still sat in the dining room. Cassandra had wanted to work in the lab—or the workroom, as Harry often called it—but he'd pointed out that here, with the door open, they at least had a verisimilitude of chaperonage and that he could scarcely ask Mrs. Drinkwater to waste the morning sitting in the old crypt with them. Cassandra had told him that she trusted him, and he'd bowed to her, but trust, apparently, was not the point.

"How Victorian!" she'd exclaimed, and found her remark rather hard to explain.

She next suggested that they at least move to the library so that he wouldn't have to keep running back and forth for books and the voluminous notes he'd made at meetings of the Royal Society of London for Improving Natural Knowledge, the Philomathic Society of Paris, and the newly founded Royal Institution.

"We already have a fire here," he said stiffly.

"Why don't you light one in the library?" Cassandra asked, then blushed and answered her own question. "Oh, it would be too much trouble for Mrs. Drinkwater, right?"

She should have realized last night, or that morning at breakfast. Harry was poor, or at least impoverished. Barons don't live alone with only four servants in a house which is half-empty of furniture unless they are eccentric or impecunious. Coal was probably expensive.

Harry Font seemed a bit obsessed with electricity, but not mad. She was very impressed with him, not just because he had a quick mind and memorized what she told him with ease, but because he had no difficulty in using a quill pen, and quickly covered sheets of paper with a neat copperplate, while she made blots and nearly upset the ink pot.

He'd been singularly unimpressed with her efforts at penmanship, but a short digression on fountain pens and ballpoints—she had let him take hers to the attic for the sake of security—typewriters and word processors had done much to redeem her. By evening Harry was writing nuclear equations.

All day Cassandra had been too excited to feel tired, but when she went to bed, she fell asleep at once despite the chilly room.

Martha woke her the next morning when she came in to light the fire.

"What time is it?"

"Not much more than seven, ma'am. His lordship said you'd want to be called early."

"That's all right. Is there somewhere I could have a bath?"

"Now, ma'am?"

"Yes, if it's not too much trouble." Cassandra had a feeling it would be since there was no running water in the house.

Mrs. Drinkwater and Martha brought in screens to cut the draught, mats for the floor, and a tub—a tin basin about six inches high, scarcely wide enough for her to crouch in. Martha carried in cans filled with cold and hot water, then brought in a second one of hot water, saying, "You'll never rinse all that hair with one, ma'am."

Cassandra was left alone, at her insistence, with a jar of green soft soap, a linen towel, and an old rag for a washcloth. As soon as the door closed she undressed, got the rag wet and soapy, and started to scrub herself. It seemed the best use of the resources at hand. So much for dreams of a good long soak, but she wasn't about to complain. She heard Martha, who'd promised to wait outside in case she called, carry a chair from another room. Most likely she was going to sew by the window at the end of the hall.

As Cassandra craned her neck trying to wet her hair, she heard Mrs. Drinkwater's footsteps and then her voice.

"With such long hair you never can tell, it may look as though she just washed it, but it may well have been a month. You're not complaining I hope, Martha, for Mrs. Brown is what you might call an old friend of his lordship. It is considered perfectly respectable as long as the lady is a widow. Augusta Tate—you wouldn't know her for she was serving Mrs. Font when she stayed here, and that was before you came—but Mrs. Tate was telling me all about it. His lordship must have met her—"

There was a pause; apparently the quieter voiced Martha was speaking.

"No, he met Mrs. Brown, not Mrs. Tate, in London when he went there for one of his Royal Society meetings. No, Mrs. Tate didn't tell me this, it's obvious. Sometimes, Martha, I think you pay as little attention to me as Drinkwater does. I told him this all last night, and I don't think he listened to a word I said. This story about her being a cousin is just to keep old gossips quiet. I daresay they've been in love for years. . . ."

Cassandra heard the whole story of her and Harry's romance while she washed her hair. She was dressed again before Mrs. Drinkwater finished the tale and went back downstairs. Cassandra called for Martha, and spent the rest of the morning letting the maid towel-dry her hair while Job emptied the bath and carried everything away. She suggested that Martha put it up wet, but the girl had insisted that would lead to "congetation of the lungs."

In Cassandra's mind the morning was a toss-up. She'd

been glad of the bath, but it had never occurred to her that one could spend a whole morning at it. In the meantime, she had acquired a new appreciation for blow-dryers and showers.

5

"I AM A PIGEON," Lord Font announced as Cassandra came in to breakfast the fourth morning after her arrival.

Martha had told her that a groom had brought a letter over from the Dove and Willow. Apparently Anna Font, Harry's sister-in-law, sent her letters down with the stagecoach driver.

In London, at the end of the twentieth century, it could take over a week for a first-class letter to go across the city. Harry and Mrs. Font could exchange letters within twenty-four hours. But, Cassandra reflected as she buttered her toast, in her time, you could send an overnight letter, or even a fax, to the States. Here—or should she say now?—it took weeks for a message to cross the Atlantic. The Battle of New Orleans, she recalled, had been fought after the Peace of Ghent.

"I am a wooden-headed pigeon," elaborated Harry. He didn't even look up as Cassandra took her place next to him.

"Good morning, Cousin Font." Cassandra thought his remarks were rather affected, but still wondered what disturbed him so. She'd never seen him be so rude as to read a letter in front of her. "Harry?" she said when he still ignored her.

He began to read the letter again. Cassandra could see from her chair that it was closely cross-written, and she wondered how he could read it at all. Harry turned the paper so he could make out the vertical lines and adjusted his spectacles.

Cassandra felt like the wife in a comic play. She wondered if she should just keep bleating his name, or wait and see if he'd explain all in his own good time.

"Oh, dear," he said after a third reading. "Mrs. Font writes to remind me of my promise to visit her. She's sending her chaise for me in a week."

"Where does she live?" Cassandra asked, a little worried.

"She has a house on George Street. In London," he added, apparently noticing that Cassandra did not know where George Street was.

London. In Cassandra's day Font Hall was in London. Now it stood seven miles from the southern edge of the city. "You'll be gone all day?"

"For about six weeks, I think. I agreed to go for Christmas."

"But that's not for a month. Could you wait until I'm back home?" The thought of being stuck at Font Hall, with the only person who knew who she really was miles away, filled Cassandra with panic.

"*That* could take a month," Harry said without concern.

Cassandra had to agree. Although they had a fairly good idea of how she had been transported—or transtemporalized, to use Harry's favourite expression—the *why* continued to escape them. Cassandra had been leaning towards an explanation involving string theory, but a few well-placed questions from Harry led them to abandon that line of reasoning. That seemed to be their *modus operandi*: Cassandra would suggest a line of enquiry. As she was explaining the necessary background to Harry—a process which required her to think it through very carefully—one or the other of them would see a flaw.

"But you can't leave me here alone! Think what it would do to Mrs. Drinkwater's rationale." Cassandra laughed. "I expect half the neighbourhood is seething with righteous indignation after she tactfully explained who I *really* am, and the other half can't imagine why you would take a mistress who 'looks as though she'd been dragged through a hedge backwards,' to use Martha's phrase."

"I'm pleased to see you've kept your sense of humour. And you really do look quite respectable now."

So respectable, thought Cassandra, that you're no longer afraid to be closeted for hours in the workroom with me. I suppose I've become an honourary man.

"Besides," he continued, "I very much doubt that anyone takes any notice of what I do at all."

Cassandra remembered how everybody had surreptitiously craned their necks when she'd walked into church on his arm the day before. Martha, who had an ambition to become a dressmaker and so preferred sewing to any kind of housework, had cheerfully altered one of the dresses to fit Cassandra, and made her a plain cap. The day after Cassandra's arrival, Harry sent her to the village of Leigh Font with Mrs. Drinkwater to buy new gloves and a black bonnet, as the ones she'd been using were disreputable in the extreme, and to call at the shoemaker to have a pair of slippers quickly made up. They had also brought her a set of stays from the little general shop. Cassandra found them uncomfortable, but not unbearable.

Cassandra had worn her new finery on Sunday and felt that she did look very respectable, but that changed neither the fact that despite Harry's indifference or wishful thinking, the people in the village and surrounding farms *did* take notice of him, nor his plans for departure.

"If you stayed for a week or two longer, we could work on the equations together, and you could go to see your sister-in-law as soon as I've gone home. It *is* a month until Christmas, after all."

"She'd probably come to fetch me herself, out of friendliness, and if she speaks to any of the servants . . ." Harry shook his head. "Well, there would be no way to keep her from learning about your presence. And I have no doubt that she would invite you as well!"

Cassandra found the idea of visiting his sister-in-law with him preferable to remaining at Font Hall without him, but not by very much. "Why not tell her you've got a cold or something, that you'll come when you feel better?"

"If I take to my bed, I can hardly do mathematics for you."

"You wouldn't have to be that sick. Tell her you don't want to expose Edmund to your cold."

"You don't know Anna. She'll send me conserves and arrowroot, and perhaps even come to see me herself. If she gets word that I'm not really ill, she'll assume I'm snubbing her and be very hurt."

"Surely she's learnt not to take Mrs. Drinkwater's word for things."

"She'll rely on Drinkwater for news of my health. Would you be so kind as to pass the dish of ham?"

Cassandra set it down forcefully in front of him. "You just don't want to stay here with me."

"I don't want, madam, to arouse anyone's suspicions, nor do I wish to cause Mrs. Font any worry. I am no more pleased at this turn of events than you are. But had I not been suffering from the shock of your appearance in my laboratory, I would not have agreed to go."

For all his sputter he sounded a little contrite, but Cassandra was too indignant to notice his tone of voice. "You locked me up, and then blithely made arrangements to go away for more than a month."

"I did not blithely agree. When Mrs. Font put the idea to me, I was not attending. I was thinking about you, and wondering if I had become a lunatic, or if you were one. I was answering that question out loud."

"And who did you decide was crazy?"

"I decided that either I was, or you were—it did not occur to me that we both might be. Then I'd feel your calculator in my pocket and wonder if I'd imagined its properties." He grinned. "It was not a comfortable meal."

He seemed to have made up his mind to go to London.

"*Would* she mind if I came? Believe me, I wouldn't invite myself in normal circumstances."

"Not if the world believes, as you assure me it does, that you're my mistress."

"I thought you just said that no one even noticed me."

"I said that no one here takes any notice of me. But Anna's mother, Mrs. Chubbs, lives with her, and they have their own circle of friends who'd wonder about us. That cousin story isn't really a very good one, you know."

"I am sure it was the best you could manage at the time," Cassandra said as mildly as she could, for she did not want to antagonise him.

There was an icy silence, broken when Harry said, "In any case, I hardly think you know how to go on in society."

Cassandra nearly told him to go to London and be damned, but she quickly realized that he had a point—even if he had made it rudely.

"If I don't know the conventions of polite behaviour in your time, you had better teach them to me, for I will not be left here. We are almost certain that I could spend a century in your laboratory, waiting to be transported home. There is no reason for me to stay here, without you to"—she almost said protect—"advise me."

"I am sorry, but it is out of the question." He sounded almost remorseful. "I do not like it any better than you. Please, believe me."

"Harry, try to see this from my point of view. I feel the way you would if someone dropped you in the midst of a group of . . . of Africans and told you to make sure no one noticed you. Assume that you look like them and almost speak the language correctly, but you don't have the slightest idea of what's going on."

"But you speak English very well."

"You're not seeing the point!"

"The point is, my dear Miss Brown, that I cannot bring a strange woman into my sister-in-law's house. She is a respectable young matron."

"Are you suggesting that I'm not respectable?"

Harry took off his glasses. "No, of course not. But you wouldn't seem respectable."

"Then think of a way in which I would. Look, I know you didn't invite me here or anything, and that you've had to buy me things, and I'm sorry, but you're the only person I can trust."

"You would be perfectly safe here with Drinkwater."

"I can think of a hundred things that could go wrong. If you're here and I make a slip, you can cover for me. Without you, I could just go on until I'd talked myself into real trouble. Remember yesterday, when we talked about the Congress of Vienna, and you said that if I mentioned what I told you about Tsar Alexander making secret deals to anyone else, that I'd be hanged as a spy, and you for harbouring one?"

"I was jesting."

"You were deadly serious."

Harry ignored her charge. "But there's no one here for you to talk to."

"What if the minister came to see me? He just might. I know that if nothing out of the ordinary happens, I should be fine. But we can't count on it. The very fact that I'm here proves that."

"Which minister are you referring to? Or perhaps you think the First Lord of the Admiralty would call on you."

"You know exactly what I mean. I mean the parson, the vicar, your local man of the cloth." Cassandra glared at him.

"All right, I shall think of something."

Cassandra spent the morning working alone in the laboratory. At three o'clock Harry himself came to escort her to dinner.

"I'm sorry I was unpleasant this morning," he said.

"That's okay—all right, I mean. I think I should finish this by tomorrow. We can do the measurements then, and start on the calculations. Whoever would have thought it was this simple?"

"It seems a lot of trouble to me."

"Oh, not this mess, I mean time itself."

As they sat down to boiled beef and barley Harry announced, "I have a plan, Cousin Brown, a great plan. Mrs. Font is convinced that little Edmund is a prodigy. He is actually a very clever little boy. She also worries that she spoils him, although he's really very well behaved. She told me several times that she doesn't want to teach him herself because she'd be too indulgent, and because he's too intelligent for her, and it will be a few years yet before he is old enough to go to school. You can come with me and be Edmund's governess."

"How old is he?" Cassandra had several reservations, not least among them the fact that she knew very little about children.

"Three years."

"What can I teach a three-year-old? I would think he'd need a nanny."

"Oh, how to count and his letters. His mother thinks he could learn to read if he had a clever teacher."

"I don't know a lot about children."

"I'm sure instinct would guide you. I'll write to Mrs. Font this morning and explain to her that I've engaged you."

"Won't that seem a bit high-handed?"

"As I am little Edmund's guardian, Mrs. Font expects me to oversee his education."

"Will I still be your cousin?" Cassandra asked.

"Yes, because I offered to take Job with me to help Mrs. Font's servants, and of course, he knows you as my cousin. I thought we'd ask Mrs. Drinkwater to give us a tea tray in the library, and we can practise introducing you to people. You seemed a little . . . unsure at church."

"How *kind* of you to let me come," Cassandra chimed.

"A bit too effusive, I think. Perhaps you should speak in a more natural tone of voice."

Harry, drawing on memories of having to play the part of the countess, the bishop, or even the Queen herself, as his countless female cousins prepared to enter society, had just finished guiding Cassandra through the sometimes tricky business of being introduced and making introductions in turn. This had not been his favourite part of his cousins' lessons. As a little boy, he'd greatly enjoyed the part when everyone had sailed around the room pretending to cut each other. As he grew older, he came to prefer helping the young ladies practise dancing.

"It's from a play," Cassandra explained. "All about a flower girl who wants to be a lady, and a professor who teachers her. A bit like us."

"Does she marry her lord?"

"She doesn't want to marry anyone, actually. She wants to work in a flower shop, but she has such an awful cockney accent she can't get a job—a position, rather. She goes to the professor, who teaches her to speak so well that when they go to a ball, she's mistaken for a princess."

Harry looked thoughtful. "I fear that Anna's going to drag me to a ball. In fact, I think I even agreed to let her find me a wife."

"Don't you want to be married?"

"No. I'd have to change." Harry trimmed the candle wicks.

"How?"

Could it be, Cassandra wondered, that men have always been afraid of commitment? It seemed unlikely. Cassandra had the impression from her admittedly poor knowledge of social history that Regency gentlemen went their own way after marriage.

"Be more congenial, not spend my whole life shut up in the laboratory." He sighed. "Yet I *ought* to produce an heir. It would please Anna if I did."

"But it wouldn't please you. Are you sure it would be so bad? With the right woman, of course." He sounded so serious that Cassandra couldn't help teasing him.

"I'm not sure I could find the right woman. And if I did, I've not got a lot to offer her aside from the title. I'm not sure I want to marry a woman who only wanted to be my Lady Font."

Cassandra wished she knew him well enough to ask what the right woman would be like. To fill the silence, she said, "If you and your wife were in love with each other, she wouldn't mind that you didn't have a lot of money, and you might even find you enjoyed spending time with her."

"You're worse than Anna."

"Tell me about her."

From the few things he'd said, Cassandra had formed the impression of a silly woman who doted on her son, who was, Cassandra *knew*, a spoiled, dim-witted cry baby.

"She's very pretty, very sweet." Harry smiled fondly.

"How old is she?"

"About your age; she'll be twenty-one in the spring."

"Child bride." Cassandra was amused to notice that Harry had misjudged her age and given her nearly four year's grace.

"She was only sixteen, and Edmund twenty-one, when they wed. She was widowed very soon after. They met when he was on leave and were married very quickly. My mother didn't like it very much, but Ed was of age, and Mrs. Chubbs did not object. She had married off four other daughters, so I suppose she thought she could trust her eye at picking sons-in-law. Mother soon came to see what a dear Anna is, and before Mother died they were good friends."

That gooey look in his eye is really disgusting, Cassandra thought. I wonder if he even knows that he's in love with his sister-in-law. Well, at least I know who the right woman is. I wonder how long it's been since Edmund died. I suppose Harry has to wait a year before he can propose.

Harry, who'd been lounging in the window seat, leapt to his feet. "Why don't I teach you how to waltz?" He stood before her and bowed. "Mrs. Brown, would you honour me with this dance?"

"I thought you didn't like balls."

"I don't. Dancing is the only thing which makes them tolerable."

Cassandra stood and made her very best curtsey, one of the results of the evening's work. "My lord."

Cassandra thought she could waltz. One simply stood stiffly about six inches from a man's chest, and walk, more or less in time to the music—step, two, three, step, two, three—around the room, trying to avoid other bored couples. She'd always thought the old biddies who seemed to run London society in the Regency must have been a pretty repressed lot to find something that staid exciting. It was nothing compared to the close dancing of her own age. The sight of blue-jeaned couples pressed together with their hands rammed into each other's back pockets would have most likely given Lady Jersey the vapours.

However, the waltz Harry taught her was anything but boring. The steps were very lively and quick, and much more complicated than step, two, three. They didn't just face each other, clasping shoulder and waist, but often danced side by side, his right and her left hands forming an arch. Harry knew how to lead. Before long he was twirling her around the dimly lit library, skilfully avoiding the desk and chairs and singing a love song in a very pleasant tenor.

Cassandra let herself be caught up in the moment. She could imagine a large ballroom, lit by hundreds of candles in chandeliers. She was dressed in green silk, with pearls in her hair.

Then Harry's song ended, and he bowed again. "If you can manage that, I could teach you country dances in no time. You're very nimble. We could start with 'Gathering Peasecods.' "

"I used to fence. You get used to moving your feet quickly."

"Good Lord, do your ladies fight duels over the gentlemen?"

"When necessary," Cassandra said airily, "but it's more a sport than anything else. I expect you'd find it very bloodless. We wear masks and protective clothing, and we fight for points, not to the death, or even first blood. I don't think there's been a duel for well over a hundred years."

"Would you like to see my sword? It's a naval officer's blade, actually."

"I'd love to."

Harry brought it downstairs to her. Apparently he kept it hanging in his wardrobe. He let Cassandra hold it, making only the slightest correction of her grip. It was heavier than she expected and wickedly sharp. With very little encouragement Harry demonstrated cuts, thrusts, and parries for her.

He was, Cassandra mused, really very graceful. He was also tall, and strong looking. As the candlelight glinted on his blade, she saw another side to him—one removed from the rational scientist, a man who was dangerous and wilder than the men she'd known before. He'd been taught to use that sword to kill—and although she very much doubted he ever had, it gave him a virility that Cassandra was forced to admit intrigued her.

The next few days fell into a pattern. During the day they worked on the problem of returning Cassandra to her own time. Cassandra had expected to spend a few weeks at least teaching Harry the advanced calculus they would need for the tedious work of constructing the equations. Fortunately, Harry had studied mathematics, and the knowledge that he had provided an excellent basis. It took only a day's work before he was ready to tackle the equations.

In the evenings they sat in the library, with a small fire, and practised conversation. They were supposed to talk about topics of the day to help Cassandra become more familiar with them, but they often found themselves talking about other things, from women's rights to quantum physics.

When they got chilly, they danced. Country dances, Cassandra learned, were something like square dances, but there was no caller. At the beginning of each dance, a chord was played and the instruction, "Honour your partner" was given, but after that, the dancers had to rely on their memories. Some of the dances needed only two couples, others three, or six or even eight.

"If you learn the basic steps," Harry assured her, "the others can just pull you through."

Cassandra had her doubts. Harry's instructions were full of phrases such as, "You stand there, while the third couple does the same thing," and he spent a lot of time leaping about trying to take the parts of all the men.

Finally he decided to content himself with teaching her dances such as "Haste to the Wedding" and "We Won't Go Home 'til Morning," for "as many as will, long ways," which meant they could be danced by however many couples fit into the room.

"We won't have to worry about what the rest of the set is doing."

"That's the Virginia reel," Cassandra said, recognizing it from high-school gym classes, when Harry set about teaching her "Sir Roger de Coverly."

"You know this dance, cousin?"

"Or one very like it, H—cousin. I'm sorry. I find this sort of family courtesy rather hard to follow. Would it upset anyone if I called you Harry and you called me Cassandra."

"I would be honoured." Harry bowed.

"In my time, well, maybe a generation before me, people used to talk about our cousins across the sea when they referred to England. I always thought they meant that we and the British were getting closer—oh, Harry, what about the War of 1812? I was thinking about it a week ago, and it never even occurred to me that it might still be going on. Are people going to be hostile to me because of it?"

"I wouldn't worry. People here know that it was based on a misunderstanding, although I imagine that those hotheads in America might be less tolerant of an Englishwoman than we of an American lady."

"Harry, I can't say anything to that without being unpatriotic or rude. Why don't you ask me to dance again, and then you can tell me about English and American relations."

"After a pun like that, I'm not sure I have the heart to dance."

The evening before they were to leave for London, Cassandra, who had tried several times to turn the conversation to the topic of money, finally asked outright. "How poor are you? I know you're short of funds, but you have that very fancy-looking carriage, and you have books and scientific equipment. I worry about the money you spend on me. I wish I could repay you.

"Maybe we could pretend to invent something together, something which already exists in my time. Not the internal-combustion engine. It would have to be something with fewer ramifications."

Cassandra glanced around the room for inspiration and noticed the coal scuttle. "What about the safety lamp—a lamp for miners that would help prevent explosions in mines because it doesn't have an open flame?"

"I am afraid that someone else has already done that, Cassandra." Harry stood up, and his hands went into his pockets. "I was in London three days before your arrival, and had the privilege of hearing Sir Humphry read a paper on firedamp—the accumulation of combustible vapours in pit mines. Afterwards he very kindly showed me his diagrams for such a lamp. I believe he completed the design some three weeks earlier, in response to a letter from the

Reverend Dr. Grey, lamenting the large number of lives tragically lost in mining explosions." He paused to take a breath.

Cassandra seized the opportunity before he could successfully turn the conversation to the details of Sir Humphry's lamp. "Perhaps we should invent something else."

"No, that would not do," Harry said firmly. "I am certain that you mean well, but it would be dishonest, even if I were merely to take the credit for something which you had discovered entirely by yourself. Does not a natural philosopher in your day feel anguish when another publishes his idea without permission or acknowledgement? As any man of business could tell you, it is the manufacturer of an item who becomes rich, not the man who invents it."

"But I really feel I must repay you in some way. I am sure that I am a drain on your resources."

Cassandra knew that Harry wanted to bring the subject to an end, but if there was any possibility of her paying her own way, she wanted to do so.

"I shall endeavour to make my financial situation clear to you, Miss Brown. I have sufficient money. I'm just short of the ready. I have some income, but I spend most of it on the fabric of the house. When the Font fortune is restored, I want the family to be able to live in the Hall."

"How do you expect to restore the fortune? Invent something yourself?"

"I have to do nothing but wait for the mortgages to run out. My grandfather mortgaged nearly all the income from the various estates and sold everything that wasn't entailed to dower my eight aunts. He hoped one of them at least would marry a man willing to support him in the style to which he was accustomed." Harry's good humour had already restored itself. "Most of my father's first wife's money was spent on my cousin Charles, and his son, Arthur. My mother's portion went on my education and Edmund's. I have some money, I just choose to spend it in what seems to others an odd fashion. The curricle was

Edmund's. Anna asked me to take it after he died, but it's so much fun to drive, even though I make do with the farm horses, that I might have bought one for my own use."

"Will you take it to London?"

"No, Drinkwater needs the horses here."

"And the money you spent on my clothes . . ."

"Payment in kind for the lessons you give me."

"But—"

"I don't want to hear another word about it, Miss Brown. The knowledge you give me is worth a great deal more than the trifling expenditures you've allowed me to make."

His tone had become so stiff and remote again that Cassandra felt she had finally to let the subject drop and bid him good-night.

6

MRS. FONT SENT her chaise—a square, black carriage. It arrived just after ten in the morning driven by Daniels, her groom-cum-coachman, who left Job standing with the horses while he drank ale and devoured seed cake in Mrs. Drinkwater's kitchen. Drinkwater made heavy weather of strapping Harry's trunk, Cassandra's valise, and Job's tin box to the back of the chaise. Then, Daniels emerged from the kitchen and drove the chaise to the front of the house.

Martha had knitted Job a new muffler for the occasion of his visit to London. When she tried to wrap it about his neck, he evaded her and managed to escape to the stable with the scarf trailing from the shoulders of his enormous greatcoat, a hand-me-down from Drinkwater. Cassandra, who'd been instructed to warm herself at the stove before they set out, heard Martha complaining to Mrs. Drinkwater.

"I've been telling him I'd make that old coat over for him. He looks like a scarecrow. He'll be an embarrassment to his lordship. But he won't let me touch it. He hardly said thank you for the scarf!"

Ah, young love. At least the girl doesn't have a crush on Harry, Cassandra thought—not that Harry's love life is any of my business.

Finally Harry handed Cassandra into the carriage, draped a rug over her lap, and took his place next to her. Drinkwater placed a hamper of food and several hot bricks on the floor, put up the step, and slammed the door. Job ran from the stable and scrambled up on the box next to Daniels. Martha and Mrs. Drinkwater waved from the front door, and the coach was off . . . travelling, Cassandra estimated, at the rate of about three miles an hour.

The interior of the coach was padded with red velvet and would have been fairly comfortable if it had not been for the constant swaying and jolting, and the cold. Her breath formed a cloud of vapour.

Harry was wearing his sword. "Too difficult to pack?" Cassandra asked.

"I have no wish to alarm you, but there might be highwaymen."

"Not really."

"Yes, really, although not very likely. Still, if we do run across any, my sword won't do me much good unless it's in my hand."

"But you said that your sister-in-law drives out to see you every month."

"Daniels carries a pistol. I doubt he could hit anyone with it, but the noise would scare the louts off. We can't let riffraff bully us into staying at home."

"Have you ever seen a highwayman?"

"Not on the road."

Cassandra decided that he was teasing her. She had *real* things to worry about.

"I thought of something last night. Won't Mrs. Font recognize her dresses?"

"I doubt it. Martha seems to have done something to them."

"Yes, she made them to fit me," Cassandra replied dryly. "But I still think they'll look familiar to her."

"How many women make, or have made, black gowns each year? There must be thousands in London alone."

"But this one has bands and bands of ribbon around the cuff. I expect she'd remember something like that."

"If it was the fashion that year, every gown would have

them." Harry patted her arm. "Trust me. Anna will be eager to welcome you. Have you noticed the view?"

Cassandra looked dutifully out of the small window as the carriage jogged along through Leigh Font. To her discomfort, the women bobbed curtseys and the men tugged on their forelocks as the carriage passed by. Harry let down the window and called something about a ditch to one of the men.

"Did I tell you that the village used to be called Lays du Font—Font's Fields—hundreds of years ago. It was right against the castle walls, and is listed in the Doomsday Book," he said, as if that were a very ordinary thing. "Bit by bit, as houses fell down, new ones were built farther and farther away from Font Hall, and the village simply moved. Would you have ever thought something like that could happen?"

"Does the village belong to you?"

"The land does, and some of the people are my tenants."

The carriage veered onto the turnpike and the horses picked up the pace a little. When they stopped to pay the toll, Cassandra was delighted to see that a bar was set across the road, and turned on pivots so that they could pass. They drove past ploughed fields and leafless trees, until Daniels stopped the coach.

Cassandra's first thought was that there might be highwaymen after all. Harry opened the window and stuck his head out.

"All right, but tell him to be quick about it," he shouted in response to something Daniels said.

Harry pulled his head in, and Cassandra saw Job running toward a thicket, clutching the front of his coat.

"Do you think he's all right?"

"Too much breakfast, if you ask me. Do you want a drink now that we've stopped?" Harry opened the hamper and took out a leather flask, which he passed up to Daniels. "Have some ale. Would you like something to eat?"

"I could do with a meat pie. Thank you, my lord."

Harry handed up the pie, then closed the window. "Mrs. Drinkwater was born in London, you know, but after living at Font Hall for twenty years, she has become convinced that the journey is so long and perilous that we're in danger of starving."

"The driver seems well aware of it. Did Mrs. Drinkwater pack anything else to drink?"

"One should refer to him as the coachman, cousin. There is no need to look so downcast. There's a bottle of wine for you. Would you care for a meat pie, too?"

Cassandra had worried a great deal about typhoid and cholera at first. Finally, to give herself some peace of mind, she'd decided she'd insist on either boiled water or alcoholic drinks and trust that fermenting would have sterilised them. At this time of year she doubted anyone would be offering her fresh fruit. She let Harry pour her a glass of wine.

Daniels passed the flask back. "Thank you, my lord."

"Is Job coming?"

"I don't see him, my lord."

Harry opened the door and leapt down. "I'll hold the horses. Go see if he's ill. I don't want to stand here all day."

The carriage lurched as Harry swung onto the box and Daniels climbed down. An anxious five minutes passed. Harry leaned down and tapped on the window.

Cassandra opened it. "Is something wrong?"

"Do you think you could hold the horses?"

"Only if it were a matter of life and death."

"Nonsense. You could do it easily. Just stand by their heads and hold the leaders' bridles."

Cassandra opened the door, kicked the step down, hiked up her skirts, and went out backwards so she could hold on to the side of the doorway with her free hand.

The horses were large, very large, and she approached them with caution. She grabbed two handfuls of reins, and nearly dropped them as one of the horses rubbed a slobbery mouth against her shoulder. When Harry got down, one of them took a step forward and the other three raised their heads. Cassandra's heart leapt to her throat. She had visions of being dragged along as the animals galloped away, or of letting go and having to face Harry's laughter or anger—she wasn't sure which would be worse—when they were stranded on the road.

Harry adjusted his sword, sketched a salute, and strode off in the direction Job and Daniels had taken. A couple of minutes later Cassandra heard shouts. Then over the hill came a half-grown terrier with a rope trailing after it, Harry, running full tilt, his sword banging against his legs, and in the rear, Job with his open coat flapping, and Daniels, who had a firm grasp on Job's ear. The puppy dashed under the chaise and cowered against the wheel as the three men came to a stop.

"Lego m'ear!"

"I'll give you what for!"

"I demand an explanation."

Cassandra, who was afraid that all the noise would frighten the horses, said so.

"He's me dog, me lord."

"Kept the horses standing twenty minutes—and on a hill or as good as."

"Didn't I say that animal was *not* to come to town?"

Cassandra repeated her observation in a louder voice.

"He'll be champion ratter, I was just going to take him to the pits."

"No knowing how long the little devil would have made us wait."

"There is a limit to *my* patience, Job."

Cassandra shouted: "I want someone else to look after these horses."

"It's not me fault Tiger got away, missus."

"Why, ma'am, you shouldn't of bin left with 'em."

"Now you've upset Mrs. Brown."

Cassandra understood then why generations of women

had resorted to hysterics. "Then perhaps, Daniels, you would be so kind as to find someone to hold them."

"Yes, ma'am," he replied as Cassandra gladly let him take the reins.

She turned to Job and Harry. "Let me guess. You had that dog hidden under your coat."

"Yes, missus. He's not very big yet, but he's a fighter. Give any dog in London a run for its money. But I didn't think Tiger could hold on all the way to London, so I thought I'd better let him down. Only he jumped right out of me arms, and I couldn't catch him. I didn't want to call him, 'cause his lordship might hear."

"Odd, how this entire debacle can be laid at my door. Job, you are to take that dog and go straight home!" Harry's expression was grim.

"But we must be halfway to London," protested Cassandra.

"I'm sure Master Job can walk two miles before dark," Harry retorted.

Job darted for the dog, which ran around to the other side of the carriage. Job tried from that direction, with the same result.

With a sigh that clearly said, "Do I have to do everything around here?" Harry shooed Tiger towards Job. Just before the boy could grab his dog, it turned and ran back towards Harry, making a tight circle around his lordship. The muddy rope smacked his legs, marking his coat. With great presence of mind, Harry stepped on the rope, which slid along the muddy ground and from under his feet. Then the dog was under the chaise again.

"Damnation! Job, you stand here, and I'll poke it out with my sword."

"May I try something first?" Cassandra opened the carriage door and took out a meat pie from the hamper on the floor. "If you would be so kind as to stand back?"

It took all of three minutes to coax Tiger into her arms and wipe the mud off him with a napkin. Harry might have no qualms about sending Job back alone, but in the half hour they had been standing here, no one had driven or walked by, and this, she assumed, was a major road. The countryside looked pretty wild and lonely. If anything did happen to Job, no one would suspect he was missing until a message could be sent to the Drinkwaters asking if he'd arrived safely. But judging by the look on his face, Harry wasn't about to be reasoned with. She'd have to try outflanking him.

"I'm sure that if you apologized to his lordship, Job, he would forgive you and allow you to come. Tiger can ride inside with me." She smiled at Harry. "He really is a very nice little dog."

"I didn't mean no harm, me lord. And didn't mean to cause no upset. And I didn't mean no disobedience, but you didn't say that I couldn't carry him—just that he couldn't come in a basket. And I am sorry"—he looked at his feet as if they might whisper to him any sins he'd omitted—"for everything."

"All right, but if anything else goes wrong, you're walking all the way back from London. Mrs. Brown, give the dog to Job. It isn't going to dirty the inside of Mrs. Font's coach."

Tiger was handed up to Job, and Cassandra was installed inside the carriage once again. Harry looked at her for so long that she finally asked, "Are you very angry?"

"I was thinking that perhaps you should have ridden on the box and Tiger inside. You wiped his paws, but you have an inch of mud around your hem."

"Are you being odious?"

"I rather think it suits the cruel baron who was going to force a poor lad of sixteen or so to trudge three miles carrying a dog which must weight at least five pounds."

"I never know if you're teasing or not."

"Like Anna, if you really thought I wasn't, you wouldn't ask. And it was not your cozening which made me permit

Job to continue to London, but my wish to spare Mrs. Font as much trouble as possible."

"I'm not sure that letting Job come will prevent trouble, but I don't think he meant any harm."

"You have no idea what Job's going to do with that dog, have you?" Harry asked with some impatience.

"I suppose he shouldn't have brought it with him, if you told him not to, but Martha told me he's an orphan, so it's reasonable he would become very attached to something he loved. It hits some kids that way." Cassandra used the soiled napkin to brush the dirt on her cloak, but only made a worse mess.

"He's going to—or was going to, for I shall not let one of my servants go near such a hellhole—take him to a rat pit. Job's so green he'd have agreed to let Tiger face fifty rats, and that would have been the end of that."

"I don't believe something like that would be allowed," Cassandra protested, but even as she said the words, she thought of the various societies for the prevention of cruelty to animals that existed in her own time.

"It's illegal, but like cockfights and bull baiting, it happens all the time. However, I apologize. This is not a fit topic for a lady's ears."

"You don't have to shelter me so."

"You picked a poor time to visit, cousin. My aunts would tell you that. There are two generations between me and them. Aunt Tavie especially, laments the passing of her youth, when a lady drank like a duke, gamed like a gentleman, and—or so they tell me—swore like a sailor."

As they approached London, the road grew more crowded with carriages, wagons, and pedestrians. Once they crept through a herd of cows. Twice Daniels pulled up as other vehicles overtook them.

"Look," cried Cassandra, pointing to two young men dashing by in a ridiculously high carriage, "Regency bucks!"

They came in through Kennington and across Blackfriars Bridge. Cassandra stared in fascination. The streets were lined with small stalls and shops. Signboards swung in the wind. She recognized a barber's pole.

"What does the golden pineapple stand for?" she asked. "A greengrocers?"

"A confectioner."

"And those yellow balls?"

"The three brass coins of the pawnbroker."

The air was filled with street cries as broom peddlers, muffin men, and women hawking stockings and bobbins of lace competed for customers. All the men, even the labourers building houses and the beggars, wore hats. Only the most ragged women did not wear bonnets, and they covered their heads with shawls. Even the children did not go bareheaded. To Cassandra's great amusement, they were dressed almost exactly like the adults—the opposite of modern times, when the adults dressed like children in blue jeans and sweatshirts.

At Mrs. Font's house on George Street Cassandra at last found the elegance she had expected to see in Regency England. The house itself was built of brick and had a white painted portico. A footman hurried out with an umbrella, and as soon as they were in the tiled hall, a maid took Harry's coat and Cassandra's cloak and led them up the wide staircase.

Before they reached the landing a child dressed in a long blue coat flew at them and climbed into Harry's arms. "Uncle, Uncle, I saw you coming all the way from the square. Oh, how do you do, madam. Put me down, Uncle, so I can make my bow."

With a sinking heart, Cassandra said, "You must be Edmund."

"Little Edmund, please, for Edmund is my lost father."

A very pretty woman in a white dress joined them and took the child's hand. "Why don't you go with Uncle

Harry, my pet. I'm sure you would like to help him hang up his sword. It is just like Papa's."

"I rather wanted to present Mrs. Brown to Mrs. Chubbs," Harry protested.

"Oh, I shall take care of Mrs. Brown. Little Edmund, my dear, go with your uncle." The boy obediently let go of his mother, grabbed Harry's hand, and tugged him upstairs.

The woman turned to the maid. "Augusta, go see if Mrs. Chubbs needs anything. Mrs. Brown, be so kind as to come with me."

She led Cassandra back down the stairs into a large, elegant sitting room dimly lit by candles, and stood in the middle of the room.

"I am Mrs. Font, and I must ask you to leave at once."

"But didn't Lord Font explain; he said he'd write you a letter."

"My brother-in-law is not a worldly man."

"I don't understand."

"I understand very well. You, madam, are an adventuress. There you stand in one of my gowns, carrying my reticule. I wonder what else you have tricked him into giving you. You have cozened him into believing you are perfectly respectable, but I shall not allow you near my precious little boy."

"I'm, that is, my husband was, a cousin—"

"Stuff and nonsense. I heard from my friend, Miss Henderson, that I supposedly brought Lord Font a letter announcing your arrival from America. You may expect me to provide you with an entry into society, but you are sadly in error."

"Mrs. Drinkwater often makes mistakes." Cassandra faltered.

"Lord Font himself told Miss Henderson of this letter. In church. I do not know what Banbury tale you told Lord Font"—she raised her hand—"nor do I wish to know. It must have been a very affecting story to cause such an upright gentleman to lie." Mrs. Font's eyes flashed, but her voice was quiet. No one passing the door could have known of the drama that was taking place inside the room. "If you do not leave at once, I shall have my footman force you out."

Cassandra had no doubt that she meant it. She thought of making a dash for the door and running to Harry, but since she wanted this woman to let her stay in her house, it seemed best to give her every chance to save face by creating as little uproar as possible.

"Lord Font has some of my things, papers and money," she said.

Mrs. Font looked at her for a moment, then rang the bell. She sent the servant for Harry. When he entered, she said, "Mrs. Brown is leaving. Please give her back her belongings."

"Cassandra, are you out of your mind?"

"Mrs. Font thinks I'm not your cousin's widow."

"Is she?"

"Well, not exactly, Anna, but . . ."

With great dignity Mrs. Font said, "I know you will not lie to me, Brother Harry, and I know that your detachment from the world has left you ignorant of many of its unpleasant aspects, but suffice to say that Mrs. Brown—if that is indeed her name—is not the sort of person you would wish me to know."

Harry ignored Cassandra's warning nod and burst into laughter. "You think she's a fashionable impure! Oh, Annie, that's rich. She's a bluestocking. I know she's not my cousin, although she must have done something pretty foolish to give it away to you so quickly."

"Mrs. Font recognized her dress. And her friend, Miss Henderson wrote to her after you told her all about the letter Mrs. Font supposedly delivered to you," Cassandra interrupted desperately, almost stuttering in her haste to explain.

Harry ignored her. "In fact, I know all about her. She's

quite respectable, but for reasons which you wouldn't understand, she's forced to assume a role."

"How do you know I wouldn't understand?"

"All right. Ah, Mrs. Brown, who is, er, fleeing from her wicked—"

Mrs. Font stamped her foot. "You are shameless. Just because I read novels doesn't mean I think I am in one. I demand to know the truth."

"You don't need to worry about it."

This, Cassandra decided, was the moment for sisterhood. "Mrs. Font has a right to the truth." She turned to the other woman. "If I assure you that nothing I tell you will endanger you, or your son, or anyone else, in any way, will you promise not to tell *anyone*, not even your mother?"

"If it endangers no one, but I hope, Mrs. Brown, that you are not bamming me as Harry was."

"Unfortunately not."

It took some time before Anna would believe them, but Harry was able to explain to her that Cassandra was a visitor from the future. Anna was sure that clever Harry had brought her to the past all by himself, for she stuck firmly to the view that something which hadn't happened yet couldn't have any effect, but she was willing to welcome Cassandra into her house, and even to lie to her mother and Edmund.

"Aren't you still worried that people will mistake Cassandra for an adventuress?" Harry asked.

He seemed to find the whole idea of Cassandra being taken for anything other than a frumpy widow amusing. Cassandra had to admit he hadn't seen her at her best, but still found his attitude annoying. She wondered if he'd be so cavalier with a woman of his own time.

"Not at all. I wasn't foolish enough to deny having delivered a letter. The very fact that you've brought Mrs. Brown to stay with us will tell everyone that the whole matter is unexceptional."

7

"Are you quite sure you're comfortable, Mrs. Brown?" Mrs. Chubbs asked, for the third or fourth time that morning. "If you need anything, you must ask my daughter, for this is Mrs. Font's house."

"I have everything I need, thank you. Now, Edmund, can you put the blue marble in the blue cup?"

"He's been able to do clever things such as that for some time, Mrs. Brown."

Edmund dropped the blue marble in the blue cup. "Mrs. Brown, I expect that the ducks are expecting me."

"What ducks, Edmund?"

"The ducks on Mr. Sprightly's ornamental pond. He did expect swans, I understand, but keeps the ducks to please me."

Cassandra looked to Mrs. Chubbs in hopes of a more detailed explanation, but the old lady said only, "Yes, yes, my darling," and fussily put away the purse she was netting.

Edmund climbed down from his chair and took her hand, "Thank you, Gran'mo'ver, for you know they do rely on me. Good morning, Mrs. Brown. Thank you for playing with me."

"Good-bye, Edmund, Mrs. Chubbs."

Cassandra wondered if the child ever went anywhere without having his hand held. He wasn't a bad little boy, in fact he had lovely manners, but he was used to being the center of attention and well practised in making precocious and adorable remarks. He reminded Cassandra of a story she'd heard about the infant Boswell (or was it Dr. Johnson?) who'd had coffee spilt on him. When a woman asked if he was all right, he replied, "Thank you, madam, the pain has somewhat abated." Cassandra wasn't about to pour boiling liquids on Edmund in an effort to reproduce the same result.

But she'd cheerfully spill coffee on Mrs. Chubbs if it would get the old lady to leave her alone for five minutes. Mrs. Font had sensibly left Edmund alone with her, and gone shopping. As soon as the front door closed, Mrs. Chubbs slipped into the room and hadn't been quiet for a moment.

Cassandra would have much preferred to have no audience, for she really had no idea what she was doing with Edmund. Last night, after Mrs. Font tried to throw her out and Cassandra and Harry explained the true story, Mrs. Font had given orders for the child's education. She insisted she was not particularly clever and so would not presume to tell Mrs. Brown how to go on, but she would like little Edmund to receive two hours of gentle instruction each morning in the nursery. Since Cassandra's only memory of kindergarten was of poking beans into a paper cup full of wet dirt, she wished that Mrs. Font *had* presumed to give detailed instructions.

She went over to the fireplace and held her hands to the blaze. Even the toothless, complaining Mrs. Chubbs seemed not to notice the cold, but it bothered Cassandra.

"Has your scholar run away already?" Harry came into the room, carrying a parcel wrapped in brown paper and tied with string.

"Mrs. Chubbs took him out. Something about ducks."

"He feeds Mr. Sprightly's ducks every morning. About six months ago Mr. Sprightly had a mad idea to create a Chinese garden. He got as far as having the pond dug, then changed his mind. I believe his latest idea is to build a miniature theatre, but since little Edmund adopted these ducks, I suppose the pond will stay no matter what happens. Mr. Sprightly is devoted to Anna."

"Oh?" Cassandra studied Harry closely, looking for signs of jealousy.

"Yes, he's her godfather."

Cassandra idly stacked a few of Edmund's blocks.

"How went the lessons?" Harry asked after a moment of silence.

"I'm wasting his time and Mrs. Font's money."

"Have you tried teaching him his letters?"

"His mother made him a set of blocks with letters and pictures pasted on them. And he knows all their names. He can count to one hundred. He knows his colours."

"See if he can tell you the names of the letters when you draw them. If he's like any other child, he's memorized the pictures. And see if he can recognize numbers." Harry unwrapped the package. "A slate and coloured chalk. We might as well protect little Edmund from your handwriting for as long as possible."

"Thank you."

"A small token to make amends. You were quite right. Women indeed know their own gowns, and I shouldn't have been so effusive when I spoke to Mrs. Henderson. I confess I was enjoying the romance of the moment."

"Romance?" Was Harry interested in Miss Henderson?

"The intrigue, the excitement. The moment was, I fancied, somewhat like an incident in a novel, but much tamer, of course."

The English language, Cassandra reflected, hadn't so much changed as diminished. "How is it that you know so much about children?" she asked, to change the subject. After Harry had admitted that he'd been wrong, she wasn't going to force him to dwell on it. "I think you'd do a better job with little Edmund than I."

"I have thirty-four first cousins, most of them much older than I, but they produced a large number of children who are my age and younger. Although my mother had only two children, I grew up in a large family."

"I was an only child. To tell the truth I'm scared of babies. When they cry, there isn't any way to tell what's wrong."

"Well, you can practise on little Edmund. That ought to keep the pair of you out of trouble for a day or two."

"When are we going to work on the equations? We can't closet ourselves away for hours like we did at home."

"Maybe we could meet at breakfast. Anna and her mother always eat it in their rooms."

"How many servants do they have?"

"Daniels and James the footman, and a boy to help them. Augusta, and two other maids, and Walter the cook has a girl in the scullery. And Hester, who, I am certain has the easiest lot of any nursery maid in London."

"The cook is a man?" Cassandra's information about cooks came mostly from *Upstairs, Downstairs*. "I thought cooks were always women."

"Not so, Mrs. Brown, a she-cook is quite an inferior creature."

"So there are nine servants altogether?"

"Yes; why do you ask?"

"This house has six bedrooms, a dining parlour, and three other good-sized rooms, as well as attics and servants' quarters and a kitchen, I assume. But two people and a child live here, with nine people to look after them." Cassandra's twentieth-century sensibilities were outraged.

"You have to look to Anna for that. She keeps hiring the most unlikely people as servants because she feels sorry for them. That's how we ended up with Job. She saw him begging outside St. Paul's and took him home with her. The next time she drove to Font Hall she presented him to me. He told her that if he stayed in London, his beggar master would find him and kill him. I think he was hoping for passage money to the Indies, and instead he got Font Hall."

"Well, I'm glad he knows his way around London. Since I'm here, I might as well see the sights."

"You can't go about with *him*."

"Why not? Mrs. Font took the footman with her this morning."

"That's different."

"Why?"

"It just is. I'll take you around myself. That way we can talk privately."

When little Edmund and his grandmother returned, Harry deftly removed Mrs. Chubbs from the room by deferentially asking if she still had time to oversee the linen closet and saying that his Aunt Seppie had always admired her needlework.

Your uncle really loves you, little boy, Cassandra thought, looking at Edmund.

To her amazement, Harry was right, and the child really didn't know his letters. By the time Hester came to take Edmund to comb his long brown curls before luncheon, he could tell E, A, B, and C apart, and Cassandra was ready to endorse all kindergarten teachers for sainthood.

The noon meal was little more than a cold snack, although Harry had explained that it was becoming fashionable to serve a more elaborate meal if there were guests. Edmund graciously offered his place at the head of the table to his uncle, who equally graciously refused. Edmund had his own seat, a captain's chair with a padded board fixed across the arms so that he could reach the table. The footman waited on them, and had to cut the boy's food for him. Mrs. Chubbs proudly announced that until recently his mother had cut up his food, but little Edmund had objected because it was babyish. Cassandra felt like cheering. There was some hope for the boy after all.

After lunch, Mrs. Chubbs, Mrs. Font, and little Edmund left in the carriage to make their morning calls.

"But it's afternoon," Cassandra pointed out.

She and Harry were in Anna's sitting room again, with their notes spread before them.

"Well, they're called morning calls. I don't know why. Tomorrow I'll have to go and make my leg to the aunts. And you'll have to come, too, since you're a relation. If we call upon one each day, it will only take a week."

"Oh no. I was so pleased when I realized that Mrs. Font doesn't want Edmund doing lessons for more than two hours in the morning. I thought I'd have all afternoon and evening to work. Do you really think a distant cousin by marriage is all that much of a relative?"

"I'd like you to meet my family. The old girls aren't going to eat you. I'm dining with my cousin Tom tonight in his rooms, and I've made an appointment to see Sir Humphry tomorrow morning."

"Harry, it seems that between visiting your friends and relations, and one thing and another, you're trying to avoid working on the calculations. They're my only hope of getting home. I almost think you're doing it on purpose."

Harry stacked Cassandra's papers neatly.

"I preferred them spread out like that. Stop fiddling, and tell me why you don't want to help."

"Madam, I am doing my utmost to help. I have taken you into my home, shabbily foisted you off on my sister-in-law, accommodated you in the matter of Job's dog, in short turned my life upside down. I cannot like the fact that you are suggesting I am attempting to detain you. Good day."

His bow set Cassandra's teeth on edge. Slamming the door might be less civilized, but at least it was more honest. Instead, Harry left the door open, and she could hear him in the hall, instructing the servant to tell Mrs. Font that he would not be in until very late.

I hope he gets drunk, and has a shocking hangover, thought Cassandra as she picked up her papers and went to her bedroom. She laid them out again, relieved to notice that Harry had left her the calculator, and tried to start work. She wasn't about to work in Anna's sitting room since she had no idea how soon the lady of the house might return.

The bedroom was beautifully decorated in blue and cream. The furnishings had obviously been designed to evoke images of ancient Athens. The bed had simple head- and foot-boards, decorated with a frieze of urns and laurel wreaths, which gave it a faintly funereal air. There was a large dressing table, with a woden armchair before it. When Cassandra had pushed the hairbrush and other oddments to one side, there was just enough room for her to work, but for the first time since her arrival, she found it impossible to concentrate, and it wasn't just that she kept thinking how much more quickly a computer would do the work. She kept wondering how she would live if she were really trapped here.

She heard Anna's carriage return, and a few minutes later, Anna called to her through the door. "May I come in?" Cassandra gathered up her notes and hurried to open the door. "Of course."

Anna closed the door behind her and sat down on the bed. "I know it's bad for the mattress, dear, but it reminds me of home. My sisters and I shared a bedroom, and when we were all gathered in it, if some of us didn't sit on the beds, there wasn't room to turn around. I was the youngest, and the elder girls were very much of an age. I used to watch them dress for the evening, and they were always borrowing each other's clothes. I noticed that you seem rather chilly, and I wore those gowns in the summer...."

In the historical novels Cassandra had read, replenishing the heroine's wardrobe was always a simple matter. Either her lover, or husband, or guardian was so fabulously wealthy that he could keep seamstresses sewing all night until all manner of clothing was delivered the next day. Or it just so happened the dressmaker had a customer with a figure exactly like the heroine's, who had ordered but not paid for clothing that the heroine could have. Or—and this particular device always made Cassandra cringe—the farsighted modiste had discovered the concept of off-the-rack clothing a few decades ahead of her time. And now, transparent Anna was offering Cassandra the clothes off her back. She wondered how long it had taken her to think of moving her conversation from sitting on beds to her sisters to hand-me-downs.

"It's terribly kind of you, Mrs. Font, but I feel that I have imposed upon the kindness of your family too much already." Cassandra wasn't satisfied with this speech; it sounded so stiff and cold. "I mean, I don't want to be any more trouble."

"Nonsense, it is merely that I don't see why you should be cold. Silly Harry didn't even see fit to provide you with a shawl. I had several gowns made after I was married and before my husband died that I am sure could easily be made to fit you. Pray come with me."

Anna stood, took Cassandra's hand in her own, and led her into her own bedroom. A number of dresses were carefully laid out on the bed. Cassandra, who recalled that Harry had told her that Anna always wore white because she was still in mourning, made a last effort to dissuade her. "But won't you need them again when you've finished mourning," then she realized that she had been tactless. "When your period of mourning is over, that is?"

"I shall never put off mourning, for I shall never forget Edmund. But Harry is right. Whilst I have the living reminder of his son, I do not need a few garments."

"You mean you were saving these as keepsakes?" Cassandra gestured to the gowns on the bed.

"Yes."

"And Harry, I mean Lord Font, knew?"

"Oh, yes, Mama often remarked on it."

"And now he's asking you to give them up?"

"He is right, Mrs. Brown. Keeping them locked away won't make my loss any easier to bear, nor my husband's memory any fresher."

Even though she was less than pleased with Harry right then, Cassandra had to admit he had a point. In her opinion Anna's obsession with her late husband wasn't healthy, and anything she could do to lessen it would be doing the young woman good. And, she thought wryly, further Harry's suit, although it seemed that his sister-in-law was less smitten with him than the baron might hope.

Anna selected a woolen gown, made of soft rose fabric, with brown trim. "This should suit you very well, Mrs. Brown, better than it ever suited me, for it will show off your brown hair." She giggled. "Is that why Harry chose the name for you?"

"No, Brown really is my name." She took the dress from Anna, conscious of the effort the younger woman was making to please her, and Harry. "This really is lovely. Do you think it will fit me?"

"Oh yes. The hem is very generous. Mrs. Simpson, Mama's dressmaker, was quite certain I would continue to grow, since my sister Bella did until she was twenty. And you are much slimmer than I ever was. Do look, there is a pelisse to match, and we can easily trim a bonnet for you."

Anna's enthusiasm was boundless. Soon she had selected several gowns she thought would look well on Cassandra and put the others aside.

"For years I had to wear my sisters' old gowns, whether they suited me or not. I don't see any reason why you have to do the same."

"If you believe some of the books written about the Regency, you'd think that ladies had a new gown for every day." Cassandra commented.

"Only if you're incredibly rich, or a queen, I suppose. They say that Bonaparte wears a new silk shirt every day. I have the impression, Mrs. Brown—"

"Cassandra. Please call me Cassandra, since I am your cousin by marriage—or rather playing that role."

"Very well." Anna smiled. "I have the impression, Cassandra, that you think we who live now are like so many lead soldiers, all cast from the same mould. Surely, in your age those who are born to a particular station in life conduct themselves differently from those above and below them."

"You're absolutely right."

Anna was cleverer than Cassandra had originally imagined. She had been quick to notice how Cassandra made assumptions, yet she had little confidence in her own abilities.

"I read a couple of Jane Austen's novels in high school, and now that I think about it, the women didn't have *that* many gowns," Cassandra said.

"Oh, are Miss Austen's books still read in your day!" Anna exclaimed. "Edmund knew her brother well, and when I first met her, no one knew that she was an authoress. When we did find out, I was very surprised because she is so quiet and still and never puts herself forward, but then I remembered how quick her tongue is, so I decided it wasn't so extraordinary after all."

"Do you like her books?"

"No, I really do not care for them because they are so ordinary, and if any of her characters travels, they go only as far as the next county. If I traveled, I would like to go very far away. Edmund used to joke that when he was captain of his own vessel he would take me to China."

Anna pressed her lips together firmly, then said brightly, "Here, try this shawl." She held out a rich paisley wrap—rose, brown, blue, and gold mixed riotously. "I think it will cover nearly all the gowns we've put aside for you."

"No, I really can't accept this. It must be very valuable."

Poor fat Jos in *Vanity Fair* had given his mother and sister paisley shawls, and Cassandra remembered that everyone had remarked on their cost.

"Then I shall lend it to you, for as long as you stay with us. I have one very like it which Edmund gave me. Would you care to see it?"

Cassandra admired the shawl, and several other gifts the young groom had given his bride. Anna showed her the miniature she wore in a locket around her neck, and Cassandra was struck by a similarity between the features of the brothers. Edmund looked so young it was almost impossible to believe that he'd been a lieutenant. Cassandra found herself blinking back tears.

"I'm sorry, Anna. How old was he?"

"Almost twenty-four. He'd been a midshipman at fifteen and passed his lieutenancy examination when he was nineteen. He was posted to *The Indefatigable* as second lieutenant almost immediately. He said he loved the Navy, although I would have been proud of him no matter what he did. I'm sure that under any circumstance he would have been a gentleman."

"I'm sorry," Cassandra said again, feeling helpless. She remembered only too well the sickening sorrow she'd felt when her parents died, and how little it had mattered what people had said. Just their presence had helped. Those comforting words that time heals all pain were only half-true. In the years that followed, Cassandra had realized that one spent less and less time immersed in grief, but that when one remembered, the pain was as sharp as ever.

Anna closed the locket. "I wish I knew how he died. His captain sent a letter, but it was so cold and short." She withdrew a folded piece of paper from her writing desk, and showed it to Cassandra.

> Madam
> With the deepest regret, I must inform you of the death of Lieutenant Edmund Font, on the fourteenth instant. He will be remembered by all for his exemplary conduct and lively disposition.
> Yours, etc.
> Captain J. Matthews

Cassandra had to agree, it did seem very heartless. "Perhaps he had a great many letters to write," she suggested, hoping to give a little comfort.

"Captain Matthews might at least have let me know if he suffered greatly. There was, I learned from the newspapers, an engagement, and I have spoken to several of his friends, who believe he was wounded, but none of them had served on the same ship, and so I do not know for certain. It would mean so much, Cassandra, for me to know of his last days and hours. Still, I must be thankful for the time we had together, for I know that we almost always gave each other joy. Certainly, he never caused me a moment's sadness."

"I'm sure you made each other very happy," Cassandra said awkwardly.

Anna shook her head, and seemed about to speak when there was a scratching on the door and Augusta entered.

"Begging your pardon, ma'am, but there's a gentleman to see you. James told him you weren't receiving, but the gentleman said he was a member of the family—Mr. Arthur Font."

8

HARRY MARCHED SMARTLY through Manchester Square, then down to Oxford Street. He was irritated, not angry, he told himself—not even annoyed, but irritated—by Anna and that dratted Miss Brown. He had realized for some time that Anna saw him as a charity case. It was natural, given her odd notion that little Edmund must not succeed him to the title, that she would do her utmost to see that Lord Font married. Still, Harry had the uncomfortable notion that Anna felt that he possessed certain qualities that would make the task of finding him a wife more difficult than it might be for another man.

He understood better now how his cousin Celeste had felt when her mother insisted that she would never marry unless she changed her character—or appeared to do so at least—into one more pleasing to men and showed less resentment toward their natural superiority. In short, Anna seemed to feel that he needed to be made more presentable. Their conversation before luncheon had been rather uncomfortable. Anna had chatted gaily about her plans for introducing Harry to various young ladies, until he began to feel rather overwhelmed.

When she suggested a certain Miss Larchmont, pointing out that her sweet disposition would be ample compensation for her rather small fortune, Harry had decided to make a stand.

"My dear," he interjected firmly, "I understood the purpose of the campaign was to provide me with a lady who would in turn provide me with sons. You know, my dear, that I have nothing to offer a bride, save the promise of a title for her son. The mortgage against the income from the property in Devon will end in ten years. Frankly, I'd be in a much better position to wed then."

"Ten years, Harry! And how old will little Edmund be in ten years? Thirteen, old enough to be bitter at the loss of his prospects. I'm almost certain that I can find a respectable girl from a good family—and with a little money, too—even if her parents don't move in the highest circles."

"Well, since I am hardly on intimate terms with the Prince, I don't suppose her background will matter very much, but remember that life in the country can be very flat. This imaginary miss had better have inner resources as well as wealth, for there'll be no Seasons in London."

"But Brother Harry, you could always stay here."

That was the last thing Harry wanted. True, he was fond of Anna and his nephew, and he enjoyed their company. Mrs. Chubbs was tolerable. But he did not like the fact that when he visited Anna he was very much dependent on her. Rather than refuse Anna's offer outright, he returned to the main subject of their conversation.

"Be that as it may, the poor girl had better bring with her the means of raising a family, at least for the first few years. Find me a bride who likes dogs or sketching, something to fill her days, and we'll run along well enough, but if you don't think me ungrateful, perhaps this visit could be a scouting expedition, not a full-fledged campaign."

Anna, who was sewing the neckband of a shirt for her son, put down her work. "I am surprised, Harry. You sound as though 'out of sight, out of mind' is your maxim for taking a wife."

"Not at all, so pray don't scold me. I shall greet her every morning at breakfast, and at dinner on Sundays. On quarter days, when we go over the household bills, I shall engage her in lively conversation for a few minutes. Too much time in each other's company is the ruination of many a good match."

Anna took out her handkerchief. Edmund had spent less than five weeks of their marriage on land.

"I beg your pardon, my dear." Harry took her hand in his.

"No, no. It would be a sad life if one could not make a jest. Pray, do not speak of it again." She tucked her handkerchief into her sleeve. "But I shall not let you return home unwed."

"If you insist, Anna, but before you begin the search in earnest, I do have one request."

"Let me see if I can guess the sort of bride you wish? Blond, I expect, for gentlemen seem to favor a yellow head of hair, and—"

Harry raised a hand in protest, and Anna fell silent. "I did think, Anna, that perhaps a not-so-young lady, someone who has passed her twenty-first birthday, and will not have unrealistic expectations."

"Oh, Harry, don't concern yourself. I have already thought of all that. I know exactly what sort of man you are, what are your virtues, and your faults."

"My faults?" Harry asked unwisely.

"You do have some, you know, from a woman's point of view," Anna said matter-of-factly.

"You mean my scientific notions and impoverished estate."

"No, they would mean little to a woman who loved you. Everyone knows that you have little money, and all men have separate interests from their wives. I mean such things as your spectacles. You are very handsome without them, although you look more like your cousin Tom than Edmund."

"If I did not wear them, I doubt I could find any young ladies at all," Harry teased.

"Then there is the fact that you give lectures. You tuck your hands in your pockets and start explaining things. Of course, you are very careful not to bore people now, but as you grow older, it will become more of a habit," Anna said seriously.

"Oh really, Anna. That is hardly a hanging offence."

"You dance well," she offered.

"I thank you."

"But you tend to return your partner to her chaperone too quickly and find a man to talk to."

"Well, men say interesting things," Harry replied.

"So do women, if you let them. And you must be more dashing, Harry, show more verve. Be guided by me, Harry. You remember how careful Celeste was when she came out, and how completely she relied on her mama?"

Now, as Harry pushed through the crowd on Drury Lane and turned onto The Strand, he remembered only too well how Celeste had changed from being a tomboy into a little china doll. She had spent a decorous, miserable Season in London, and then returned home to marry a neighbours' son just as she had always said she would.

Harry didn't have an ace up his sleeve, as Celeste had. No girl was waiting for him at home. Anyway, their situations were quite different. He was a grown man, not a schoolroom miss who needed to be pushed and prodded into attracting a man's attention, then bullied and bated into keeping it. Sometimes Anna was too romantic for anyone's good.

And Cassandra had had the effrontery to accuse him of wanting to keep her here—as if he hadn't already recognized that some men might be tempted to do such a dastardly thing, lured by the storehouse of knowledge she offered. He'd already learnt so much from her. It would be difficult not to allude to the facts she had taught him. He would have to be ever vigilant. He wondered if she knew how difficult she made things for him.

Tom lived in lodgings in the Temple, and as Harry left Fleet Street and passed under the handsome arch built by Wren, he began to feel better. There was nothing worse for a man than to be trapped in a house full of silly females, he thought, forgetting that he'd spent the morning out and had passed hardly half an hour in conversation with each of the women that day.

Tom was not expecting him until much later, but he was a capital fellow, and no doubt would find some amusing way for them to occupy the afternoon.

Tom was still in bed when Harry arrived, but heard him talking to the servant, and shouted through the door for Miller to stop being a blasted fool, let Lord Font in, and bring hot water and breakfast. Miller ushered Harry into the room, which served as dining room and sitting room, and took himself off to procure some breakfast. Tom entered a moment later, coatless and in stockinged feet, his unbrushed hair sticking straight up.

He crushed Harry in a bear hug. "Want to watch me cut the old throat?" he asked, as nonchalantly as if he saw Harry every day, and went back into his bedroom.

Tom's idea of a well-furnished sleeping chamber held a bed long enough to accommodate his six-foot stature in comfort, a tripod table to hold a washbasin, and walls hung with sporting prints. Harry brought in a straight chair from the living room while his cousin worked up a lather.

"Why do you still live as if you were on campaign, Tom?"

"Don't. Shaved the old mustachios the day I resigned my commission in the Royals."

"I mean your rooms."

"Didn't have rooms. Lived in a tent."

"Well, your bedroom looks like a tent. Don't you ever have a fire?"

"Can't hang pictures on a tent, Harry. No walls." He gestured with his open razor to a print of hounds streaming through a gap in a hedge while horses and riders leapt over them. "Like that one? Engraved by Howett. Think he used to be a coachman, most of these painting fellows are."

"It's very pretty." Harry gave the print a cursory glance. "Tom, what was it like?"

"What was what like?" Tom asked, and promptly splashed water on his face.

Harry did not take the hint. "The war. Being a soldier." Anna's words about virility still rang in his ears.

"Lot of fun, really. All those French madamozelles. Lots of wine. Did I tell you about the time we had a race through the Louvre? We were riding in relays and old Bentinck—"

"That's not really what I meant."

"All right, tell you about the Iron Duke and the men's pigtails. The First Dragons had always had them. Wellington didn't like them above half. Had his way in the end, but when he first said they were to be cut off, Captain—"

"Damn it, Tom! I'm not little Edmund, I don't want to hear funny stories."

"Then stop thinking like him, and use your imagination. What do you think it was like?" Tom flung his towel on the floor and savagely snatched a coat off a hook.

"I'm sorry," Harry began, for he could tell that Tom was more hurt than angry.

He didn't understand why Tom couldn't share some of the horror with him. He knew that war was not the long game of wagers his cousin pretended it was. Edmund, whom Harry freely acknowledged to be a brave man, had been more than willing to tell his brother about his experiences and had claimed that doing so helped him put them behind him. Harry would have liked to offer a sympathetic ear to his cousin. He was certain that Tom spent his days boxing and practising swordplay and his nights in such pastimes as laying odds on who could leap over the most chairs with his cronies from the army in an effort to avoid memories of slaughter and suffering.

"Don't mention it. Can you smell those pies? Old Miller must have gone to the cookshop, bless him."

Harry enjoyed a second nuncheon of pigeon pie and small beer, while Tom broke his fast on the same.

"Thought I might go to Tattersall's," Tom informed him. "Delighted if you'd join me."

"My pleasure. Buying a horse?" Harry grinned. It didn't take long in Tom's company before one began to speak in the most shocking fashion.

"Looking. Still happy with Hector and Achilles."

"However did you acquire a matched pair named after mortal enemies?"

"Didn't. Already had Hector, you know. Saw the other when I went to visit old Smith, matched Hector's paces exactly. So I bought the old charger—Smith called him Alligator—and a week later he went lame. Make a long story short—don't want to hear about heroic days and nights in the stable with bran mash, do you?—didn't think so—well, cured him, named him Achilles after his heel, and unless some silly fool takes it into his head to tell the beasts that one's a Trojan and the other's a Greek, I don't expect any trouble. You know, last month I was going to race old Bentinck from Land's End to John O'Groats. Might have won, too, but we both upset ten miles into it, never did set a rematch. Can't say I'm sad, though, bit hard on the horses."

"If anyone knew that you were soft on your beasts, Tom, you'd be the laughingstock of all your friends."

"You won't tell them. I still have that electrical generator—let's have a few friends up for a shocking party tonight. I'll just tell Miller to get in a case of champagne and something for us to eat, and we'll be off."

They spent the afternoon admiring horseflesh. Tom, who seemed to know every half-pay officer in London, invited nearly fifty young men to stop by his rooms for a shocking experience that evening. Those who knew Harry laughed. When the others asked what this experience might be, Tom just smiled and said, "No ladies, that's all I ask, no females," and refused to say more on the subject.

"Can't be too careful," he explained in an aside to Harry. "Don't want any of them bringing their lightskirts. Spend the whole evening looking after fainting damsels, and we'll want to go out afterwards, to Boodles."

"You might be able to game at your club all night Tom, but I'm an old man."

"If I'm going to be old in five years, I'll live all I can now."

Tom's arrangements for meals tended to be impromptu, and Harry was not surprised to learn that he had made no plans for dinner. As it was, they joined three officers from Tom's old regiment at a coaching inn for a meal of porter and steak.

One of the men was getting married in a fortnight. They solemnly drank his health and insisted that these were his last weeks of happiness. They played cards for half crowns until eight when Tom decided it was time to get ready for his party and called for his phaeton.

"Don't worry that you're not dressed," he told Harry, apparently noticing for the first time that Harry was not in evening clothes.

"I don't think I've ever gone anywhere with you that I'd want to dress for, Tom. I wasn't about to carry my glad rags across London on the off chance you would take me to the opera."

"Heaven forfend," said Tom piously. "So what do you think about old Pilkington getting leg-shackled? Never thought he'd step into the parson's trap."

"Everyone does sooner or later."

"Think you will?"

"If Anna has her way."

"Oh, Anna. She was so happy with Ed, you know. Shame she's built a shrine to the old boy—not that he wasn't worth a hundred."

"I've often thought, Tom, that the only way to persuade her to marry would be to convince her that Edmund would have wanted it, but she's given so many people the impression that she'll never have a second husband, even that course might prove too difficult."

"Wouldn't be too sure of that. If she does make up her mind to marry again, she'll be stubborn. Remember, she decided she'd marry Edmund before *The Indefatigable* sailed, and she did, although it wasn't five weeks after she met him."

"I remember. Damn it, Tom, I remember."

"Had thought of her myself, but I was nineteen then, couldn't see myself taking on a wife—thought I'd look her up in a year or two—came home, and found she was taken."

"You're not the only one."

"Carrying a torch?" Tom stared over the horses' backs, but Harry heard the concern in his voice. "No, I'm not wearing the willow for Anna. That would be rich. What a fool I'd be!"

The horses stumbled.

"Lord, Tom. What a fool I am. But you didn't really expect to come back and find Anna waiting for you."

"No, I'd forgotten her, really. I was terribly in love with her for a few weeks, and then the whole thing faded, as it does when you're young. But when I came home, I met her again. You know what the family's like, we live in each other's pockets. Everywhere I went I'd see her and the little boy—look sharp, Harry, we're here! Hop down and go inside. I'll take the horses around to the mews myself."

There were already half a dozen of Tom's friends waiting in his rooms. The sideboard was covered with glasses and champagne bottles, and as Harry entered Miller was carving roast fowl.

The generator stood in the place of honour on the dining-room table. When Tom asked Harry to make him one several months ago, Harry had known exactly what his cousin wanted it for, and so made a small and very sturdy machine that, even when fully charged, gave only a mild shock. While travelling on the continent, Harry had heard stories of people being killed playing games with electricity, and he had no wish to see Tom make such a mistake.

Over the next couple of hours young men arrived in various states of drunkenness, drank a glass or two of champagne, took a turn cranking the generator, and placed bets as to what would or would not conduct electricity. Champagne, Harry was not surprised to learn, conducted the spark excellently. As the hour grew later, the room became noisier. At eleven, Harry decided to leave and found Tom sitting in a corner quietly listening to a tipsy young man explain how he'd been trapped in a burning farmhouse outside Brussels. Tom excused himself to see Harry out, promising to return.

"Shall I send Miller to find you a pair of catch farts?" Tom offered.

"No, I'd rather walk than have a chair thank you."

"I'll come to the corner with you, then. I want to clear my head. Poor old Will."

"The young man who was talking to you?"

"He'll be all right. Funny thing, seems that anyone who is caught in a fire needs to talk about it. He'll tell you over and over again what it was like. Use the same words even, and then he'll never mention it again. It's as though talking cures the horror."

"Tom, do you ever talk to anyone?"

"Why should I? Never been in a burning house in my life. Keep an eye out for footpads, my lad, and my respects to Anna."

Harry walked slowly home, turning north to avoid the crush of carriages gathered around a house where a ball or rout was being held, and wandering past a row of half-demolished buildings that were being removed for the making of Regent's Street. At the rate the buildings were coming down, it seemed the street would never be finished.

So, Tom had fallen in love with Anna. When he'd first realized it, Harry had been less than pleased, for Tom hardly seemed the sort of man who'd make a satisfactory husband. But just now, after seeing his willingness to listen to another man's fears, even though Tom would have died rather than admit to having any himself, Harry wondered if there was more to his cousin than met the eye.

It had always seemed foolish that Anna refused even to consider the possibility of marrying again, but Harry had little idea how to change her mind. Nonetheless, if he could sound Tom out a bit more, and if Tom were as solid as Harry hoped . . .

Harry laughed out loud. Anna might have made him feel like a debutante being launched into society, but here he was thinking like a matchmaking mama.

9

"Mr. Arthur Font? Are you certain, Augusta?"

"Yes, ma'am. Should I ask James to bring his card upstairs to you?"

"No, of course not. I hope you're not being pert, Augusta."

"No, ma'am." The maid curtsied.

Anna turned to Cassandra. "What should I do? I do wish Harry was here."

"If you don't want to see him, I'll tell him to go away."

"No, you cannot do that. I could ask James to tell him that I will not receive him, but although Edmund's father and Arthur's father were . . . not on good terms, we've never snubbed them. In fact, we invited Arthur to our wedding. The late Lord Font insisted that the estrangement wasn't Arthur's fault. I must receive him, or if he's anything like his father, he will spread the story in no time. Oh, do come downstairs with me, dear Cassandra. Maybe he won't stay long."

Cassandra was about to point out that Anna didn't have to do anything she didn't want to do, but Anna had already left the room. Cassandra caught up with her on the stairs. Augusta had hurried ahead to open the door for them. As they passed her, Anna murmured, "That will be all, thank you." Cassandra expected that the maid would be polishing the keyhole if the footman didn't beat her to it.

A very elegant gentleman—for all Cassandra knew he might be a dandy—stood before the fire, looking intently at the china figurines on the mantelpiece. His pale breeches fit like a second skin. His boots shone as if they had been varnished. He wore a blue coat which bore all the marks of expert tailoring, and a yellow-and-blue-striped waistcoat. His collar was the highest Cassandra had yet seen, although she was willing to admit that her experience was limited. And his cravat, or cravats—for it seemed to Cassandra that he had a black one and a white one wrapped around his neck—really did look as if they had taken an hour to tie. But when he made his bow, it was not as elegant as one of Harry's.

"Mrs. Font, I beg you, forgive this intrusion, but I hoped, indeed, I must rely upon our family connection. I trust that you can receive me now."

"Good afternoon, Mr. Font. I have a few moments. Mrs. Brown, allow me to present Mr. Font. Mrs. Brown is a cousin by marriage and is recently arrived from Boston in Massachusetts."

"I am delighted, Mrs. Brown. Had I known that the American shores boasted such beautiful ladies, I would have ventured there long ago."

I bet you would have, Cassandra thought, and offered him two fingers, as she imagined Lady Catherine de Bourgh might have.

Anna sat on the sofa and gestured for Cassandra to join her. "Pray be seated, Mr. Font."

"You will forgive me, ma'am, if I come directly to the point, although I must say that this matter concerns your late husband's father. Indeed, I took the liberty of ascertaining from your servant that you were not engaged, for I wished to speak to you alone."

"I am sure, Mr. Font, that you can say nothing about Mr. Edmund Font, nor any member of his family, that I would be ashamed to have another hear."

"I wish I could say the same about my own relatives. However, I rely on your assurance that we may trust the charming Mrs. Brown."

Cassandra wondered how he could defend either of his assertions, since Anna had said nothing about her discretion, and she herself had done nothing that could be considered charming.

"Then I shall come directly to the point—I trust Mrs. Chubbs and your delightful son are well."

"Yes, thank you. And your own family?"

"My mother is well. But my father, my father is not well at all; indeed, this may be his last illness." Arthur Font paused. "I trust I do not distress you, ma'am."

"I am sorry to hear that Mr. Font is not well," said Anna, her puzzlement clear in her voice. "Is there anything that you wish us to do on his behalf?"

Cassandra fully expected him to ask for money, but instead he said, "If I could ask you to intercede with Lord Font. As you know, my father's behavior . . . Perhaps you are aware that at the time of your husband's birth . . ."

"Yes, Mr. Font, I believe I understand you."

"He has always been an excellent father and husband, and his many friends speak highly of him. I know that my own actions at that time were reprehensible. Indeed, I'm told I made rather a cake of myself." He gave a nervous laugh, but broke off when he saw that neither lady was even smiling.

"I beg your pardon. I meant merely to say that it is difficult to judge the actions of one's parent, but my father hopes to completely heal the breach that he created."

"I am sure that Lord Font would not hold a grudge unjustly, but I am in no position to speak for him."

"Dear lady, I would not ask it of you. But I know well how a word from a beloved sister can soften a man's heart. While my father's uncle lived, it seemed there was no hope of a reconciliation. My father is well aware that there are some actions for which no apology will suffice, but now, he is an old man, Mrs. Font, and very ill. . . ."

"Of course I will speak to my brother-in-law."

"Then I shall detain you no longer." He stood.

When Anna rang for James to show the visitor out, Arthur Font turned to Cassandra, who had remained seated. She wished now that she had stood, for she hated to have people towering over her, but she was not going to leap to her feet simply because this man was about to speak to her.

"I feel quite confident, Mrs. Brown, that our fair peacemaker will succeed, do you not agree?"

"I really can't predict."

"Perhaps that is wise, madam, although I am certain that I would take any word which passed your lips as a true oracle. Good day." He made another bow, then took his leave of Anna, thanking her profusely for her valued assistance.

"Well," said Anna, sinking into an armchair. "He was not at all what I expected. The poor man. It is so difficult to lose a parent. And how touching that old Mr. Font wants to make up the quarrel. Aunt Seppie tells me it was such a scandal at the time, but if he is genuinely repentant, it is wonderful. I wonder if Harry should go and see him."

"Didn't you find him a bit slick?"

"How so?"

"Well, he was very effusive."

"Some gentlemen are."

"Not just that. Did you hear what he said to me?"

"I didn't pay particular attention. It sounded like a harmless compliment. I do hope he wasn't rude."

"He made an allusion to my name. The mythological Cassandra struck a bargain with Apollo. If he gave her the ability to foresee the future, she would sl—grant him her favours, so he did. But she reneged, and to get even, he fixed things so that no one would believe her. When I said I couldn't predict whether or not you'd get Harry to forgive old Mr. Font, Arthur said something about regarding anything I said as the truth. But, Anna, you introduced me as Mrs. Brown, and you never mentioned my first name, did you?"

"It could be a coincidence, or maybe someone told him your name. Don't worry, my dear, I am sure he is a gentleman."

Cassandra recognized the faintly patronizing tone of a married lady advising her younger, unwed friend, and decided not to press the matter.

Anna went to sit with her son while he ate his supper. Cassandra stayed downstairs, warming herself by the fire. It soon grew dark, and James came in to light the candles for her.

"May I ask you something, James?" she said impulsively.

"Yes, ma'am."

He came to stand nervously before her. He was a short man, in his late thirties, and already balding. Cassandra knew that three fingers on his right hand were badly crushed, but his white gloves hid the deformity.

"Did you let Mr. Font into the house?"

"Yes, ma'am."

"What did he say?"

"He asked for Mrs. Font."

"Anything else?"

"Then he asked if she had any callers, and I said no, but that she wasn't at home. Then he said that he was Mrs. Font's cousin. I only bin at the house two months, and there's a powerful lot of cousins, so I went to ask Mrs. Tate."

"Who is Mrs. Tate?"

"Mrs. Font's maid, Augusta."

"Thanks, *thank* you, James."

He didn't move.

"Yes?"

"Is something wrong, ma'am?"

Cassandra was in a quandary. If she said no, she would look like the worst sort of gossip and snoop, but if she said yes . . .

"I don't know, James. I didn't like the look of Mr. Font, but obviously he hasn't done anything wrong. I know that

I ought not to have been asking you awkward questions, though. May I ask you not tell anyone about my silly notion?"

"Of course, ma'am." His expression was impossible to read.

Dinner was a somewhat dreary affair. There they sat, Mrs. Chubbs, Mrs. Font, and Mrs. Brown, while James served soup, and fish, and beef and vegetables. Mrs. Chubbs read aloud a letter from her eldest daughter, then explained at length to Cassandra why she couldn't go and visit her, even though both she and Margaret longed for a visit, and Anna kept saying plaintively, "But Mama, I have Edmund to keep me company, I would not miss you for a few weeks, and Margaret would dearly love to see you."

They ate their blancmange in the drawing room and then Anna played the old spinnet, and Mrs. Chubbs told Cassandra all about Mr. Chubbs' last illness. Then Cassandra, calling upon half-remembered piano lessons, played "The Merry Peasant" and "The Minute Waltz" while Mrs. Chubbs loudly whispered that Anna was a fool to give her gowns away and that she should stop playing at being a ghost, go into colors, and marry again while she was about it. At half past nine Anna announced that it had been a long day, and they all must be tired, so they went to bed.

Cassandra lay shivering between icy sheets. One of the maids had run a warming pan between them, and there was a hot brick for her feet. She was wearing her stockings and a long nightdress lent to her by Anna, and was wrapped in the borrowed paisley shawl, but she was still freezing.

She had no qualms about letting Anna give her the dresses. It was a positive step in overcoming Anna's grief for her husband. And any sign of independence that Anna showed was, in Cassandra's mind, to be encouraged—even if it did lead to her marrying Harry. And what would be wrong with that? Unless, of course, that tiresome business of Edmund and the title would create a complication.

Harry was an infuriating man. Consider the way he'd stormed out of the house, and was no doubt in some gaming hell doing whatever Regency bucks did there, while she lay in a cold bed after an evening dismal enough to give anyone indigestion. She dreamt that night that she was back in the Center, dressed incongruously in her old sweats and a mink stole, feeding data into the computer and getting the same error message over and over again: HARRY FONT/NO FILE.

In the morning there was a warm fire and a cup of tea in bed and, after breakfast, several quiet hours to work on the calculations. Cassandra was finding it the most frustrating work she'd ever done. If she had access to a mainframe computer, it would have taken her only a few days to write a program to do the work. If the program had already been written, she could do it in minutes. Instead, here she sat with every step clearly written out before she started, punching number after number into the little calculator, painstakingly setting up each differential equation and checking everything three times, while Harry worked independently on the same material. Only when their answers agreed did they go on to the next step. Cassandra was devoutly grateful that she had the calculator. The thought of doing this work with a slide rule made her feel positively ill.

At ten o'clock she went to the nursery. This time Mrs. Chubbs stayed away. At noon Anna collected Edmund for his daily visit to the ducks and told Cassandra that Harry was in the sitting room. "He asks that you join him there."

Cassandra's first reaction was that Harry shouldn't use Anna to run his errands and that he might have come to her instead of sending for her, but upon reflection she decided that he might be giving her a chance to avoid seeing him if she was still angry with him. So she went directly down to him.

"That's a very pretty shawl," he said as soon as he had greeted her.

"Thank you. Anna lent it to me."

"It's not the one Edmund sent her?"

"No. You know that she's given me a lot of her clothes? One of the maids is altering them."

"So she said. Cassandra, I know that you think I'm not doing my share of the calculations, and I promise that I'll do my bit tonight, but will you pay a call with me this afternoon? Today is my cousin Tom's day for looking in on Aunt Seppie and Aunt Tavie, and I'd particularly like you to meet him."

"Why?"

"I'd like a woman's view on him, that's all."

"Ask Anna."

"I rely on your judgement. Any man who can pass the exacting standards of the future must be sound."

Since Harry wouldn't tell her why he wanted her opinion, wild horses wouldn't have kept Cassandra away. If there was any kind of mystery, she wanted to get to the bottom of it, but she merely said, "On one condition."

"Name it, madam."

"Tell me why your aunts are called Seppie and Tavie."

"They were christened Septima and Octavia. When my grandfather was presented with female twins after six daughters, he didn't take much interest in naming them."

Anna was delighted at the prospect of Cassandra meeting the family. She obviously found it very difficult to accept the idea that Cassandra came from the future, and preferred the fiction that Cassandra was a visiting cousin. To tell the truth, at times Cassandra would have preferred to believe it herself.

The alterations on one of the dresses, a royal blue gown, were finished in time for her to wear it to go visiting. Augusta had started work the night before, and Cassandra had been concerned that she had sat up all night with it, but Anna assured her it had taken only a few hours' work. Cassandra, who could only just manage to sew on a button, considered it a minor miracle that anyone could make a garment without a paper pattern and a sewing machine. Anna had tried to explain to her that the alterations were just a matter of letting down the hem and putting in a few darts, which somehow avoided something mysteriously called "setting the sleeves in anew," but Cassandra was still in awe of the whole process.

Anna, Cassandra, Edmund, and Harry drove to the aunts' house in the chaise. The sisters, both widows, lived in a small Georgian house. As soon as Cassandra entered the hall, it was obvious to her that two women with very different tastes resided there. On one side of the hall hung a tapestry showing a deer cornered by several hounds—on the other, an oil painting, in the style of Sir Joshua Reynolds, of a large number of children.

The drawing room was full of women and their children, with a scattering of men. Edmund, after he had made his bow and been kissed by his great aunts, went to play with two little girls who were arranging dominoes under a table.

Cassandra was introduced, and installed in the place of honor, on the sopha between the two old ladies. She could not tell if they were identical or fraternal twins, for whatever attributes nature had given them, each had wrought her own changes. Octavia, Lady Bestor, known in the family as Aunt Tavie, was bent over, twisted so that one shoulder was noticeably higher than the other. She had a sharp face and wore a full, red gown trimmed with gold braid, which contrasted sharply with her plain cap. Her sister, Mrs. Clutterbuck, was taller, or at least not as bent. Her full, round face smiled under her ornate cap, and her plump hands were busy as she embroidered a baby's smock.

"Do you ride to hounds?" asked Aunt Tavie.
"No, Lady Bestor."
"Do you have any children?" asked Aunt Seppie.
"No, Mrs. Clutterbuck."
"I did, until I was sixty. There used to be good hunting

around Font Hall." Aunt Tavie persisted in her own conversation.

"Don't bore Mrs. Brown, sister." Aunt Seppie paused for half a breath. "I expect you noticed the portrait of my grandchildren in the hall. They are all grown now and have children of their own."

She launched into a list of names, and Cassandra half listened, paying more attention to the tumult around her. The room was noisy and rather warm, both from the large fire and from the number of people in it. Anna was sitting with a woman her own age, so carefully wrapped in a shawl that it took Cassandra a few moments to realize that she was pregnant. Harry was listening attentively to an old gentleman, nodding politely. Suddenly they both burst into laughter, and the old man slapped Harry on the back, nearly knocking his glasses off.

The talk all seemed to be about various members of the family, no more interesting than the genealogy that Aunt Seppie was pouring into Cassandra's ear.

"And now I shall show you something, Mrs. Brown, our coat of arms. Eliza, my dear, unlock that little desk, please, and bring me the large envelope inside it."

The coat of arms proved to be a shield that was quartered so many times that Cassandra could hardly make out any of the emblems. The helmet drawn above would never have fit on any knight's head. Aunt Seppie was off again, explaining how various heraldic heiresses had added their fathers' coats of arms to the mess.

Cassandra caught Harry's eye and mouthed "Tom?"

Harry made a reply that could have been, "He's not here yet."

Cassandra admired the achievement of arms. It was returned to its proper place, and Aunt Seppie gave Cassandra a chance to explain that she didn't have any brothers and sisters.

"It is a shame that you have no children, Mrs. Brown, for it is a woman's calling. Indeed, I say a woman is not a woman until she is surrounded by her family. Don't you agree?"

"I think a person can do other things of worth."

"Oh no, Mrs. Brown. A man, of course, may do many things, but all a woman's accomplishments are for naught if she has not fulfilled her natural role." She glanced slyly at her sister. "Even a childless woman will find someone to mother."

"Would you say that a man had wasted his life if he had no children?"

"It would be very sad, but not wasted as a woman's would be."

"I'm afraid I cannot agree with you, Mrs. Clutterbuck. I think that a woman's worth has nothing to do with the children she might or might not have, and depends on her own—actions." Cassandra had nearly said career.

Aunt Seppie sighed. "Look how happy Anna is with her son, and how lonely she would be without him. Lucinda—she is Alice's second child, remember—is expecting her first babe in March. She is radiant. You will understand one day, God willing—" She broke off as the door opened and looked to see who the new visitor was. "Oh, it's only Tom."

Aunt Tavie was struggling to her feet. "Lend me your arm, Mrs. Brown, if you please," she asked, shaking away the young men who offered help, and hobbled across to embrace the man who had just entered wearing a multi-caped coat. "You look like a coachman, Tommy," she announced delightedly.

"I know, Aunt. I'm just going to kiss Aunt Seppie, and then, if you like, we could go for a drive."

"You've never brought your phaeton?"

"Never, for you'd persuade me to let you handle the ribbons, and then create a scandal by racing every young blood in the park. I've borrowed Uncle Guy's rig, since it's a mild day."

Tom made his way across the room. Harry hurried over

to Aunt Tavie and said something to her in a low voice. "Very well," she said. "Mrs. Brown, you are to come with me." She took Cassandra's arm again, more as a means of dragging her from the room than for support.

A maid brought a large, fur-lined cape with a hood. "Russian wolf," said Aunt Tavie, and gave Cassandra a wicked smile. "Given to me by a grand duke."

"Indeed?"

"Indeed."

Uncle Guy's rig proved to be a low carriage, with a seat for the driver and one behind for passengers. Tom lifted his aunt into the vehicle, despite her protest that she wasn't crippled, then handed Cassandra in and carefully tucked rugs around both of them.

"Do you have your gloves, Aunt?" he asked.

"Do I have my gloves? God's blood, boy, you sound like a governess. Drive on."

Tom let the horses go.

"Ought to make you known to Mrs. Brown. Mrs. Brown, this is your cousin Thomas Font. Tom, your cousin Cassandra Brown. Ask Seppie how the pair of you are related. And while we're on the subject of Seppie, that achievement of arms isn't worth the paper it's painted on. The Fonts have the right to a shield, half-blue, half-silver. Don't know the fancy names for the colours and don't want to, though we have a fine motto: Ever Loyal. Seppie made the rest up out of whole cloth to amuse her old age."

Cassandra found the ride most diverting. Aunt Tavie might be in her eighties, but her eyes were as sharp as ever. She looked out for horseflesh and the male form, and criticised them loudly. Both, she assured Cassandra, had diminished in quality since her young days.

"That's why I like young men like Tom. Bruisers, they call them, or Corinthians. Men, I call them. So what if they are a bit rough at the edges? Tom, tell Mrs. Brown about Hector and Achilles."

"That old story, Aunt, I scarcely remember it."

"Oh yes, you do, you were visiting your friend Mr. Smith."

With much prompting, and digressions into the breeding of each animal, Tom told her the story. Cassandra responded with a carefully edited story of one of Will's pranks, which sent Aunt Tavie into a fit of laughter.

Once they were in the park, Tom stopped, and carefully moved Aunt Tavie onto the box. As soon as he was settled beside her, she took up the reins.

"My legs may be worn out, but there's nothing wrong with my hands," she called tartly to Cassandra. "But don't mention this to my sister, Mrs. Brown, or I shall call you out."

"I wouldn't dream of it, Lady Bestor."

Cassandra's experience of being driven was limited, but she thought that the old lady did an excellent job. She could pass another vehicle with exactly six inches clearance.

"See those young bloods harassing that poor girl." Aunt Tavie pointed to a very high carriage driven very slowly by a young man whose companion leant over the side firmly clutching the brim of a girl's bonnet. She looked no more than fourteen, and a boy younger than she walked next to her, crying in a high voice, "Please sir, let my sister alone!"

"I'll bump his wheels!"

"Careful, the way that lout's tipped, you'll have them over," Tom cried.

"Nonsense, it's too poorly balanced for that. If it were properly made, he'd have turned it himself." She whipped up the horses and they cantered smartly by, brushing the wheels of the phaeton. "Pigs!" yelled Aunt Tavie at the top of her lungs. "And you've got hands like lead."

As the phaeton lurched, the driver nearly dropped the reins and the carriage rocked perilously. His friend let go of the girl's bonnet and grabbed the reins out of his hands. The horses stopped and the young men nearly fell off their perch. They both lost their hats.

Aunt Tavie slowed the horses and turned them neatly to

stop before the young brother and sister. "You, sir, be so good as to hold the horses."

The boy stepped forward, "Th-thank you, madam," he stuttered.

"God's teeth, don't loll about, Tom, help me down, and hand the young lady in."

As soon as Aunt Tavie was settled, she ordered the boy to take his seat next to Tom. "Give your direction to my nephew, and we shall set you down near your home."

"Ought to speak to their parents," objected Tom. "Tell them not to let the young ones out alone."

"You don't have the sense God gave a goose. They escaped from the schoolroom and were having an adventure, I'll be bound. Don't worry, children, I have better things to do with my time than run to your mama with tales."

"Thank you," the girl murmured, her words coming out in a rush. "Thank you for everything."

"Well, don't start crying, or you'll have some explaining to do at home. And the next time someone tries a trick like that, miss, bend his little finger back."

Before they reached her house, Aunt Tavie had fallen asleep with her head on Cassandra's shoulder.

10

THE NEXT MORNING Cassandra took her breakfast in Anna's room. Anna sat propped up in bed, wearing a charming silk dressing gown, sipping hot chocolate, and nibbling a biscuit. Cassandra, dressed in her made-over blue gown, was by her side in an armchair, almost inhaling her coffee and eating scrambled eggs on toast.

"We shall go to the shoemakers today, for you need boots. You cannot wear those slippers all winter."

"But I won't be here all winter. Just a few more weeks, at most."

Anna frowned. "Yes, I suppose Harry will return you to your own time eventually, but while you remain, you need boots for winter, and I would like to make you a gift."

"I don't think I need any, thank you."

"You'll want another pair of slippers for evening, for I want to see Eliza O'Neille. They say that as a tragedienne she rivals Mrs. Simpson. Mrs. Eliot vows she was moved to tears—"

Anna seemed happy to prattle on, with the transparent object of distracting Cassandra from the subject of who would buy her shoes. Cassandra was certain that Anna had no intention of going to the theatre.

Cassandra interrupted without a qualm. "Anna, I can't afford—"

"I shall take it out of your wages."

"I don't even know what my wages are."

"I haven't decided yet. Please, Cassandra, the weather won't stay dry forever."

Cassandra wanted to settle the matter of her wages and was trying to formulate a sentence to that effect, when Augusta entered, peering around two bunches of hothouse flowers.

"Oh, orchids!" cried Anna. "But whoever would send us flowers?"

Augusta handed her mistress a card.

"Mr. Font. Arthur Font. Thank you, Augusta, please put them in water and come back directly, for I want to get up."

Augusta left and Anna set down her chocolate cup and toyed with the card. "How very kind of him to remember both of us. I noticed when he took his leave that Mr. Font did not provide any direction, but now we have his visiting card. I must speak to Harry. It is a very urgent matter, and Mr. Font called the day before yesterday. Yet how to broach the subject. Cassandra, my dear . . ."

"Anna, I really don't think it is my place to interfere. This is family business."

"If you would just mention the visit to him, then I could explain. It is getting started that I find so difficult. I would baldly say, 'Your cousin Arthur called on me.'"

"Well, that's exactly what I would say, Anna, so I can't be much help. I'll leave you now, though, so you can get dressed."

"Coward," Anna said, laughing, then sobered. "Oh dear, I ought not to make merry while a man lies dying."

Anna had her way in one thing that morning. After Edmund's lessons, Cassandra went on the duck-feeding expedition. She was introduced to seven ducks, with such names as Emperor Quack and Ping-Ping, and was chucked under the chin by Mr. Sprightly. As he was only in his fifties, she rather took exception to that. As soon as the last crust had been cast upon the waters, they went to the shoemakers, and Cassandra was measured for both the boots and the slippers.

Cassandra thought that since Anna had prevailed in the matter of the shoes, she would capitulate in the matter of Mr. Font's request, but after nuncheon, Anna neatly trapped both Harry and her in the sitting room and blithely announced, "Your cousin, Mr. Arthur Font, called upon me."

"Whatever for?"

"Oh, Harry, I thought you would be cross."

"Why? *You* didn't call upon *him*. Did you show him the door?"

"No, I received him—Cassandra was with me. I didn't want to snub him, Harry; he told me the sorriest tale."

"I hope you didn't give him money." His voice was very bland.

"Harry!"

"Anna." Harry smiled. "You *do* give money to anyone who tells you a sad story."

"Be serious. Mr. Charles Font is dying, and he wishes to make his peace with the family. The younger Mr. Font asked me to intercede with you."

"Did he indeed? The scoundrel can do his own dirty work. Did he leave you his direction?"

"I have it here, Harry, please do not be cross."

"I'm not cross with you, Anna, only with him. You ought not to be bothered with such things. I shall write to him at once, and tell him so."

"But what about old Mr. Font?"

"I shall take that up with his son." There was a tone of finality in his voice, and while Cassandra might have challenged it, Anna merely said, "Yes, Brother Harry," and left the room.

Harry rang for paper and ink. "Are *you* going to start on me, Cassie?"

"My name, sir, is Cassandra, and no, I'm not about to start on you. It's your family."

"Good. I'll send Job round with the letter, and then we'll go out. What would you like to see?"

"What about the Tower of London? I've never seen that. Not even at home."

"Tom's promised to take Edmund to see the bears, so we'll all be visiting the Tower soon." He balled up the sheet of paper he'd been writing on and threw it onto the fire.

Cassandra tried to think of another landmark old enough to have been standing in 1815. Her taste in sight-seeing had always run to observatories and museums, but she had seen the British Museum in her own time and wasn't even certain if it was open to the public now.

"Westminster Abbey?" she suggested. It had been built in 1050, so it was certainly old enough for them to visit, but she had no idea whether it was considered a suitable attraction for a lady to see.

"Excellent." He fingered his quill for a moment, then dashed off a couple of lines. "There, now James can get us a hackney and we'll be off."

The hackney was cold and poorly sprung, but Cassandra made no objection since Harry obviously didn't like having to depend on Anna letting him use her chaise all the time. Cassandra wondered if he realized that in many ways he and Anna reversed the traditional roles of men and women, for Anna's relative wealth and the fact that he was living in her house gave her a certain power. Perhaps he was looking forward to the change which would follow their marriage.

"Now I shall be your courier," Harry announced, interrupting her reflections. "Did you know that Westminster Abbey was built on an island?"

Cassandra kept a straight face, waiting for the punch line.

"No, really, it was built on Thorney Isle. Have you heard of London's lost rivers? There are about a dozen. Fleet Street is named for one, and Walbrook, although that is a dead river."

"How were they lost?"

"At first they were piped into reservoirs. I believe Tyburn Conduit is the first example of this. Queen Caroline had the Westbourne dammed up to form the Serpentine. There used to be a number of deep-water ports where these rivers met the Thames. And you'll find that trades such as tanners and brewers, those which need water in large supply, line the streets where the old rivers ran, now that the rivers have been diverted through pipes or built over. There used to be any number of grist mills, or so the antiquarians say. I understand that Westminster Abbey owned one which made use of the flow of the tide."

When they entered the Abbey, several scholars from the Westminster School offered their services as guides. Harry agreed to pay one of them as long as he didn't tell any whoppers.

"The present Abbey took nearly four hundred years to build, it was started in 1269," the boy informed them.

"True enough," Harry said.

"The first church on this site was built in A.D. 616, by the first bishop of London."

Harry considered. "Doubtful, but I'll accept it."

"And over there," he said, pointing to the elaborate tomb of Edward II, "is the very spot where King Edward confessed everything and expired."

Harry shook his head and tipped the boy before sending him on his way. "You have to go through the motions," he told Cassandra, "or they mob you like starlings. Let's go to the Chapter House; I want to show you something. The murals of the Book of Revelation. They say that Newton loved to look at them."

As they rode home in silence, Cassandra realized how little she missed modern life. For many years, she'd concentrated solely on her work, and she did miss that. But she had no close friends. It was, she knew, a subconscious result of losing both parents suddenly—a desire to make herself invulnerable to bereavement by the simple device of not caring enough about anyone to miss them if they suddenly vanished from her life. Yet in less than a month, she had become attached to Harry and Anna. Putting the matter firmly out of her mind, she looked out of the small window and commented on the first thing she noticed.

"You know, Harry, there are an awful lot of homeless people here." She was looking at a group of men lounging against a wall. They were literally dressed in rags. Several even had rags wrapped around their feet—and they passed a bottle among themselves.

"Discharged soldiers or sailors, most likely."

Cassandra was about to make a scathing comment, when she remembered that in her own time disabled veterans begged on the subways and runaway children slept on the streets.

"There are various relief committees," Harry said, "and Tom told me about a scheme to settle some men with families on plots of land in Canada. I tried to persuade him to serve on one of the committees, but he said something about being more of a hindrance than a help. Cassandra, what did you think of Tom?"

"I liked him very much. He's very kind to his aunt."

"Did you notice anything else?"

"Was I supposed to? Is there something wrong with him?"

"Did he seem at all shallow?"

"Harry, I spent half an hour with the man, and frankly I noticed your aunt Tavie much more. She's something else."

"I don't take your meaning."

"She's unbelievable, then."

"She's an original. When we go to the bear garden, please take particular notice of Tom."

"You're being positively gothick," she told him, using one of Anna's favourite phrases and wondering what was behind Harry's request.

Harry laughed and told her to read Mrs. Radcliffe's

novels if she wanted gothick, but refused to say another word about Tom. There was a note waiting for Harry when they returned home, and he read it standing in the hall, then sent James running after the hired carriage to call it back.

"Cassandra, please be so kind as to tell Anna that Mr. Font has replied to my letter, and I am going to call upon him. I should return in time for dinner."

"Is something wrong?"

"Nothing that need concern you ladies." Harry closed the front door behind him.

Cassandra unfastened the tapes of the old black cloak and took off her bonnet. Blasted men! They *made* women hysterical, by not telling them what was going on. She found Anna in the drawing room, surrounded by relatives.

"Mr. Arthur Font called again. I am sorry that you missed him," said Anna.

Before Cassandra could reply, Aunt Tavie hobbled up to her. "I see you have recovered from yesterday's adventure, Mrs. Brown. I have brought my woman to see to you."

"I beg your pardon, Lady Bestor?"

"You need a crop. Anna, send someone for Culpepper. Mrs. Brown is taking me to her chamber."

"Are you ill, Aunt?"

"I am never ill."

Cassandra was soon seated before her dressing table with a towel wrapped around her shoulders. "I'm not sure, Lady Bestor . . ."

In fact, she was certain: she could arrange her return for a second after she had left her own time, and knew that her fellow scientists would assume that their eyes had played a trick on them if she hadn't been there for a blink of an eye, but if she turned up looking different, she might find things very awkward.

"Nonsense," said Aunt Tavie. She snatched the scissors out of Culpepper's hand and sliced halfway across the braid Cassandra wore pinned to the back of her head. "Now something will have to be done about that birds nest. Culpepper, bring me a chair. I want to talk to Mrs. Brown."

Cassandra was far from speechless. "How dare you?"

"Very easily. You look like a frump. And you are in fact a very beautiful young woman. In my day women would have slain for a complexion such as yours. It is obvious that you have never suffered from smallpox. Anna had Edmund vaccinated this autumn—more of Harry's philosophical nonsense. You want to enjoy life for a long as you can, so we shall take some steps to ensure that you do."

"What are you talking about?"

"Sit back down so Culpepper can reach your hair." Aunt Tavie lowered herself onto her own chair. "You have made no effort to find a new husband."

"Oh." Cassandra was nonplussed.

"If you listen to me, my girl, we'll have a fine new husband for you by the new year."

"But I don't want a husband."

"If you please, ma'am." Culpepper finished brushing Cassandra's hair and tipped her head forward.

"Don't be missish. Unlike Anna, you can ill afford the luxury of remaining unwed. Do you plan to spend the rest of your life as a guest in another woman's house? You may feel secure now, but think of your position if you and Mrs. Font quarrel. And a few years from now, when her boy is a man and married—his wife may put up with his mother and grandmother, but a third female! It is my belief, Mrs. Brown, that you have no money of your own. Don't you want a household, an income?"

Cassandra took advantage of the fact that her chin was pressed against her chest to mutter something indistinguishable.

"I can tell you're not grief-stricken, although something troubles you." Aunt Tavie's voice was a little softer. "Just because one husband didn't please you doesn't mean the next won't. I shall tell you something I learned long ago:

ugly men make much the best lovers. The mamas will go for the rich men, and the girls for the handsome ones. That leaves the well-to-do and plain ones for us. Now, you have no money. Did Mr. Brown leave any debts—for those would pass to the second husband?"

"No, ma'am."

"Well, that is to the good. We must make the most of your beauty and your wit. Fortunately widows aren't expected to be bread-and-butter misses. I was never beautiful, but I was handsome, and I knew my own mind. Other girls had more suitors and admirers, but I had my pick of the best. Let Mrs. Font take you out and about—and when you see a buck who catches your eye, let me know. If I don't know his family, my sister will. Then we'll see what can be done."

"Thank you." Cassandra breathed a sigh of relief. As long as the old lady didn't take a more active role, she could string her along nicely until she and Harry returned to Font Hall, and then, with any luck, she'd be home free.

"The trouble with you young people is that you have no spirit." Aunt Tavie sighed. "I had a friend once, married the wrong man. Well, some women would have martyred themselves, and others would have run off with their lovers, but not Helena. Now I'm not saying that what she did was were right—but God's teeth, it was a gesture. She and her lover were so flagrant that they forced her husband to challenge him to a duel. Helena attended, dressed as a page, holding her lover's horse. What do you think of that?"

"Who won?"

"Husband got himself killed. Helena and her lover went to Italy. She abandoned him for a count. I'd say that Helena did well." She chuckled. "I admire you, Mrs. Brown, becuase you have some spirit. I like what you said to Seppie about a woman's worth having nothing to do with her being a brood mare. But you have to learn that the world is arranged for men and their convenience. Accept that, and learn to manipulate them. It is the best a woman can do. If she does it well, she may contrive a great deal of freedom for herself." She pushed herself to her feet. "Well, Culpepper, let's see what you've done."

Cassandra looked at herself in the glass. Her hair, which had not been cut since she was nine, was cut to fall between her shoulders and her elbows. "Hack the front short," ordered Aunt Tavie, "some of those Grecian curls."

Culpepper gathered most of Cassandra's hair into a loose knot on top of her head and arranged the rest in loose curls spilling down her back. The fringe in front was teased into tight little curls. Cassandra had to admit she was delighted. "It makes me look almost mysterious."

"That is the idea. I shall lend you some combs and a strand of pearls."

Culpepper made a sharp noise in her throat.

"Be quiet, woman, she's not going to hock them, are you?"

"Nothing could be further from my mind."

"See. You can set Cleopatra or whatever it is that Mrs. Font's maid calls herself to twine them in your hair. I shall give you a silk gown, a green one. Don't make a fuss about it, it will cost me next to nothing. In my day a gown had a decent amount of stuff in it." Aunt Tavie shook out her full skirts. "You young misses might as well be in your shifts. Come along, Culpepper, I'm leaving now. Don't come down with me, Mrs. Brown, or everyone will remark on your hair. Wait until dinner, it won't be so noticeable then."

Cassandra sat at the dressing table and laughed. Aunt Tavie was so high-handed, but it was impossible to be cross with her, for she meant well. When she returned to her own time, she'd just have to keep insisting that she'd had her hair cut the afternoon before and tease everyone for not noticing.

Harry was as good as his word and was back in good time for dinner. He smiled warmly at Cassandra. "Is that a new gown?"

"No."

"It looks different."

"No, Cassandra looks different," Anna said. "Since she is a relative, you might as well come out and say that her new crop suits her."

"Indeed, Cassandra, you look very fine."

Mrs. Chubbs sniffed.

As they dined on trout and saddle of lamb, he told them about his visit to Arthur Font. "I was surprised by my cousin's address. He's a little effusive, but I think he genuinely regrets all the unpleasantness."

"It is gratifying to think of the old gentleman, his heart eaten by jealousy for many years, able at last to reconcile himself with his loved ones—or at least, with the son of the man he must once have loved as a father. I am sure that many who wish for such an opportunity are denied it."

"Yes." Harry looked thoughtful for a moment. "I shall call upon him tomorrow. He lives at Bristix Minor, so I shall have to hire a horse."

"No, Harry, pray take my chaise. None of us shall need it tomorrow."

"Thank you. Are you certain, Mrs. Chubbs, that I shall not be depriving you?"

"You are too kind, but it is my daughter's carriage, although she allows me to make use of it."

"Take it, Harry, and Daniels to drive you. I hope it keeps fine for the journey. If it rains, put up somewhere for the night. If you have not returned by the following day, Tom will procure a conveyance for our outing to the Tower."

"How far away is Bristix Minor? Cassandra asked, wondering how you spelled a word that sounded like "brick sticks."

"Oh, a good fifteen miles, I would say, but no more than twenty."

Cassandra hoped to have a private word with Harry before he left, but the company assembled in the drawing room after dinner. It would be scandalous, she suspected, if the two of them went off alone, so she sat in the dim light and unpicked the hem of the rose-colored gown while Mrs. Chubbs netted a purse, Anna sewed a shirt, and Harry read *The Quarterly Review*.

Cassandra took care to be down to breakfast early. Harry was already there, helping himself to haddock.

"Good morning," she said sweetly, although she planned to be as tough as necessary over his neglect of the calculations.

"Good morning, Cassandra. You look very well. May I pour you some coffee?"

"Yes, thank you."

"Look on the table. There's a packet with your name on it."

Cassandra took the cup from him and went to sit down. "More toys for Edmund and me?"

"No. Just a few mathematical scribblings."

"Thank you." Had she been back in the informal twentieth century, she would have hugged him; he had finished the set of calculations. "It must have taken you a hundred hours without the calculator. You can't have slept for days."

"The slide rule, in the hands of one who has made himself proficient, is almost as rapid. We should compare our answers before I leave, and then we can each begin the next series."

Cassandra ran upstairs to get her own papers. All the resentment she had felt earlier was gone.

11

A HUGE HAMPER filled with food and wine packed in straw, the beginning of the Christmas preparations, had arrived earlier from Fortnum and Mason. The carters carried it into the hall, and James had emptied it where it stood. It was too heavy for one man to carry, and there was no one to help him with it. The boy who normally helped him had been sent to the butchers, Job was nowhere to be found, and Anna refused to let the maids lift anything so heavy. The basket stood waist high to a man, and was so large that Cassandra's arms could not stretch halfway around it. Anna planned to follow the German custom, which the Duchess of York had recently introduced, of giving gifts to children at Christmas. She would have the basket filled with bran and have gifts of sweets and clothing buried in it for the children at a nearby charity school to hunt for.

Cassandra leaned against the basket, while Anna peered under the furniture and called her son's name.

"No, he is not under that table," Cassandra said.

There was a muffled giggle from the basket.

"Nor is he behind the umbrella stand. Really, Anna, have you forgotten what a big boy he is. He could never hide there."

Just then Harry let himself in, and Anna hurried to greet him. "A wasted morning," he said with vehemence, flinging his greatcoat over a chair.

"Are you all right?" Anna asked anxiously. "I would

have thought you halfway to Bristix Minor by now. I do hope you did not overturn."

"There was no accident, just a misunderstanding of sorts. If you'll come into the sitting room, I'll tell you both all about it. I am not very happy with your Mr. Font, Anna. And if it's Job's blasted Tiger you're hunting for, I'll drown the pair of them."

"He is not *my* Mr. Font," Anna said with dignity. "And I can't come until I find little Edmund. I wonder if the gypsies could have stolen him?"

"No, Mama, I am in here!" Edmund could scarcely choke the words out for laughing.

"Did you hear someone call?"

Cassandra said that she had not. Although she was anxious to learn what had happened, she felt that if Anna wanted to continue the game, it would not do for her to end it.

Harry suggested that he should make himself useful by carrying away the hamper while the ladies continued to search. As he heaved it, he exclaimed, "Why, there is something in here!" and lifted out Edmund, who was crowing with laughter. "How ever did you get in there? Are you a little boy, or a pork pie, or"—brushing the straw out of his hair—"a scarecrow?"

"Mrs. Brown was so kind as to lift me in when Mama wished to play hide and go seek, and no one knew I was there!"

Edmund was praised for his cleverness, and Hester came to take him upstairs to the nursery. The three adults repaired to Anna's sitting room. Harry, who seemed willing to play Anna's delaying game, waited until the ladies were seated, and then rang for some ale. It wasn't until he'd enjoyed a long pull and set the tankard down that Anna's patience finally gave out.

"You cannot have reached Bristix Minor, brother."

"No, I did not." He took another sip of ale.

"Did something prevent you?"

"Yes." He set down his tankard again. "It was most vexing. Mr. Font came galloping after me, and overtook me just outside the city. Daniels drew up in a veritable quagmire. I wasn't about to get out, and Mr. Font refused to dismount and join me in the chaise, for which I was grateful. He must have ridden like the very—very hard, for he was covered in mud. So we had a most confused conversation shouted through the window. When I left him last night, I had not decided if I would go to his father or not—"

"Oh, Harry, how could you have been so heartless?" cried Anna.

"Because, my dear, I wasn't certain if it was the father's idea or the son's, and I had no wish to intrude. But as I made my way home, it occurred to me that it might please old Mr. Font whether he had asked for me or not. I know that my own father always regretted the break—even though it was not of his making. My cousin Charles had been like a son to him for many years. And your remarks last night, Anna, bore much weight in the matter.

"Well, this morning I wrote Mr. Font—Arthur Font—a note about my intention to visit his father, and sent James to deliver it, but apparently Arthur Font did not spend the night at his house and so had not received it. When I spoke of my letter, Mr. Font kept assuming that I meant the one I'd written yesterday, for he did not know of my later note. And I couldn't imagine how he knew to seek for me on the road if he hadn't received the second one. Finally, we established that he had, by chance, run into one of your servants this morning and learnt of my departure from him."

"Did Arthur tell you to go home?" Cassandra asked.

"Yes. He explained that late last night he received a message from his mother to the effect that her husband had taken a turn for the worse, and the physician had stated that the slightest shock might end his life. She felt that my arrival might well prove such a shock. So I came home, and left Mr. Font to ride on to his father."

"How did he get the message from his mother if he was out all last night?" Cassandra asked. "And how did his mother know that you were coming?"

"I expect a servant took the message to him, and that it was really he who did not wish me to attend his father after all. Really, Cassandra, I am fed up to the back teeth with the whole business, pray give over. Anna, might we have our luncheon a little early? I am famished."

Cassandra watched Anna ring for a servant and arrange for Harry to have a fortifying snack. Cassandra was half-annoyed that his sister-in-law fussed over Harry so, and idly wondering why Arthur, who had made such a point about the deathbed reconciliation, had suddenly called it off. If Mr. Font really was in such a precarious state, why had Arthur prevented what was likely to be the last opportunity for Harry to see his father? Perhaps he had wanted a reconciliation without an actual meeting.

That afternoon Cassandra and Harry set up the next series of calculations. They had mentioned to Mrs. Chubbs that Harry was teaching Cassandra mathematics, and although the old lady did not approve, it gave them an excuse to spread out their papers in the public rooms. They were still very careful not to discuss the actual problems in front of anyone.

As Cassandra had told Harry when he mentioned that the servants wouldn't have the slightest idea of what they were doing, "If we start making exceptions, we'll make an exception in front of the wrong person, and at the very least end up looking like fools."

They were alone in Anna's sitting room. The door, as Mrs. Chubbs's sense of propriety demanded, was ajar, even though she had gone to visit a friend. Little Edmund had been taken with some of his young cousins to a children's party, and Anna was belowstairs, closeted with Walter and James.

"And, like magic, we will have solved yet another variable. Do you realize Cassandra, that I am the only man in Britain to whom this makes sense? Unfortunately, I can never talk to anyone about it."

"Harry, if I hadn't had you to discuss things with, I'd still be chewing my nails at Font Hall."

"And once you're gone? Cassandra, I spent a recent morning with Sir Humphry. I have always admired him enormously, and he has been very kind to me. Indeed, he arranged for me to accompany him to France and Italy as his secretary so that I had to bear almost none of the expenses of the journey."

After it became clear that he wasn't about to speak without prompting, Cassandra asked, "Did he say something to trouble you?"

"Everything he said troubled me. His is one of the greatest minds of the age. Yet, thanks to your teaching, I know that almost everything he holds to be true is false."

"That doesn't make his own accomplishments any less," Cassandra stated firmly.

"I know that. What troubles me—and it is very selfish of me—is that my own few years as an experimenter are over. I shall not be able to continue my own investigation into electricity and magnetism because I would be too influenced by what you told me about the discovery Monsieur Ampère will make in a few years. I fear I will find no pleasure in listening to others report their discoveries, for I already know what they will say—and in what particulars they are false."

"I haven't covered every little discovery between now and the year two thousand, Harry. I'm sure—"

"Cassandra, even if you haven't, don't you see that I can't enter into the discussion which surrounds a new discovery, for fear that I will inadvertently say something which reveals my greater knowledge. I came to know that as I spoke with Sir Humphry. Once you leave, I shall have no one to talk to."

"Even if I stayed, I'd eventually run out of things to teach you. And I wouldn't dream of trying any experiments—except those connected with my returning home."

"I am sure I wouldn't ask it of you," Harry said coldly.

"I'm not going to apologize for being here again. It was just as much your fault as mine, and unintentional on both our parts. I understand what you're saying, believe me. I'd be heartbroken if I had to give up science."

Even as she said it, Cassandra knew it wasn't true. Her brilliance in science lay in mathematical applications of physics, and she suspected that like most mathematicians, she would make one contribution to the field at an early age and never again equal it. She had long expected to start a second career at thirty, although she had no firm idea what that would be.

"I am sorry, Cassandra, that you were brought here without your consent—without even knowing that it might ever happen. I am very, very pleased that we have met, yet I would have forgone it gladly to spare you the fear and discomfort of your . . . journey. And I'm sorry for acting like a bear with a sore head for the past week," he added ruefully. "The impatience that I feel from the gap between my new knowledge and what my contemporaries hold to be the truth,"—his voice was scornful—"is immense."

"Harry, the very fact that I was conducting an experiment ought to show you that *my* contemporaries don't have the final word on the truth. As for your other problem, I know that giving up science will be a blow, but I can see why you feel it would be both dangerous and painful to continue being active in the field. You must find something else to do." Cassandra offered the universal panacea of her time. "What about going to law school, or whatever you have to do now to be a lawyer?"

"Become an articled clerk and study jurisprudence? Oh, Cassandra, I don't think I could bear it, law is so dry."

"Well, go into finance, and restore the family fortune."

"I don't have any capital, and no one in his right mind would back me."

Cassandra decided that anything she suggested now would be rejected, and resolved to bide her time for a few days while she found out what she could about careers open to barons at the beginning of the nineteenth century. She was about to make a cheering remark when Anna entered the room, carrying a handful of invitations.

"The Larchmonts have invited us all to dinner next week, the evening of the twenty-third. When I was helping Mrs. Larchmont with the invitations, she kindly urged me to go and to bring Mama, but I reminded her that Mama will not go without me and that I would not be able to accept, but now Mrs. Larchmont has sent invitations for us all."

Cassandra noticed how Anna blushed when she mentioned that she had helped with the invitations. No doubt she had advised Mrs. Larchmont which women to invite for Harry.

"Very civil of her," said Harry. "You remember the Larchmonts, Cassandra, you met them at Aunt Tavie's. They are my mother's relations."

Cassandra remembered them. Mr. Larchmont seemed a bit dour, and his wife talked incessantly of her husband's gout. Aunt Seppie had pointed out the elder daughter, who was married, as an example of a contented young bride expecting her first child, and the younger girl had sat on a sopha with a hard-eyed man and agreed with everything he had said.

"Why did you refuse?" Harry asked.

"Because there is to be dancing after dinner, and you know I am still in mourning."

"Annie, it will only be an informal hop."

"Oh, no," said Cassandra, "and I was trying so hard not to pollute you."

Harry looked at her in amazement. Anna turned a giggle into a cough, and blushed.

"Sock hop," elaborated Cassandra. "It's a modern phrase. I don't know when I could have used it."

"I don't know about the sock part," said Harry, "but I've used the word 'hop' to mean a dance for years." He got up from the table and went to sit by Anna. "You are only in half-mourning."

"I *dress* in half-mourning for the sake of my child. That is different."

"I still think you should go. Mrs. Larchmont obviously does, or she would not have sent another invitation card."

"Either Mrs. Larchmont made a mistake, or she is interfering in a matter outside her province. A private matter," Anna said emphatically.

Harry opened his mouth to speak, but before he could, Cassandra asked, "Did you say Mrs. Larchmont had invited me? Do you think there will be waltzing?"

"Here is your card. The Larchmonts always have waltzing, because it is so avant-garde. Mr. Larchmont's brother is a Low Church clergyman. He tried to forbid it once, and since Mr. Larchmont will brook no interference, he would have the waltz played if the King himself were to forbid it."

"Harry taught me to waltz," Cassandra said wistfully. "Do you think, Harry, that we might go?"

"Of course you must," said Anna, "and I am sure Mama will go with you."

"Out of the question, I'm afraid," Harry said. "I would be honoured to accompany Mrs. Chubbs, but Cassandra may not go."

"Why ever not?" demanded Anna. "However long ago her husband is supposed to have died, it is obvious that she is wearing colours again. I know she was not really married—I mean she is pretending to have been married—I mean, under the circumstances, Cassandra, although you may not seem to need a chaperone, my mother will be there, so you will have one after all."

"I understand," said Cassandra.

Harry laughed. "That isn't the problem, you goose.

There will be no one to tell Cassandra how to go on. I know that Mrs. Chubbs will do everything that is proper, but she does not know Cassandra's secret. And the conventions that will govern society in her day are so different from ours that unless she has someone who knows what to watch for and how to guide her nearby, I cannot permit her to go."

"Perhaps Aunt Tavie . . . ?"

"No, we cannot put the old lady in such danger."

"Tom . . . your cousin Tom."

"He would suffer from the same disadvantage I do. Mrs. Larchmont would expect him to stand up with the other young ladies. I fully expect that Cassandra could hold her own in the conversation that takes place on the dance floor, but if she were left alone among a group of women—why, they would be asking questions and taking notice of every little thing she did."

Cassandra wanted to come to the defence of her gender, for she did not like the implications Harry was making, but since Anna seemed on the point of weakening, she decided to let the charade continue.

"Would you be very disappointed, Cassandra?"

"Of course she won't be. You're not disappointed, are you, Cassandra?"

"No, not really."

"See." Harry almost crowed. "I knew she wouldn't mind. She's not in the habit of going to dances anyway, Anna. She told me that she'd not been to one in years."

That was true enough, unless you counted a faculty-student New Year's party at M.I.T. as a dance.

"Then we cannot deny her this treat. Cassandra, we are going to dinner. I shall write to Mrs. Larchmont this instant, and accept on behalf of us all. There is no reason why I have to dance, I am sure. Pray excuse me."

As soon as she left the room, Cassandra gave way to quiet laughter. "We were shameless, Harry. I hope you realized that I would never let a man tell me what to do, except in a good cause. Isn't it funny that Anna can only stand up to someone in support of another person. When she alone is involved, she has no spine."

"You're wrong. Everyone thinks she is very meek and mild, but she saves herself for the big battles. You should laugh more often. You are very pretty when you laugh."

That made Cassandra laugh harder. "I think Mrs. Chubbs would scold you for making personal remarks."

"She'd only sigh. And you ought to say, 'Thank you, sir,' and blush."

"Very well, Harry. If another gentleman tells me that I'm pretty when I laugh, I will do just that."

12

THE FOLLOWING MORNING Aunt Tavie arrived just as Cassandra and Anna were finishing their breakfasts. She hobbled into Anna's bedchamber, leaning on Augusta's arm, and immediately demanded that the maid stop offering to show her into the drawing room. "You can make yourself useful by fetching me a dish of Bohea. Be quick about it. Mrs. Font will be getting up directly."

Cassandra stepped forward to help her, for the old lady did not have her walking stick with her. Aunt Tavie bid her good morning, then turned her attention to Anna. "I always rose before seven, even when I was breeding, and you have no such excuse."

Anna responded indirectly by begging Aunt Tavie to be seated and asking how she could be of service to her.

"We are going to the dressmakers. You, Anna, are accompanying us because Tom will want someone to talk to, and I shall be occupied with Mrs. Brown."

"But I teach Edmund in the morning," interjected Cassandra, who felt that someone should at least go through the motions of standing up to Aunt Tavie.

"Give the boy a holiday."

"Is Tom to join us, Aunt?" Anna asked timidly, putting aside her tray and climbing out of bed.

"Tom is downstairs. Did you wish him to come up with me?"

Anna blushed.

"I thought not. I brought my own coach, and you would

do well to be ready in ten minutes, as I told my coachman to return in a quarter of an hour, and I will not have the horses kept waiting."

"But I shall have to get little Edmund ready," Anna said.

"The child will stay at home. Harry can amuse him," said Aunt Tavie with the air of one who will brook no further opposition.

Aunt Tavie's tea was brought to her, and Cassandra excused herself while Anna dressed.

As she descended the stairs, she heard whoops of laughter coming from the dining room, where she found Edmund, still in his nightshirt and armed with his great-aunt's walking stick, reenacting a cavalry charge against the French. His hapless foe was played by Harry, who scuttled away on his knees, vainly trying to defend himself with a spoon. Tom sat at the table, enjoying a chop, issuing orders to his troops, reviling Harry's cowardice, and making Hester giggle by paying her exaggerated compliments. When he noticed Cassandra, he greeted her warmly and hastened to usher her to the table.

"Come on, grimikin," he said to Edmund, disarming the victorious hero and depositing him in the arms of his nurse. "Can't have bloodshed in front of the ladies."

To Cassandra's surprise, Edmund allowed himself to be borne away without a murmur of complaint, although he did insist that Hester wait while he assured Cassandra that he wouldn't really have harmed his uncle. Harry picked himself up, dusted off his knees, and left the room, saying that he had letters to write, and with such a significant look at Cassandra that she realized that she was to use this time to form an opinion of Tom.

To make conversation, she asked if he often accompanied his aunt on errands.

"Not often, exactly. Thing is, it's a bit dicey letting the old dear out on her own. She won't listen to the servants, and she will overdo things and get herself fagged. Don't like going to the dressmaker's, though."

"You can blame *me* for that. Your aunt wants to give me a dress as a present. I feel rather bad about it."

"Don't. One of her greatest pleasures is giving people things. Know how you feel, though. The estate and all that."

"Which estate?" Cassandra asked.

"Uncle Bestor's. Great-uncle, really, by marriage. He adopted me, and left it to me, to put his brother's nose out of joint. Aunt Tavie has the income for life. One of these days I'll get the capital—in no hurry, though. Old dear offers no end of amusement."

"So you'll be Lord Bestor one day."

"No, though if I was, I'd be Sir Thomas—her husband was a baronet—baronetcy went to his brother, adopted children can't inherit rank—and none of his own made it out of the nursery. Don't care much for titles anyway—and that's not a dog in the manger talking. I don't see how Harry could be a finer fellow if he were plain Mr. Font."

"So Sir Bestor—"

"Sir Giles, actually. Aunt Tavie won't take kindly to you making such mistakes about her husband."

Cassandra gave up trying to frame a tactful question and said bluntly. "You get the money and the other man gets the title?"

"More or less—I get everything that isn't entailed. It bothers me sometimes, though, because everyone thinks I hang on the old girl's coattails to further my expectations. But I'm damned—beg pardon—if I'll turn my back on her to quiet gossip. Specially since there's nothing she can do to prevent me inheriting. Sorry, not much you can say to that. Don't mean to be so morose. It's the hour. Too early. I know, I'll ask you how you find London. Your first visit to our capital?"

"Yes," said Cassandra, with no concern for the truth. "I've not see a great deal yet. Are we still planning to go to the Tower today?"

"Of course. Wouldn't disappoint Edmund. After you've

done with your furbelows I'll see Aunt Tavie home and call here again at two as we first planned."

Just then they heard the two ladies on the stairs. Tom hurriedly swallowed the last of his coffee and picked up the walking stick. As they left the room, Cassandra said, "I think that you and I are the only two people who don't call him little Edmund."

"He won't be little forever. No point in his growing up in his late father's shadow. Knew Ed myself, fond of him, really, but no reason that the lad has to be a pale image."

Aunt Tavie's carriage was an enormous vehicle, painted blue with red-and-gold trim. The door was emblazoned with a coat of arms. It was drawn by six horses, and even Cassandra could tell that they were of superior stock. Tom lifted Aunt Tavie in and helped Cassandra and Anna take their places on each side of her. Although the seat would have held four people in comfort, he sat across from them with his back to the horses.

Aunt Tavie was silent, and since neither Anna nor Tom spoke, beyond his enquiring if the ladies were comfortable and her assuring him that they all were, Cassandra did not like to start a conversation. She looked out the window, until a bit of byplay caught her eye.

Anna would surreptitiously look at Tom, until he noticed her doing so, at which point she would look away. Tom would pretend to stare out of the window, but in fact be looking sideways at Anna, until she realized what he was doing. Then both would look at the floor until Anna's gaze again wandered to Tom's face. They repeated the cycle seven times in the half-hour ride, and Cassandra was particularly amused, since they could have both stared directly at each other and attracted less notice.

Did this mean, she wondered, that Harry had a rival? If Harry thought so, it would explain why he wanted her opinion of Tom. He was probably looking for ways to defeat his rival.

The dressmaker's shop was empty when they arrived. Either she did little business or most people shopped later in the day. Aunt Tavie was obviously a well-known and valued customer, for the proprietress hastened from the back room to greet her and fussed over the placing of a chair in front of the fire and a screen to cut the draught.

Aunt Tavie bore with this for about a minute, then said firmly, "If I am cold, Madame Prévost,"—she pronounced the name as if it were an English word—"I shall tell you. I have brought my friend, Mrs. Brown, to you. It is obvious that her hair, her eyes, her figure, and her complexion are fine, so there is no need for you to exclaim over them."

"Indeed, milady." The woman's tone was grave.

"You are to find some green silk to suit her. Tom, Mrs. Font wishes to walk about. We shall want an hour, so escort her to the lending library."

Tom and Anna departed with good humour. Remembering that Tom had told her he was to inherit his aunt's money, Cassandra wondered how large a fortune demanded such patience as gratitude.

The old lady seemed more acerbic than ever. When Madame Prévost left them while she fetched a bolt of fabric too delicate to be entrusted to her assistant, Aunt Tavie stated, *sotto voce*, that nothing annoyed her more than a man smelling of April and May without the wherewithal to do something about it.

"Indeed, Mrs. Brown, I am quite out of patience with them. Anna, as you can see, is cut of a different cloth than you and I. She is one of those females who dote on being led about. If Tom were to order her to the altar, she would burst into tears and comply at once. I know you have qualms about accepting a gift from me. Well, if you do anything to further a match between those two, I shall consider myself well paid. Hush, here comes that Prévost woman, and I don't want her to hear you gossiping of family affairs."

Cassandra was given a sheaf of French fashion plates to

look at, but soon found that she was to have no say in the matter of her gown. Green silk was chosen for the overskirt, white silk shot with gold selected for the body of the dress. Madame Prévost herself took Cassandra's measurements, and she discovered the meaning of the expression "a speaking glance" when that lady saw Anna's made-over shift and drawers.

Cassandra stood shivering as the cloth was draped and pinned around her. There was a looking glass, but her wavy reflection gave her little idea of what the gown would look like, as the pinned material bore little relation to a finished garment.

Finally she was allowed to dress again in the rose gown and pelisse. When she emerged from the fitting room, Anna had returned and sat with Aunt Tavie and two other ladies, one who seemed to be in her late thirties, the other a little older than Anna, before the fire. Aunt Tavie called to her to join them.

"Tom has gone to fetch the coach. Anna, make your friends known to Mrs. Brown."

Anna introduced Miss Jane Austen and her niece, Miss Fanny Knight. "Miss Austen is in London visiting her ailing brother, Captain Austen. I met them in the lending library, and when I learned that they would pass along this way as they returned home, I asked them to be so kind as to step in to meet you."

As the ladies greeted each other, Cassandra studied Jane Austen carefully. While she was not a fanatical Janeite, it was always interesting to meet, though sometimes not to talk to, a famous person; and Miss Austen had the additional attraction of being someone Cassandra had never dreamt it was possible to meet. Anna must have remembered her mentioning Jane Austen's novels.

Aunt Tavie glared at Jane Austen. "Hear tell, Miss Austen, that you recast one of your books into French. Waste of time, madam. You ought to be writing a book about hunting. What do you say to that?"

"You are mistaken, Lady Bestor, my aunt did not write *La Raison et la sensibilité, ou les deux manières d'aimer.* Some other person *translated* the novel," Fanny Knight said earnestly. "And she cannot undertake to write a novel about hunting, because a *certain* gentleman, a gentleman at Carlton House, has asked her to write about entailment and tithes."

Jane Austen smiled. "And a fine job I should make of either subject, Lady Bestor, for I do not write well on serious topics, and I fear that hunting is a passion I could not do justice."

"I could write such a novel, Miss Austen, if I cared to."

"It is a very difficult undertaking, Lady Bestor," Fanny Knight said. "My aunt encourages my cousin, and even with her guidance, Mrs. Lefroy achieves only indifferent results. I am sure that if you were to try—"

"Did you know that when my husband was a midshipman he served aboard *The Unicorn* with Captain Austen?" Anna said quickly.

Miss Knight ignored the interruption, but it had served its purpose. Aunt Tavie did not hear that she lacked the genius necessary for writing novels.

"I often feel, Fanny, that writing novels is not a matter of genius, but of time and inclination. And while a married woman might have plenty of the latter, it is most unlikely that she would have much of the former." Miss Austen sounded amused by her niece's comments. "May I enquire, Lady Bestor, if you are keeping well?"

"Naturally. And does your brother's health improve?"

Tom returned with the news that the coach was waiting outside, and after Miss Austen hastily assured Aunt Tavie that her brother was much better, they took their leave.

As Anna helped Aunt Tavie fasten her cloak, Cassandra asked him, "Where does the coach go while we're inside shops?"

Tom gave her a funny look. "It's driven around the square."

"You mean around and around?"

"Yes. Why ever shouldn't it be?"

"Oh, I'm not used to having a coach. In Boston I walked."

"Well, don't think all London coaches are like Aunt Tavie's. This monstrosity is really her travelling equipage, but she likes to go about in style."

Aunt Tavie concluded her business. Cassandra was to return in a week's time for a fitting, and the gown would be ready for the Larchmonts' dinner.

As they drove home, Cassandra, who had used the time in the fitting room to compose a suitable speech, said, "I cannot tell you, Lady Bestor, how grateful I am for your kind attentions—"

"I am sure that your sentiments are everything they should be, Mrs. Brown. But I don't care to be hearing them. I do not like to be thanked for pleasing myself, do I, Tom?"

"No, you don't, ma'am."

"So you may simply say thank you, and we shall hear no more of it."

"Thank you very much, Lady Bestor."

"Thank heavens that is out of the way."

Cassandra expected that the return journey would be as full of sidelong glances as the outward one, but Anna now turned to Aunt Tavie and said, in the tone of one determined to make general conversation, "I have always liked the Austen family. Indeed, Miss Austen is a very fine woman."

"Her cheeks are too round," stated Aunt Tavie with a smile. "Tell me who else you saw in the library."

Anna chattered away until they reached home.

Augusta was waiting in the hall. "Oh, ma'am. Oh, ma'am."

"Is something wrong? Little Edmund?" Anna went pale.

"No, ma'am. Oh, ma'am."

"I think you had better come into the kitchen with me, Augusta. Has something been broken?"

"No, ma'am, not the kitchen. There is a man there, a sailor, oh please, ma'am, let me fetch James!"

"Is Lord Font here?" cried Anna. "He will know what to do."

"No, ma'am, he took little Master Edmund to his ducks and Mrs. Chubbs went with them."

"Is the man dangerous?" asked Cassandra.

"No, ma'am."

"Then," Cassandra said firmly, "we shall go into your sitting room, Anna, and Augusta shall fetch James."

James came almost immediately, looking grave. He closed the door behind him and came to stand in front of Anna. "While you were out, ma'am a sailor came to the back door. His name is Jack Peters, and he told us that he had served on *The Indefatigable*. I questioned him closely, and he knew the names of the officers and corrected Daniels when he falsely described some of the incidents Mr. Font used to tell." He paused, apparently wanting to see how his mistress took the news.

When Anna did not speak, he continued. "Peters says that he was with Mr. Font at his final hour, and that Mr. Font entrusted him with a message to be delivered to you, ma'am. If I might take the liberty of saying so, he seems an honest fellow."

"Of course I must see him. Please bring him to me directly."

James bowed and left to do as he was bid.

Anna, agitated and flushed, began to pace the room. "Oh, Cassandra, do you think, perhaps some mistake . . ."

"No. Anna, please don't get your hopes up."

"I know I should not, but—" She pressed her handkerchief to her face, then put it away, and sat down again.

Cassandra was amazed at how quickly the young woman was able to compose herself. When James entered with Peters, she was in full command of her emotions.

Peters was a painfully thin young man, dressed in widely cut, dirty white trousers and a shabby blue jacket. He wore clumsy shoes on his stockingless feet. He had a long scar across his brow, and his hair was scraped back into a pigtail, which—Cassandra realized with distaste—had been painted with tar. He clutched a grimy stocking cap in his hand and made serveral clumsy bows over it.

"I am Mrs. Font. This is my friend Mrs. Brown. I understand that you knew my husband."

"Yes, ma'am." His voice was a throaty whisper.

"And you were with him—at the end."

"Yes, ma'am."

James, who had remained by the door, said, "I believe Mrs. Font would like to know whatever you can tell her."

"There was an engagement, ma'am. You won't want to hear about that. An' I was struck in the face by splinters from a spar an' as I fell, a ball went right through me leg. I thought I was blinded, ma'am, an' they carried me below. An' they put me next to Lieutenant Font. I knew it was him, 'cause when they put me down, he said, 'Wipe the blood from his eyes. Let him know if he can see.' So they did, an' even though every man, be he sailor or gentleman, is supposed to wait his turn for the surgeon as he's carried down, he told them to take off his neckcloth and bind up me head. So Jemmy, our powder monkey, he did that.

"An' I said, thank you sir, an' had a good look at him, and I knew he was a goner, ma'am, because his stomuch was all blood. But he didn't seem to have no pain, no pain at all. Now, mostly that's a bad sign, because it means they're dying, but if they're going to die, best that they don't feel it loike." He licked his lips.

"Pray continue."

"It was right noisy down there. You can hear the guns an' the men running an' officers calling their orders, an' it's dark too, but I could see that they had propped him up comfortably and the chaplain gave him sommat to drink.

"An' the lieutenant says to me, 'I'm going out, Peters.'

An' I says, 'Never say die, sir.' An' he says, 'Belay that. I want to ask you something.' So I says, 'What?' Well, he tried to sit up a bit more, but it starts his bleeding faster, so he lies back, an' says, 'Are you a married man?'

"Now, I can see he's sinking fast, so I says, 'No, I ain't, and begging your pardon, sir, you'd best ask me whatever you want done right sharp, or you'll be asking St. Peter.' Now, I only says it so impertinent like to cheer him, for he is going fast.

"An' he says, 'Peters, I am married, an' I want to write to my wife. You must write a letter for me.' I ken see he's out of his mind, which happens with bleeders. I ken't write me name, an' there wasn't a pen or a scrap of paper, but I only says, 'Tell me what to put down.' So he tells me where you live, ma'am, and says, 'Put down, "I love you." ' Then he says, 'Read it back to me.' I says what he sayed. Then he says, 'She's young, you know, young enough to find a better fellow . . . someone to take care of her and the little one.'

"He closes his eyes, and I think he's gone. Then he come to again, an' says to give you this." Peters drew a scrap of folded paper from his pocket and, stepping forward, handed it to Anna.

She unwrapped a signet ring as Peters leaned forward and whispered something in her ear.

"Edmund," cried Anna, and fainted.

13

CASSANDRA HAD NEVER seen anyone faint before. She imagined that a swoon was accompanied by a dramatic sigh and resulted in the overcome lady falling gracefully into the arms of a handsome man, who placed her tenderly on a couch. Her female friends then restored her with smelling salts and burning feathers and sal volatile, although Cassandra was not certain if the last was inhailed or imbibed.

Anna had merely crumpled and was sliding ungracefully from her chair as Cassandra, James, and Peters all rushed forward to help her. James supported her in the chair with an arm about her shoulders. Peters, apologising all the while, brought a footstool, and Cassandra lifted Anna's legs onto it. Anna regained consciousness almost at once, and said in a weak voice, "Do not let him go . . . I shall feel myself in a moment . . . Pray do not let him go."

"Of course not, ma'am," James said comfortingly. "Mrs. Brown will stay with you while I fetch Mrs. Tate, and Peters will wait belowstairs."

Peters made another of his clumsy bows, muttered something inaudible, and followed James from the room.

Anna began to sob. Cassandra urged her to lie down on the sopha, but she only cried harder. "You should put your head between your knees."

"Feeling much stouter," Anna sniffed.

"At least undo the buttons at your neck." Cassandra herself unfastened the three buttons that closed Anna's high collar.

Cassandra felt very much at a loss. She had some idea of how to care for Anna physically but did not know what she could possibly say to a woman who had just learned how her husband had died. Cassandra had a suspicion that it was not the sight of the ring which had caused Anna to faint, but the few words that Peters had whispered into her ear, and feared that in her ignorance of those few words, she might say something which would add to Anna's distress. So she rubbed Anna's shoulders until Augusta came and firmly suggested that her mistress be helped upstairs and put to bed.

Once in her bedchamber, Anna's fortitude reasserted itself. "Little Edmund will be home soon, and I cannot have him distressed. Cassandra, please, go downstairs, and when the others return, tell them that I have a headache, for I cannot go down with my eyes all red. Ask Harry, quietly, so that Mama will not be worried, to step up here with you. I shall lie down for a moment."

Cassandra did not like to leave her, but complied, leaving Augusta to bathe her mistress's face with rose water.

As Cassandra was descending the stairs, Mrs. Chubbs and Edmund returned. She had no sooner explained that Anna had a slight headache and, to confound Mrs. Chubbs, who wished to see for herself how her daughter was, compounded the lie by saying that Anna had just fallen asleep, when Harry also arrived. Fortunately, Mrs. Chubbs went directly into her own sitting room, and Cassandra was able to draw Harry into Anna's.

"We had some excitement while you were out. A sailor, who knew your brother, came to the house, and was able to tell Anna about his death," she said, surprised at the catch in her voice.

"What a shabby begging trick!" exclaimed Harry. "Is Anna very distraught?"

"She is—not happy, but the man is genuine. He gave her a ring which she recognized—a signet ring."

"Our mother's uncle's," said Harry. "I wear our father's."

"She is feeling much better now, but she fainted. She's lying down upstairs and wants you to go see her. Shouldn't she see a doctor?"

"Perhaps. Will you come up with me."

Anna had dismissed Augusta and was lying, fully clothed, on her bed, studying Edmund's miniature when they entered. Harry kissed her brow, then sat next to her on the bed and took her hand. "How do you go on, Annie?"

"I am better, thank you. Oh, Harry, a sailor came . . ." Her tears started anew, but she impatiently brushed them away and repeated Peters' story. Her voice broke when she recounted how her dying husband had ordered that someone bind Peters' wound, and again when she said the words "I love you." But she made no mention of those whispered words.

"He is still downstairs, Harry, and he is not to go until I have spoken to him again. He looks so very poor and hungry, yet he carried a gold ring to me. I sent Augusta down to make certain that he was given something to eat. If you go to the kitchen, you can hear his account for yourself."

"Edmund was very brave, Anna," Harry said as he got to his feet, "but we always knew that. Have you told your mama?"

"No, but I shall do so directly. Cassandra, could I trouble you to send Mama to me? Please do not tell her anything: I should break the news to her myself. Please, I do not mind being left alone."

Harry and Cassandra went out of the room and down the stairs together. "A terrible shock for her, I fear," he said. "But she is bearing up well, and it is a comfort to know, even after all this time, that he did not suffer greatly."

"I wonder why it took Peters three years to get here?"

Cassandra hated to suspect the emaciated man of an

elaborate confidence scheme, but she wondered if he had found or stolen the ring, and come looking for a reward or to look the house over prior to robbing it.

"*The Indefatigable* only docked at Plymouth a few weeks ago, and Peters would have had to tramp all the way here."

"Couldn't he have come last time he was on leave?"

"Common sailors don't have leave, Cassandra; they can't be trusted not to run away. I daresay this is the first time Peters has been on dry land since he first shipped."

Cassandra remembered history lessons about the press gangs that roamed the streets of coastal towns, looking for any able-bodied men. There had been accounts of apprentices, students, even young gentlemen impressed into His Majesty's Navy. She watched Harry, who seemed to think there was nothing wrong with a man being imprisoned on a sailing ship for the duration of a war, go down the passage which led to the kitchen.

Then Cassandra squared her shoulders and went to find Mrs. Chubbs. Once she had sent the old lady upstairs, she sat down in Anna's sitting room and picked up the first book which came to hand, a copy of the first volume of *Waverly*. No sooner had she opened it than there came a knock on the door, and Arthur Font was shown into the room by the young housemaid. Apparently the other servants were occupied with Peters in the kitchen.

"My dear Mrs. Brown, I am certain that I find you well, for you appear radiant. And Mrs. Font, how is she?"

"Well, thank you." Cassandra decided that the only way to cope with the situation was to pretend that there was nothing extraordinary happening. "And your father?"

"Holding his own, I am thankful to say. I trust that *Lord* Font told you of our *contretemps* on the road. So amusing." He gave his hoarse giggle. "I had hoped to find Mrs. Font in."

"Is there anything I could do for you, Mr. Font?"

"Alas, Mrs. Brown, but those who would have us believe

that members of the fair sex are so alike as to be indistinguishable are mistaken."

Cassandra felt uncomfortable, as though he had just said something obscene, but his face showed nothing but his usual nervous smile. "Then if I cannot help you . . ." She paused, trying to think of a polite way to suggest that he leave.

"I shall wait while you have Mrs. Font summoned." He sat down expectantly.

Cassandra was in a quandary. In her own time she would have no difficulty in sending him way, but she did not want to raise in him any suspicion that there was news of the manner of Edmund's death, for she was certain that Anna would not approve of people outside the immediate family being told so casually, nor did she want to insult him, since Anna had taken such pains from the start not to snub him.

"Excuse me, please," she said, and went to find Harry.

He was still in the kitchen. He and Peters sat at the table, tankards of ale before them and a plateful of bread, cheese, and cold beef before Peters. He was giving Harry a blow-by-blow account of the naval engagement.

"—I knew, sor, that the frog was about to strike his colours, but just then the four-pounders, what was loaded with grapeshot, went off an'—" He caught sight of Cassandra. "Beg pardon, sor, but there's the lady."

Harry hurried over to her. "Is Anna—"

"She's fine, but your cousin—Arthur—is in her sitting room, and I can't get rid of him."

"Leave him there, then. Go back in half an hour and sit in silence. He'll soon get the message."

"Thanks."

"Cassandra, I am trying to listen to this man. Pray indulge me."

Although Cassandra felt a little slighted, she reminded herself that he was undoubtedly facing the grief of his brother's death all over again as he vicariously experienced his last engagement. She decided to fill in the half hour by sitting in the dining room where Edmund was eating his late nuncheon in solitary state, but was forestalled in the hall by the arrival of Tom. Since Anna's sitting room was occupied by Arthur, and the housemaid had told her that Mrs. Chubbs had repaired to her own sitting room, Cassandra took him into the drawing room and told him of the events which had transpired since he left them. "I'll take care of His Majesty for you."

"His Majesty?"

"King Arthur. Do you care to come and see how a cavalry man despatches the enemy, Mrs. Brown?"

But the reinforcements had come too late. A grave, sympathetic Arthur sat on the sopha next to Anna, pressing her hand between his, and saying, "Too true, my dear Mrs. Font, I understand only too well the loss of a loved one."

"Mr. Font!" cried Tom. "An unlooked for pleasure."

He stood in front of him and held out his hand, forcing Arthur Font either to stand up and shake hands or appear uncivil. As soon as he was on his feet, Tom had the advantage. Arthur was propelled towards the door as Tom explained that they were about to depart to visit the Tower of London, that he had so enjoyed seeing his cousin, that his cousin would have to join them one day, for there was nothing like seeing the very spot where so many famous men had lost their heads. Arthur managed to call a weak good-bye to Anna before the door closed behind him and Tom.

"Really, Cassandra," Anna said sharply, "I don't know how you could have let Tom be so rude. I was speaking with Mr. Font."

It seemed there had been no need of a rescue after all.

"*He* may take little Edmund to see the bears, if he wishes to, but I shall remain at home. Would you be so kind as to tell him so for me. I do not care to see him just now."

"In a snit, is she?" Tom commented when Cassandra

relayed the message. "I don't suppose you want to see any bears?"

"I think I'd better stay here—unless you think I'd be intruding?"

"Not at all. I'm going to take Mrs. Chubbs if I can, for she'll only start blathering about Anna's tragedy and how she is nothing but a useless old woman, but the poor girl will need a woman of sense with her. Bear with her, Mrs. Brown, for she was devoted to Edmund. And keep a close eye on her, or she'll give that sailor boy Harry's best coats."

In a matter of moments, Tom had the chaise brought round and bundled Mrs. Chubbs, Edmund, and Hester into it, promising to have them back by six o'clock, "and not a moment before," he added in a undertone that only Cassandra heard.

As she returned to Anna, she remembered Aunt Tavie's words about living in another woman's house, and wondered if all of Anna's friendliness had been a polite veneer that had worn thin in the present crisis. But Anna thanked her so kindly for taking the message to Tom that Cassandra's doubts were stilled, and she agreed to stay with Anna while she interviewed Peters for the second time.

James was summoned and sent to conduct Peters and Harry from the kitchen. When he had ushered them into the sitting room, he withdrew. Cassandra and Anna sat side by side on the sopha. Harry stood behind them, his hand resting on Anna's shoulder, and Peters, cap in hand, stood before them. Anna made a very pretty speech of thanks and then asked the man what he would like as his reward.

"I couldn't take noffink, ma'am, thank you kindly, for doing me duty . . . 'cept, maybe . . ."

"You must take something, Peters."

He twisted his cap. "Some grub, loike, ma'am, some food, if it weren't asking too much."

"But of course. Didn't my servants give you a meal?"

"They fed me famously, ma'am, thank you, but it's for

me mates. Me shipmates, what camed with me from Plymouth."

"Are they waiting for you?"

"No, ma'am, they went to see the admiral's house, since we had to come to London. I bin see his tomb in St. Paul's."

"But I must see all your friends. They all must have something. How good of them to come all this way with you for my sake."

"No matter, ma'am, for we don't have nowhere else to go."

"Why don't you go home?" Cassandra asked.

"No work for us if we did, ma'am. But Mrs. Font, ma'am, I'd best be going along, for we have to be beyond the parish boundaries tonight, or we'll be moved on up by the parish officers, and we creep too slow for their liking. They get to know us, and keep an eye out."

"You mean you have nowhere to sleep, to live! This is impossible! We must find your friends, they can stay here."

"Anna," said Harry warningly, but Anna had already rung the bell, and James stepped into the room at once. Anna told him, "Peters is staying with us tonight. In fact I am thinking of engaging him. How many friends are with you, Peters?"

"Ma'am, we ken't invade you loike this. I don't think his lordship loikes it."

"This is my house, Peters. Now, how many friends do you have?"

"There are five of us, ma'am. Please, ma'am, if you want to do sommat to thank us, not that there's need, perhaps you could help Jemmy to a trade, for he left his legs behind."

That settled the matter for Anna. Harry was admonished for his lack of Christian charity and despatched with Peters in a hackney to find three sailors and a legless boy who would be making their way from the late Lord Nelson's house on Bond Street to Tottenham Court Road. Harry had protested that a hackney was unnecessary since the distance was not much over a mile, but Anna had pointed out that a crippled boy was unable to walk.

"He managed to get from Plymouth, I daresay another mile would not be beyond him," Harry said.

"He's got a cart, sor," Peters said helpfully.

Anna resolved the argument by bursting into tears, and Harry and Peters beat a hasty retreat.

"How could two brothers be so different?" Anna sobbed. "With his dying breath Edmund spoke to that poor boy, spared a thought for the fellow suffering at his side, and his brother Harry, his own brother, would condemn the poor maimed child to drag himself along."

"I'm sure he didn't mean anything by it, Anna."

"Then why did he say it?" Her voice was becoming more and more high-pitched.

Cassandra was afraid she was going to have to deal with a case of hysterics. Then inspiration struck. "Anna, what are you going to feed the sailors? Where will they sleep? How long will they stay? Do you think you could find a job for Jemmy?"

By the time Harry returned, Anna was in the kitchen instructing the housemaids as they turned one of the attics into a dormitory for the sailors and overseeing Walters as he prepared a huge meal for them. The other sailors were as ragged as Peters, and just as thin. Cassandra was shocked to see that they all, save Peters, were maimed. One was missing a hand, another had a bandage over one eye, and the third limped badly, using a crutch and dragging one leg.

Anna would have stayed to watch them eat, but Cassandra felt that they deserved some privacy, and after a few minutes drew her away on the pretext of making sure the maids were carrying out their instructions in the attic. Harry, his callousness now forgiven, and Cassandra were left in the drawing room with instructions to "explain everything to Mama."

"I said she could be stubborn," Harry remarked.

"Isn't there a veterans' administration, some government office that could help the sailors? Don't they get a travel allowance so that they can go home?" Cassandra asked.

"Not that I've ever heard of. It seems that they are discharged at the port and left to make their own way home."

"Perhaps they could join the merchant marine, work on a trading vessel?"

"Peters seems the only able-bodied man among them. I almost wish, Cassandra, that they had not come here, for we must do something to help them, and I can't think what."

Cassandra agreed wholeheartedly that the sailors ought to be helped, but she found Harry's out-of-sight, out-of-mind attitude a little galling. "Have you thought what to say to Mrs. Chubbs? I don't have any idea."

"She's easily dealt with."

"Excellent. You speak to her, and I'll take care of Tom."

"But Cassandra—"

"I hear the carriage now, I'll tell Mrs. Chubbs that you want to talk to her."

But as Cassandra took Tom into the drawing room for the second time that day, she felt that her leaving Harry to deal with the old lady was particularly unfair, since she herself had often been guilty of the same offence—of seeing suffering she could not relieve and then wishing she had not seen the victim.

Tom, when she explained the situation to him, whistled in admiration. "Quite an old girl, our Anna is. Perhaps Jemmy could be apprenticed to a harness maker."

"I'm worried about him. He looks awfully flushed, and even though the others were trying to tempt him, he wasn't eating. Do you think he might have something contagious?"

Cassandra bit her lip. Only moments ago she had been

castigating Harry for wishing the sailors had never come, and now she was thinking that if they had typhoid, she certainly didn't want to have to look after them.

"I'll have a look at him. Is the family planning to dine tonight, or has Anna given all the food to the sailors?"

"I expect there's a bit of old bread left."

"Then tell James to set another cover. You'll need a friend by you after playing that shabby trick on Harry."

Tom returned a few minutes later, bringing Harry with him. "As best as I can tell, the boy still has a bone fragment in the stump. It is certainly infected. We ought to have a surgeon in."

"How did a child like that get to be a sailor? He must have been ten or eleven when Edmund was killed—if he's the same Jemmy."

"He's the same one," said Tom. "They would have taken him off the streets for a powder monkey—they bring the ammunition above decks during battles, you know. He's brave, too, didn't say a word when I told him he needed another operation, though his mates were upset and Anna's beside herself. I suppose we could have Jemmy taken to the surgeon's house. I say, Mrs. Brown, you don't look well."

Cassandra did not feel well. This was, she knew, well before the days of anaesthesia. "You'll butcher him," she murmured.

"Oh, it's not as bad as all that," Tom said hollowly.

"It's that or his life," Harry added matter-of-factly. "I'll make sure he has opium."

"That's all you can say?"

"It is all we can do," Harry said.

"Wait, if we only had more time, I could try to make ether, or chloroform, or nitrous oxide—laughing gas. Harry, didn't people used to breathe it at parties? Some one famous—your friend, Humphry Davy—don't you remember?"

As she spoke, Cassandra recalled that one could not achieve deep anaesthesia with nitrous oxide unless it was under pressure, and that involved use of highly specialized equipment to prevent the patient's lungs bursting. Still, she thought, one could get about eighty percent anaesthesia with nitrous oxide at standard pressure, and that, combined with opium, would be much, much better than nothing.

"By God," said Harry, "years ago he said something to me about using it during operations since those under its influence feel no pain. I even discussed it with a surgeon, but he told me that pain is beneficial to healing. I suppose that is why Sir Humphrey—"

"Pain isn't beneficial to healing. It weakens the body. If Jemmy has to have the operation, then you'll have to get nitrous oxide."

"But Cassandra—"

"If you don't, I will. I am sick and tired of being stuck in a house full of lunatics! If Anna can have hysterics, and you can sulk, then I can have laughing gas. And you can stop laughing, Tom." She sobered suddenly, wondering what she might have given away in her outburst.

Tom only compressed his lips in an effort to stop laughing. When he had gained his composure, he said, "I'll go for a sawbones."

"You'll have to make him wash his hands," said Cassandra, "and sterilise—" She broke off and tried to bring her racing mind under control before she betrayed herself.

When Tom had left, Cassandra turned to Harry. "Well," she said, "I don't suppose you want to hear all about the wonders of modern medicine."

"Not just now. Mrs. Chubbs, overcome with indignation, has asked for a tray to be sent to her chamber, in order to cause as little trouble as possible. I suppose Hester will see to little Edmund, and we can dine after the excitement is all over."

"Do you think I'm foolish about the anaesthetic? I just can't bear the thought of someone being cut open while he's wide-awake, but I don't know how we'll explain to the doctor."

"We'll think of something." He sighed wearily. "What a long day it's been!"

"I'm thankful for it, though. Did Anna ever show you Captain Matthews' letter? He wrote one just like it to my mother. I worried about it a great deal, for it was so terse, and I could think of only two explanations. Either Edmund had died so horribly that the captain could not bring himself to write of it, or Edmund was in some kind of disgrace. But Peters tells me that Captain Matthews was dying himself after the engagement, and I imagine it was all he could do to dictate those brief notes. And Anna, too, is relieved. Now she is still somewhat overset, but I can see already the change in her."

Cassandra remembered those few whispered words and wondered what sort of change it might be.

"Well," Harry concluded, "I'll be off and see if I can find a dose or two of your laughing gas."

Tom returned with Dr. Witten, a skeletal and jaundiced-looking young man with a deprecating sense of humour. He examined Jemmy and promised to come back the next day, when the light was at its best, and remove the fragment. When Cassandra diffidently suggested the use of nitrous oxide, he said only, "If Lieutenant Bestor wished it, ma'am, I'd operate on the devil himself, under any conditions."

"I don't think he's a very good doctor," Cassandra said after he'd left. "Did you see how his hands were shaking?"

"They'll be steady enough come morning," Tom told her, "and he'd boil his own hands in oil if I asked him to, poor devil. I first knew him after the battle at Fuentes Onoro, long before he became a drunk."

In the silence that followed Tom's remark, Cassandra asked, "Are you wondering about my . . . ideas?"

"No. And since it seems that there isn't going to be any

dinner in this house, I'm taking myself off now. Good night, Mrs. Brown."

Cassandra sat in the drawing room for a long time, thinking about Harry and his cousin, and wondering which Anna should marry.

Dr. Witten returned the next morning to remove the bone fragment. Anna and Mrs. Chubbs took Edmund out and urged Cassandra to join them, but she chose to remain. Although she had not had any formal medical training beyond first-aid courses, she wanted to make sure that her instructions were followed.

Jemmy was lifted to the kitchen table, which reeked of the gin Cassandra had used to disinfect it, and was draped with a boiled sheet. Harry gave him opium, then administered a large dose of laughing gas while Tom and Peters stood by to hold Jemmy still. Dr. Witten followed Cassandra's orders and washed his hands in gin while she boiled his instruments. To her relief, Dr. Witten operated quickly, no doubt because he generally operated without anaesthesia, for nitrous oxide, she knew, robbed the blood of oxygen.

When the splinter had been removed and abscess drained, Jemmy was put to bed with a new hearth grate over his stump to protect it from the weight of the blankets, Cassandra, Tom, Harry, and Dr. Witten gathered in the drawing room for a glass of sherry.

Dr. Witten sipped his slowly. "I shall return tomorrow to look at the boy. It is good nursing that will save him now. That and good food, for he is not strong." He paused. "He came through the operation well, Mrs. Brown. It seems there is something to your theory."

"Do you want to publish?" Cassandra asked forthrightly. She saw no point in beating about the bush.

"Do you really think, Mrs. Brown, that I am in any position to challenge the medical establishment?" he said bitterly. "I would rather perish in obscurity than notoriety.

If I am called in on any other cases, I will, with your permission, I hope, use your methods." His tone made it clear that he had no expectation of this happening. "I shall call upon the patient tomorrow. Your servant, ma'am, my lord, Lieutenant."

14

IT HAD BEGUN to snow, and Harry, who had worn his thin pumps, rather than wearing his boots and changing shoes at his host's house, was shivering by the time he had helped Mrs. Chubbs, Anna, and Cassandra into the chaise. He leapt in after them and thumped on the roof to signal Daniels to drive on.

He was delighted that Anna had consented to join the party and ascertained from Aunt Tavie that Tom would be among the guests, but he was afraid that with the dinner, Anna would begin her campaign to see him wed in earnest. So far she had contented herself to opening salvos—taking him on her morning calls and watching carefully to see which mamas and which young ladies paid the most attention to him, then quizzing him mercilessly to learn which he preferred so that she might arrange for Mrs. Larchmont to invite them tonight.

He had, he had to admit, shamelessly fobbed her off with generalities about intelligence and independence and mutual respect, but he could no longer treat her so shabbily. She was right. Sooner or later, he would have to marry. Indeed, he had recently come to realize how lonely it would be to return to an almost empty house, especially after spending so many weeks surrounded by congenial company. It would be unkind and ungracious not to take advantage of the opportunity she was giving him. He would devote tonight to ascertaining whether Miss Larchmont,

Miss Catherine Ross, or Miss Pierce would suit him as his lifelong companion.

As they sat in the parlour in front of the Runford fireplace before dinner, he told Laura Larchmont about Peters and the sailor's loyalty. He paused several times to give Miss Larchmont a chance to enter the conversation, but she stared fixedly over his shoulder, apparently too shy to meet his gaze, and nodded occasionally.

"And it seems that Jemmy, the powder monkey, is making an excellent recovery," Harry finished, and by asking after the health of her family was able to gain a few minutes in which he could examine her closely.

Laura was pink and fair, with light brown hair, and large, innocent eyes. Her dress, as befitted a young girl, was white, and it became her. He concluded she had a most pleasing, reserved manner. He could never imagine her contradicting him or taking him to task for the way in which the British navy was administered.

Once she had told him that her family was keeping well, although her father was somewhat troubled by gout, she sat silent, gazing at her clasped hands. Harry, about to introduce another subject, was prevented by the arrival of another guest, Mr. Ponsonby, a man in his forties, stout and red-faced. Mrs. Larchmont hurried over and, on the pretext of finding Harry a comfortable chair, made certain that Mr. Ponsonby could sit next to her daughter.

That answered a question which had faintly troubled Harry, for Mrs. Larchmont was not known for her generosity, and he had wondered why she had consented to invite two other eligible young ladies to a dinner where he, whom Anna had apparently introduced as a suitor for Laura, would be present. It seemed that Mr. Ponsonby had a prior claim.

So Harry removed her from his consideration. Fortunately, Miss Catherine Ross seemed equally delightful and much more talkative. She sat next to him at dinner and regaled him with the plots of all the novels she had read, giving him ample opportunity to examine his dinner companions and think quietly, nodding occasionally whenever Miss Ross paused.

In the middle of an exposition about whether mad monks or displaced noblemen made the better villains, Harry caught Cassandra's gaze and they shared a smile. She sat across from him, and he had to admit, she looked very handsome in her new gown. It certainly was not overtrimmed; indeed, he couldn't say exactly what set it apart from the gowns of the other women, but there was something about that particular shade of green which made her eyes shine like burning copper. And her hair, twisted around with a strand of pearls and gold ribbons, looked as though it would tumble down her back with the slightest provocation. He firmly pushed aside the unexpected, and remarkably pleasant image of himself loosening her hair so that it flowed down her white shoulders, and attended closely to Miss Ross's engaging chatter.

Miss Amelia Pierce was a trifle less charming. She was five and twenty, but by no means an ape leader, for she made no pretence to being in her first youth. Until the death of her father a year ago, she had devoted herself to caring for him, and was now, or so Anna had told him, looking for a husband to whom she could give the same unfailing care. She was dressed neatly, simply, and unbecomingly in dark brown. Harry thought it odd that she looked so sallow. When Cassandra wore brown, she looked very well.

Harry found he enjoyed her company, nonetheless, for she neither chattered nor sat silent, but asked him questions about himself in the most delightful, natural manner, and listened attentively as he explained Dalton's system of chemistry, although it was clear that she had not the slightest idea what he was talking about. This, he decided, was a most useful trait. In the unlikely event he mentioned a bit of his future knowledge, Miss Pierce would have no idea of what he had said and, very likely, would be unable to repeat it.

As the dinner progressed and Miss Pierce asked his opinion on political issues, he felt that he might have misjudged her intelligence, she was so quick to see the merit in his ideas. But when she skilfully drew the conversation around to Font Hall and the fact that the house was in need of some small repair, he could see her already calculating ways and means. It came to him that she was one of those women who needed always to martyr herself to something . . . an ageing parent, a husband, a large house. He wondered if Miss Ross could be made interested in studying mathematics or classical literature instead of reading novels.

The Larchmont house boasted a large double parlour, and once dinner was finished, the connecting doors were flung open, the furniture removed, and the rugs taken up. The musicians, a gentleman to play the piano and two other with violins, were shown into the room.

"Do you know," Miss Ross informed him, "ten couple can stand up here very easily."

"Yes, and Mrs. Larchmont had everyone to dine first, twenty-six people altogether, although some live very close by," added Miss Pierce, intimating that an economy could have been practised by inviting only those who lived some distance to dine.

Harry danced first with Miss Pierce and then with Miss Ross, although the country dances permitted little chance for conversation. As they went through the figures of "Picking up Sticks," Miss Ross, however, did manage to whisper that she was almost sorry to be dancing this dance with him.

"Why?" he asked. As they passed into the Hey, the movement of the dance drew them apart, and he was forced to wait for his answer.

"Because," she murmured as he swung her about, "the next dance will be a waltz."

"There will be others," he said as the music stopped.

It was apparent from the flush on her cheeks that he'd said something flirtatious, though it seemed straightforward enough to him. At a small dance such as this one, no one would think it odd for a lady to dance several times with the same man, but for a couple to stand up two times in a row would suggest to everyone that an announcement of their engagement would follow.

Miss Pierce was sitting next to Lucinda Eliot and her young brother-in-law, James Eliot, chatting in a determined way that clearly indicated *she* did not waltz—a point which placed her below Miss Ross in Harry's reckoning. He saw Cassandra talking to Mr. Ponsonby and remembered the evenings at Font Hall.

Harry bowed to Mr. Ponsonby, and when Cassandra did not immediately remark that Mr. Ponsonby had kindly asked her to dance, which was how any well-bred lady would indicate that she was spoken for, Harry asked her to dance with him.

The music began almost at once, and to Harry's delight, his time spent coaching Cassandra had paid handsomely. She was as graceful as any woman there.

"Are you enjoying your party, cousin?" he asked.

"Very much, thank you. And you?"

"Miss Ross and Miss Pierce," he began, then realized that it might seem less than thoughtful to praise two other ladies while waltzing with a third, "seem to be enjoying themselves also." He would ask Cassandra's opinion of those ladies later, however, for he valued her judgment.

"I don't think Miss Larchmont is enjoying herself very much. She seems so quiet."

Harry smiled. It had not taken Cassandra long to realize which ladies had taken his fancy. "I believe that is just her manner. She should be pleased, for her betrothed is here. You were just talking to him."

"Not Mr. Ponsonby?"

"The same. There's been no announcement, but—"

"But Harry, he's a male chauvinist."

"How so?" said Harry.

"You know. He thinks a woman's place is in the home—not that you'd think anything was wrong with that. But even worse, I think he's a woman hater. Look at him glaring at Miss Larchmont."

"He does seem a little ill at ease, but then so does she," Harry said, and carefully guided Cassandra so that she avoided the corner of a table. "But if it is not a love match, they may feel shy with each other."

"He asked me how old I was when I married, so I said eighteen, which we'd agreed on, as it gave me plenty of time to have been widowed, and he said that he'd prefer a younger bride, someone whom he could bring up to his likes and tastes."

"All men wish to marry someone with similar sensibilities," Harry said a little guiltily as he remembered his plans for educating Miss Ross.

"He thinks that his wife should be an adjunct, not a separate person. She looks like a child. How old is she, Harry?"

"I have no idea." Harry was feeling a little cross; all he wanted was a peaceful waltz, and Cassandra was so stiff in his arms that he wondered how he had ever come to think she was graceful.

As soon as the waltz ended, Cassandra walked toward Anna. Harry, who did not want to look as if he were being left on the floor, went with her. Anna was talking with her mother and another old lady, but when Cassandra and Harry came over, she stood and walked a couple of steps to meet them.

"How old is Laura Larchmont?" Cassandra asked without preamble.

"Sixteen," Anna replied, looking at Harry, "but I should tell you something that I have just learned."

"Is she engaged to Ponsonby?" Cassandra asked.

She was not replying to Anna's remark, but it seemed as

if she had, and Anna responded, "Exactly. It will be made public after the New Year. I hope, Harry, that you had not—"

"Anna, she can't," interrupted Cassandra. "He's a bully. And she's too young."

"I was that young," Anna reminded her.

"But I daresay Edmund did not try to reform your character."

"Of course not. But, Cassandra, do be reasonable. If Harry has fallen in love, he can speak to her papa, since no announcement has been made, and if she prefers him to Mr. Ponsonby, her parents will permit it, I am sure. But whenever did this attachment have time to form, for I don't think you've seen her more than a half-dozen times, Harry?"

"I have not fallen in love," Harry said, affronted. "And I think she should most certainly marry Mr. Ponsonby if she wants to."

"Talk to him for half an hour," said Cassandra sweetly, "and then tell me if you feel the same."

"I can tell you something about him," offered Anna. "It seems he has been engaged twice before. Naturally, the girls cried off, or seemed to, but there is a suggestion that he may have jilted them."

"I refuse to let mere gossip be my guide as I form an opinion of a man," Harry said, wincing as he realized how pompous he sounded.

Anna just smiled, and Cassandra was already walking towards Miss Larchmont. Naturally, Harry went in search of Mr. Ponsonby, determined to find him an upstanding gentleman. He spoke first of the pleasant evening, then remarked on the handsomeness of the ladies present, noting Miss Larchmont in particular.

"Indeed, sir," replied Mr. Ponsonby a little coldly, "she is very pretty."

Harry took his tone as a sign of possessiveness, and a

mark in his favour. "A man might look for a bride like her," he said casually.

"You may drop the pretence, my lord," said Mr. Ponsonby, proudly, "and wish me happy. I understand it is all over the room that I have asked her father for her hand."

"Congratulations, sir. She has made a wise choice."

"Well, to be strict about the matter, it is not fully settled. Her father wishes to wait until she is seventeen before formally betrothing her, but since every young buck knows of my attentions, I need not worry for competition. You would do well, my lord, to take a leaf from my book, and when you see the girl you want, set your mark upon her."

Harry thought it was a most ungentlemanly trick, for if the other men thought she was all but engaged, they would never make an offer or even consider making one. Of course, Miss Larchmont might have suggested that Ponsonby behave thus since she had no wish to encourage other suitors.

Mr. Ponsonby opened an enameled snuffbox and offered Harry a pinch, which was politely refused. "You do not indulge, my lord?" His tone was so injured that one would have thought Harry had flung the contents of the box in his face.

"Took me some time to find this girl, I can tell you." Mr. Ponsonby continued taking his snuff. "It's been six years since Mrs. Ponsonby passed away, and in all that time I've not found a girl like her. Young ladies these days," he said sternly, "are too opinionated by half."

Well, thought Harry, no one could say that Miss Larchmont was opinionated. If she had strong views on any matter, she did not voice them.

"I can understand why her father wishes you to wait some little while, sir," he said, recalling the remark that had so annoyed Cassandra. "She is still young."

"Even a young girl, my lord, can be shockingly disrespectful. I have been deceived before, I am sorry to say, but I feel that Miss Larchmont is well suited to become

Mrs. Ponsonby, well suited indeed, for she is most biddable."

Harry was beginning to understand Cassandra's objection to Mr. Ponsonby. The man's bluff and blunt manner must have offended her sensibilities. He had spent a number of evenings listening to her argue that women didn't want protection and guidance, but a chance to enjoy every opportunity open to men regardless of the risks to health and peace of mind.

Harry found he, too, did not like Mr. Ponsonby, but the fact he protested so loudly that he wished to be king in his own castle led Harry to believe that Mr. Ponsonby generally found himself wrapped around the little finger of the fair sex. It was very likely, considering Ponsonby's great conceit, that his suit had been discreetly refused, and the fool had not taken the hint. He bowed to Mr. Ponsonby and went to ask Miss Pierce to make up a set for "The Lancers." Without ever praising him directly, she made such a fuss of his dancing that she was again promoted over Miss Ross.

Later that evening he found himself looking for a moment's peace and quiet so that he could weigh Miss Ross against Miss Pierce and choose which he would have as his partner in the last dance, for he knew that young ladies set much store by that sort of thing. Most of the chairs and sophas had been pushed against one of the walls when the floor was cleared for dancing. One sopha had been put at right angles to the rest, and its back was a little way from the wall. A straight chair stood behind it, in the nook formed by the corner and the sopha.

Harry sat there, hidden in the shadows. It was unlikely anyone would bother him for a little while, and the noise would not interrupt his train of thought.

Miss Larchmont, in a voice suggesting suppressed tears, was saying, ". . . that I don't know how to please him, for if I disagree with him, he is angry, and if I agree, he scolds me for showing no spirit. But if I don't take Mr. Ponsonby,

I'll never wed, for he says that no one else would put up with my airs, and I fear he is right, for Mama often says that I lack character. Oh, Mrs. Brown, you must not tell anyone this. Indeed, if you hadn't repeated his remark, I would have never known, and I should not be saying this to you, but oh, I have been so wretched for weeks. Papa will say I have to marry him, I know he will."

Harry wanted very much to stay and listen. It was too late to jump up and make himself known, for that would only embarrass poor Miss Larchmont. He stood up, intending to slip quietly away.

"Laura, I agree, you do not want to marry Ponsonby. But who do you want to marry?"

Harry sat down again quickly. He had no right to monitor Miss Larchmont's conversations, but he had a duty to make certain that Cassandra, in her ignorance, did not give the poor girl bad advice.

"Oh, I do not know, Mrs. Brown; indeed, I have never thought of it."

"What sort of men do you like? Who do you admire?"

"I have always thought that Cicero was a man of great character."

"And who do you know who is like him."

"Mr. James Eliot"—Miss Larchmont faltered—"has a very noble disposition."

"Excellent. Do you like him?"

"I really do not know him well enough to say so, for we rarely speak."

"I am going to take you over to Mrs. Font, Laura, and you are to not to worry. I am sure I can do something."

Harry slipped away while Laura was stammering her thanks. Cassandra had no right to interfere, or to make promises she could not keep. He would have to speak to her at once. Meanwhile, Cassandra went first to Anna, then to Tom, who bowed and went over to Ponsonby, and then she flirted with James Eliot until the young man asked her to waltz.

Harry was beginning to think that she was avoiding him, when she came up to him as he carried lemonade to Miss Ross and her sister and announced that they had to talk. As soon as he had delivered the refreshments, he excused himself to Miss Ross and Mrs. Brand and collected two more glasses, then stood with Cassandra in a quiet spot.

"Well," she said, "what do you think of Ponsonby now?"

"I would not say I like the man, but I daresay that Miss Larchmont will be able to manage him."

"I do not think so. Laura does not want to marry him."

"Then there is no difficulty." He wanted to scold her for interfering, but he could hardly do so without revealing that he had eavesdropped.

"He is rich, and Mr. Larchmont likes him, or so Laura says. I don't think he would listen if we tried to tell him otherwise, and Mrs. Larchmont seems firmly under her husband's thumb. In fact, Mr. Larchmont probably approves of Mr. Ponsonby's views on marriage."

"It really isn't any of your business, Cassandra, but if Miss Larchmont *were* to ask your opinion, you could tell her that he is not the sort of man one would wish for a husband."

"I tried. She explained that she couldn't be a drain on her parents' household forever, and that since they, who are so much older and wiser, had chosen a husband for her, she should be bound by their wishes. Ponsonby is right about one thing, she has very little spirit. Damn the man, I expect he's a wife beater. He has that domineering, easily wounded ego."

Harry looked shocked. "Please, Cassandra, mind your tongue."

"I beg your pardon," she said perfunctorily. "Do you think that if her father had another offer, he'd put them both to her, and let her choose?"

"He might, if it was equally good in his eyes."

"Hmmm. What do you think would measure up to cold hard cash?" Cassandra asked.

Harry saw Tom coming towards them and thought that he was about to ask Cassandra for the dance. Thankful that he had not promised either Miss Ross or Miss Pierce, he took her half-finished glass of lemonade from her hand, put it with his on a table, and led her onto the dance floor. As was traditional, the last dance was "Cellenger's Round," and as many couples as could crowded onto the floor.

As they waited for the opening chords, Harry's gaze went around room. He noticed Anna and Tom talking to Mrs. Chubbs. Suddenly Tom took Anna's hand and led her, blushing and smiling, onto the floor. Lucinda Eliot was being helped to her feet by her husband, who smiled at her tenderly, and Mrs. Larchmont was ordering the footman to adjust the footstool under Mr. Larchmont's gouty foot. Then Miss Larchmont and Mr. Ponsonby squeezed in next to them.

"Oh no, Mr. Ponsonby," he heard Laura saying softly, "I did not mean to hint that you should dance. I only meant to say that I do not think that there is anything wrong with a man not caring to dance."

Mr. Ponsonby replied, "But Miss Larchmont, you just told me that you liked very much to dance. I believe you are contradicting yourself. Again."

Harry Font put Miss Ross and Miss Pierce at the bottom of his list.

15

THE PARTY ENDED just before midnight, and as they drove home, Cassandra sat quietly, listening more to the muffled sound of the horses and carriage than to Mrs. Chubbs complaining about the rude way she felt people had treated her. When Aunt Tavie had loaned Cassandra the pearls, she had also sent over a fur-lined mantle which she had worn forty years ago. Casandra now drew it tightly around herself. For the first time in days she felt a stranger here.

She had very much enjoyed the early part of the evening. She had been admired, and men had flirted with her, but she had found it all a little unreal. The entire evening had been rather like a play. Cassandra had listened and been both amused and pleased to see how similar were the concerns of those who lived now, in 1815, and the concerns of the people she had grown up with. She'd had the feeling that if she had not expected to return to her own time in a very few days, she could have easily stepped onto the imaginary stage and joined in the performance.

Then she had danced with Harry and tried to tease him about his interest in Laura Larchmont. From that point on, the evening had been a misery. It had been very easy to get Laura to disclose her situation. A little sympathy produced a torrent of confidences.

Cassandra sighed. Not only was there the danger that the poor girl would marry a man who would treat her very badly, but if that did happen, the law would give her no protection. Divorce was almost unheard of, and wife beating was legal. From what Laura had said, it seemed unlikely that her parents would help her if she ever wanted to leave Ponsonby.

It also appeared that such callousness was normal in Regency times. Harry seemed to think there was nothing wrong with a man like Ponsonby. No doubt, thought Cassandra savagely, Lord Font believed that women ought to be miserable. No wonder he had worked so hard on the equations that all save the final step, which could only be done when the time of her departure was decided, were finished. He probably couldn't wait to see the back of a woman who had told him to his face that women were every bit as good as men and had proved it by her superior knowledge. Yet he sounded so reasonable, so willing to listen to her and treat her seriously.

Cassandra firmly dismissed Harry's perfidy from her mind. The most important question was Laura's future. She had ascertained that if Laura were ever to hold a gentleman in esteem, it would be someone like James Eliot. Unfortunately, Laura was too shy to encourage him. Cassandra had taken James over to Laura, started a conversation, then talked to Mr. Ponsonby for half an hour so that he could not interrupt them. Now she wondered if she should have done something more direct. Perhaps she should have told James the whole story.

The chaise drew up before the house. Someone, Cassandra expected one of the sailors, had been sweeping the flagstones in front of the house regularly, for although the snow was still falling, the path was virtually clear. Anna hurried upstairs to see that Edmund was tucked in safely, and Mrs. Chubbs announced her intention of going to bed.

Cassandra, too, went up to her bedroom. One of the maids was waiting and began to unpin her hair. Almost immediately there was a knock on her door, and Harry asked her to join him in the drawing room for a moment. Because she half hoped for an apology, she agreed to come down in a minute. She sent the maid to bed, finished unpinning her hair, and used one of the ribbons to tie it back before she went downstairs.

Harry was waiting for her. There was a candle on the table but no fire, and the room was cold. "I won't take a moment, my dear, but I did want to tell you that I have decided to . . . well, er, get married."

Cassandra didn't know what to say, and so kept silent.

"I thought you'd be pleased," Harry finally said.

"Why? Anna is the one who wants you to get married," she said scathingly. "I don't know why you thought it would interest me."

Before Harry could answer, Anna herself came in. "He's sleeping like a lamb, dear little boy," she said fondly. "Did I interrupt you? I am sorry."

"No," said Harry, "I'm just off to bed. Good night, Anna. Cassandra. It was a lovely evening, wasn't it? I'm certain no one thought it odd that I attended."

"I'm sure they didn't." Cassandra said.

She wanted only to go to bed, but first Harry had dropped his bombshell and gone off in a huff, and now Anna wanted reassurance that she need not spend the rest of her life in seclusion.

"I am glad I went. I enjoyed myself so much, and Harry did, too. Did you notice how much time he spent with Miss Pierce?"

Cassandra wondered how much of Anna's matchmaking had been an effort to disguise her own feelings, or perhaps an attempt to show Harry how devoted she was to him. It seemed a very anaemic way to try to attract a man's attention. Obviously, Harry didn't want Anna to know that he was planning to get married, but Cassandra no longer cared about Harry's wishes. She did want to learn *why* Anna wanted Harry to get married, and how badly Anna wanted to marry him herself before she decided how to break the news that Harry was already planning to marry.

"You worry about Harry not being married because of your son and Harry's title, but I don't understand why."

"You do realize that should, God forbid, anything happen to Harry right now, little Edmund would be Lord Font?"

"Yes."

"Well, rightfully that title belongs to Harry's eldest son—not that he has one yet, but he ought to have one before he dies and before someone gives little Edmund the idea that he will be Lord Font. Someone did that to poor Arthur's father, and it caused him no end of trouble."

Cassandra did not know if Anna meant Arthur or his father, but she decided not to interrupt to ask.

"I am sometimes afraid that Harry will wait too long before he marries, and then will decide not to merely to avoid disappointing little Edmund. My husband was devoted to his brother. He would never want his own son to prevent Harry from marrying."

"There seems little danger of that," Cassandra said dryly. She was struck by a notion that she knew at once was gothick. But once she'd thought of it, she couldn't get it out of her mind. "Anna, you don't feel that you have to marry Harry, do you?"

"Well if he has no one else to help him . . ." Anna replied in some confusion.

"No, not see him married, but marry him if no one else will."

"Marry Harry! Don't be ridiculous." Anna blushed. "What a shameful thing to say. Edmund was his brother!"

"I know."

"Think about what you are saying, Mrs. Brown!" And with that Anna stalked from the room, leaving a puzzled Cassandra to go slowly up the stairs.

She was just beginning to undo her buttons when there was a shattering scream. Cassandra ran to the door to see Anna hurrying down the hall.

"I am sorry if I frightened you, but little Edmund isn't in his bed. I went to take another look at him, and he is gone. Hester says that she didn't hear him go out, but she was sleeping so soundly that I had to shake her."

Harry came from his room, shoeless and without his coat. "Perhaps he has slipped out and hidden somewhere to tease you, Anna. It has only been a few minutes since you last looked."

"He could be sleep walking. Oh, Harry."

"He is too young to sleepwalk," Harry said firmly. "Where is Hester?"

"Searching the nursery."

"Well, the two of you look upstairs; Cassandra and I will look downstairs and in the kitchens."

After twenty minutes they had still not found Edmund. Harry sent James for the watch. Cassandra was very worried. Edmund might hide for a joke, but he was a very obedient little boy. She couldn't imagine him hiding once it was obvious that the adults were worried, unless he'd fallen asleep.

She searched the kitchen again. It seemed very likely to her that he might have come downstairs looking for a snack. She saw the hamper from Fortnum and Mason and bit back a sob as she remembered how he'd hidden there nearly three weeks ago. Then she shook her head angrily. Usually she kept her head in a crisis; but the excitement of the evening, Harry's unexpected reaction to Laura's plight, his equally unexpected announcement that he was getting married, Anna's anger, all conspired against her. You should just face it, she told herself. You've become fond of the little boy.

She did not expect to find him in the hamper. He'd never be able to climb into it himself, and it had already been filled with bran. She took off the lid anyway.

Edmund was there, half-sunk into the bran, his eyes wide with fear, and near choking on his nightcap, which had been stuffed into his mouth and tied there with a bit of rag. Cassandra pulled him out and took off the gag, screaming at the top of her voice for the others. His wrists had been bound to his ankles so that he had been unable to stand on the bran, which would have given him enough purchase to push the top off the basket and hang on the rim.

Anna took him from Cassandra's arms and Harry cut the cloth binding him. When asked how he had gotten into the basket, he first said that he didn't know, but finally stated that Mrs. Brown had put him there.

"But that was a long time ago, Edmund, when we were playing hide-and-seek," Cassandra reminded him.

Edmund looked at her, burst into tears, and said again that he didn't know how he had gotten in the hamper.

Anna turned on her. "You unnatural woman. Why? Why in God's name did you try to kill him?"

"But I didn't."

"Anna, you are overwrought."

Cassandra and Harry spoke at the same time.

The veins in Anna's wrists throbbed, and her eyes were wild. "Then how did you know he was there?"

"I didn't, it was just luck," Cassandra protested.

"Be sensible, Anna, why would she have rescued him if she'd wanted to harm him, and why would she want to?"

"I expect she was overcome with remorse. When the watch comes, I want her taken away and hanged!"

"When could she have done it?" Harry's voice was calm, but Cassandra noticed that his hands shook. "As soon as she went upstairs, I asked her to come back down and a maid was with her until she did."

"Actually, I sent the maid way," Cassandra said, knowing that it would only condemn her in Anna's eyes, but aware that if there were a trial, it would look very bad if she had concealed that fact. "I didn't do this to Edmund. But while we're arguing, whoever did could be getting away."

"Wasn't Mrs. Brown," Edmund said suddenly. "That was a lie." And then he was wretchedly sick.

An officer came from the magistrate and questioned everyone, a process which took hours. A physician was sent for, who told them that Edmund was not harmed. The child was reassured that making a mistake and confusing the time that Mrs. Brown had played hide-and-seek with this time was not a lie and his mother took him up to her bed for the night, but he was still unable to tell them who had done it. The physician said this was not uncommon in cases of shock.

Her sleeping child in her arms, Anna passed Cassandra and asked, "Do you still wish to stay for Christmas, Mrs. Brown?"

Cassandra replied truthfully that she did not.

"Then Daniels will take you wherever you wish to go in the morning," Anna said, and left the room.

"You don't have to—" began Harry.

"I do. I said something earlier which insulted her, I'm not sure why, and if she thinks that I'd try to kill a child, I'd rather not have anything to do with her just now. You don't mind if I go back to Font Hall, and then straight home. I don't want to wait until you're ready to leave."

"Not at all," Harry said wearily. "We'll talk in the morning. I can't think straight now. But don't worry. Everything will work out."

Cassandra didn't even bother to undress. She took off her shoes and lay down on the bed, wrapped in a quilt, her mind in turmoil. Someone had tried to kill Edmund, and there seemed to be no motive. That suggested a psychopath. Just as frightening was the thought that she might still be accused of attempted murder. As far as she could remember, hanging seemed to be the only punishment used at this time. Stories of the horrors of Newgate Prison crept into her mind.

It seemed to her very unlikely that she'd be allowed to leave the house in the morning. In a modern crime investigation she was sure the police would never let a prime suspect leave.

An hour later, at five o'clock, Augusta came in with a cold, weak cup of tea and a slices of burnt, dry toast. It was easy to see who had the servants' sympathies in this house.

Cassandra left London that day in her green silk gown, the overlarge boots she'd arrived in, and an ornate fur wrap. She knew it was petty, but she had no wish to wear any of Anna's clothes. She had thought the woman was her friend, and the disillusion pained her. If I did wear one of her dresses, Cassandra thought spitefully, I expect she'd have me arrested for stealing. She was immediately ashamed. She had almost forgotten that the poor woman had just seen her only child half murdered, and had no idea who had done it or why.

She wondered briefly if she should stay to help Anna, but decided that her presence would only add to her distress. There was nothing to hold Cassandra here. A freak chance had brought her into these people's lives, and she had stayed long enough.

It was Christmas Eve, and the streets were crowded. Cassandra huddled in a corner of the coach and felt like weeping. At least she didn't have to face Harry. No one had come to say good-bye to her. She fell into an uneasy half sleep, dreaming over and over that she was trying to pull Edmund from the bran only to have him slip from her hands and slide from view into certain suffocation.

Last night's snow had turned to ice in the ruts on the surface of the turnpike. The chaise crept forward, lurched, and stopped. Cassandra curled up on the seat, rocked forward, thought about waking up, and then decided not to. There was a knocking on the door, then it opened, and Harry, wearing his sword, climbed in.

"Good afternoon, Cassandra."

"Harry! What are you doing here."

"I came to tell you that you're no longer under suspicion for attempted murder."

"Thank you." Cassandra pulled herself together and sat up.

"I rode after you as soon as I learnt you left. Edmund made a clean breast of things this morning. Poor little lad. It was Job who tied him up and put him in the bran. He threatened to mutilate Edmund if he told anybody." He shook his head. "At first we had no idea why he'd put Edmund in the hamper, but later Anna and Mrs. Chubbs found that their jewels were missing. Did you send Aunt Tavie's pearls back to her? We couldn't find them."

"I left the pearls on the dressing table last night. I took the cloak, thinking that you could send it to Aunt Tavie later."

"That's all right. You can take it to her."

"Harry, I don't want to go back. We must be halfway to Font Hall. I just want to get there and go home—to my own time."

"Are you certain?"

"Yes."

"Then let me give a message to the groom from the Blue Swan who rode with me, and I'll come with you."

"Please don't," said Cassandra, but Harry had already gone.

When he reentered the chaise, he carried a small hamper. Cassandra closed her eyes. If Harry was to travel with her, so be it, she lacked the energy to protest. She slipped back into her half dream, hardly aware of the sound of the basket being opened and liquid being poured into a glass. Then Harry had an arm around her shoulders and was holding a glass to her lips.

"It's brandy. Drink slowly. I don't suppose you've eaten."

Cassandra sipped and felt the warmth of the brandy spread through her. "No. Did you say it was afternoon?"

"Just after one o'clock. We're only a half mile from Font

Leigh. I wish I had brought some food. Even though the road is fairly clear here, it may well take us an hour to reach Font Hall."

"What *did* happen last night?"

"It seems that Job robbed us. He waited until we returned from the Larchmonts, created an uproar by trying to murder Edmund, then stole the jewels and ran off. No one remembers seeing Job after midnight. It is a very odd business. If he'd wanted to commit such an atrocious crime, he could have taken the jewels first, then hidden Edmund. Why risk robbing the bedchambers when he knew people were searching for the child?"

"Has he been caught?"

"No. Anna and Edmund—and Jemmy—along with Mrs. Chubbs and the female servants have been parceled out among various relations. Tom and some of his cronies have moved into the house. They, and the other sailors, are looking forward to Job's return, but I doubt we'll see the boy again."

"What happened to his dog?" Cassandra asked irrelevantly.

"Tom's taken it in hand. I did not mean for you to leave, and certainly not alone, Cassandra, but I was out when Augusta bundled you off. As for Font Hall, I gave the Drinkwaters leave to visit Martha's mother for Christmas. Farmer Wilkin's son is feeding the chickens, but the house will be empty."

"I don't mind. I just need to do the final calculations—Harry, I never thought. How are we going to know the exact time?" Cassandra could have wept. She never wore a wristwatch. Generally she used a combination timepiece-stopwatch slung on a lanyard around her neck, but the morning before she'd been transtemporalized she'd lent it to Will.

"The exact time?" asked Harry.

"I've know all along that timing is important, but I never thought of what we'd use as a chronometer."

"My watch," said Harry.

"No, even if it keeps good time, we don't know if it is accurate enough. It was to be within a minute or so of Greenwich Mean Time, since that is what the 4-D accelerator is calibrated to. If we are a few seconds off, I'll arrive within a faction of a second of when I left, but a mistake of a moment would add thirty seconds. If we're wrong by five minutes, I could arrive half an hour before I left." She didn't even want to think about the ramifications of that paradox. A very likely outcome was that she'd simply cease to exist—or that everything else would.

"I know," said Harry. "I was wondering when you'd think of that. You're so used to having excellent time pieces that you overlooked it."

"How can you be so calm?"

"I thought of a way around it. We could use a sextant."

"How? I thought you used one to navigate."

"One does. Edmund taught me while he was still a midshipman. You take sightings at noon, and calculate latitudes and longitudes. We worked out the exact position of Font Hall."

"So when you duplicate those readings, it is noon," Cassandra finished for him.

"Exactly."

"Are sextants easy to come by?"

"I'll take care of that."

It would mean waiting a few extra days until Harry could buy one, but Cassandra's relief was so great that she didn't mind.

"Could I ask you something about last night, Cassandra?" Harry said abruptly.

She was so weary that it was easier to agree than refuse.

"Why were you so displeased when I told you that I would make an offer for Miss Larchmont? It seemed to me the best way out for her."

"Oh, Harry. I thought you were going to marry someone else. I misunderstood."

Cassandra did not like the fact that marriage seemed the only escape for Laura, but a loveless marriage to Harry would be much better than life with that brute Ponsonby. Cassandra had always discounted stories of true love blossoming from an arranged marriage as an attempt to justify a cruel institution, but she thought that it might be possible for there to be affection between Laura and Harry. Certainly, he would treat her kindly and with less arrogance than most men of his age would. There was every possibility that Laura would be happy, for Harry would be an easy man to love. The thought brought Cassandra little comfort.

16

CASSANDRA FELL ASLEEP again, leaning against Harry, and did not wake until they drew up in Font Leigh. The shops were shut, but Harry got out of the chaise anyway to see what he could do. Casandra waited, still half-asleep, while Harry roused a shopkeeper who sold him some food and a crock of milk to take with them to Font Hall.

"Would you like a meal at the Font Arms? It's a public house, but they'll give us a private room." he asked when he returned.

"I just want to get inside and lie down, but you should go."

"I'll go on to the Hall and try to cook for us there."

When they arrived at Font Hall, Harry helped Cassandra down then gave Daniels some money and sent him to eat at the Font Arms. Fortunately he had a friend in a nearby village, and Anna had already given him permission to spend that night and Christmas day with his friend and his family. In fact, Daniels could stay there until Harry wished to return to London, or sent him back because he had decided not to return.

The house was freezing cold, but Harry ran upstairs and came back with a coverlet. "Lie on the settee in the drawing room with this around you whilst I light the fire. I'll make us a pot of tea—I can manage that. It's possets which are beyond my talent."

Cassandra was only too happy to comply. She kicked off the large boots and curled up, huddled under the quilt.

Harry soon returned with the tea; and as the fire warmed the room, the hot drink laced with brandy helped to take the chill from her body.

Harry brought them a meal of fried eggs, bacon, and bread, and after eating it, she felt nearly herself again. "Shall I do the washing up?"

"It will wait until morning," Harry assured her, but he did take the plates back to the kitchen.

Cassandra knew that leaving the dishes dirty would only attract mice and resolved to wash them before she went to bed. She felt that she should get up, but it was so pleasant to lie before the fire. She had played at being a Regency lady for so long that her relief at simply being herself again was a pleasure. Alone with Harry, she did not have to watch her tongue any more than she had to with any friend. She imagined that her happiness at once again being in Font Hall was a precursor to the greater happiness that would soon follow when she returned to Font House in her own time.

It would take only a few days, perhaps a little as a week, she guessed, for Harry to find a sextant. The final calculations would be an hour's work: perhaps another hour to check them, and then they would be ready.

"Merry Christmas!" Harry placed a large leather box in her lap, making her jump.

"Thank you. Whatever is it?" She took the key he offered and opened the case's brass lock. Nestled inside, there was a piece for equipment, something she recognized from a history-of-science course. "It's a sextant."

"It was Ed's. They sent it back with his effects. Tomorrow I'll take the sightings, and then . . ."

And then she'd be home before the day was out. Cassandra pushed to the back of her mind the possibility that there might be something wrong with the calculations, but the worry must have shown on her face, for Harry asked, "What if we have made a mistake? It would be much safer if you stayed here."

"I'd stake my life on those calculations," she said, unaware of the irony.

"So would I," said Harry, "but what if the theory is wrong?"

"There is only one way we'll know. The best scientists are always their own guinea pigs—experiment on themselves."

"I'd be happy to volunteer. I'd love to see the future, even if only for a fraction of a second."

"No, no thank you. I want to be the one to go." It was her theory, and Cassandra had already decided it would be too dangerous to publish it. She did not want to be responsible for the results of meddling by people who wanted to rewrite history. "I hope, Harry, that you and I will be the only people ever to know about transtemporalization, and I can't imagine anyone else I'd rather share it with."

Harry nodded. "As long as you understand the risks involved."

"Don't be ridiculous. I hypothesized most of those risks."

Cassandra had not realized until now how much was she was going to miss his odd mixture of stuffiness, patronizing ways, and gallantry.

"I never congratulated you on your engagement," she said.

"I haven't even spoken to her father, but I will, directly I return to London. If you don't mind, Cassandra, I would rather not discuss it."

"Of course."

They sat silently watching the fire. Cassandra thought of the evenings they had spent in this room before she went to London. She remembered her arrival in this strange time, and how Harry had contrived to explain her appearance to himself by almost any means other than the real one. Imagine, preferring to believe that you've gone mad to admitting that there is such a thing as time travel. The stratagems he'd used to explain her presence to others were almost as funny.

"Blast!" Cassandra said loudly. "How are we going to explain my leaving. I can't just disappear from your house?"

"I could drive you to the stage for Plymouth, pretending that you're leaving for America, or Daniels could take you. I'd drive myself to the Hart and Hound by a different route. You leave the coach at the Hart and Hound, and bespeak a room, slipping out once it is dark—"

"Keep it simple, Harry. I'll write a note saying that I'm so distressed by Anna—by what happened at Anna's—that I didn't ever want to see a Font again, and I'm making my own way back to America. Then I'll vanish without a trace, taking with me whatever valuables I can carry. You can pretend that I did that, can't you? I don't want to take anything really."

"Someone might think that I murdered you."

"But there is a law in England, isn't there, that you can't accuse someone of murder if you can't produce a body. I'm sure there used to be one."

"True, true. Well, your scheme is simpler, and much better for that, though everyone will assume that you were an adventuress after all."

"Once I'm home, I'm not going to worry about the things people dead two hundred years and more might say about me," Cassandra said with bravado, and then wished she hadn't. She didn't much care for the idea of Harry and the other people she had known here lying in their graves.

The idea seemed to disturb Harry, too, for he stood to poke the fire. "We'll go to church in the morning," he announced.

"I can't go in this." She pointed to her crumpled gown.

"I had more than brandy in that basket. Anna sent you some clothes."

She'd have to wear Aunt Tavie's elaborate, old-fashioned

cloak, but perhaps that would just add to her reputation once she was gone. "I'd love to go with you."

Anna had sent Cassandra's nightgown and toilet articles, so she was able to spend a comfortable night on the settee, for she couldn't bear the thought of going upstairs to an ice-cold bedroom. Harry was rather nonplussed when she stated her intention. Had Cassandra been in her own time, in a similar situation with a man she knew and trusted as well as she did Harry, she would have suggested that he make up a bed for himself in the same room to get the benefit of the heat; but she was afraid that such a proposal would shock Harry to his very core.

In the morning she dressed in her rose wool gown. She was half-glad that Anna had not sent her shoes. It was a twenty-minute walk to the church of St. Anne, and if Cassandra had shoes she would have worn them instead of those awful old boots, and most likely ended with wet and cold feet. Fortunately, Aunt Tavie's cloak was so long that no one would see her feet. It was a shame she couldn't wear it while she and Harry ate breakfast. He must be getting very tired of seeing her with feet that looked as though they belonged to a clown.

She went to the bedroom she had slept in when she first arrived because there was no mirror in the drawing room. As she brushed her hair and twisted it into a knot, she looked closely at her reflection. Obviously clothes made the woman, for she was startled to see how much she looked like the other women here.

They sat in the front pew, a large box with seats on three sides which had been the Fonts' place in church for time immemorial. One day, Cassandra supposed, Laura—Lady Font—would sit beside Harry; and as the years went by, their children would fill up the benches. She hoped, for Anna's sake, that they'd have a son.

Harry knelt in prayer for several minutes while Cassandra surreptitiously glanced around the church. It was her last chance to examine life in 1815. The church was decorated with swags of holly and ivy, and the choir, many of whom played instruments as well as sang, filled the church with carols.

Cassandra did not understand the significance of vicar's adding a plea that man be kept from the vanities of this world, and since none of Harry's neighbours were rude enough to ask why he and Mrs. Brown had returned for Christmas—although Harry answered many questions about Anna's health and refused two invitations to dinner—Cassandra decided that no one thought their presence there particularly odd.

They walked home across the fields so that Harry could show her something of the estate before she left. "I have fourteen tenant families, and they use most of the land," he said. "Fortunately I do not hunt, so their crops are not destroyed, and I have not enclosed the common, so many keep cows. I sometimes think they live better than I do. Tom certainly does. He had some radical notion about the nobility farming, though you'll note he stays in town and does not get his hands dirty."

Harry took her through the ruined gardens. They had been the pride and joy of his father's first wife, five acres of lawns and paths and flowerbeds and nooks and glades adorned with fountains and greenhouses. While his own mother had been alive, she had done her best to maintain the garden, but two years ago Harry had dismissed the staff. The Duchess of Litchford thought she had lured them away, but Harry had wanted to use the money saved by not paying their wages to repair the roof.

"We'll have a picnic in the kitchen," he suggested. "I lit the stove before we went to church. There is a fried ham and the fruitcake the shopkeeper's wife gave me. Her own baking. We should be done by half past eleven. Then you can change, and I'll get ready to take the reading. Once we've established noon . . ."

He did not finish his sentence, but instead busied himself taking down one of the hams which hung from the ceiling.

He did not have to complete the thought. Cassandra knew that soon after that, if all went well, she'd be home.

She fried the ham while Harry made tea. "In my grandfather's day," he remarked, "the family ate in the hall every day, with the house servants and farm laborers all sitting along the same table. Every Christmas they'd have a Lord of Misrule, one of the servants would take the master's place at the head of the table, and now I've come to keep Christmas in the kitchen. Well, my lady, I'll bring up a bottle of wine, and at least I'll be able to drink your health."

"I'll drink yours in tea, if you don't mind," said Cassandra. "I want to be clearheaded for later."

Afterwards Cassandra could not remember what they had talked about. The conversation had been commonplace, of that she was certain, but it must have been engrossing, for as they sat over the empty plates they heard the church clock strike noon.

"Damn and blast," she cried. If Harry was to set his watch accurately, he should have been taking readings with the sextant for the last fifteen minutes. She was stranded for another day. The Freudians would say that subconsciously she feared the danger of attempting transtemporalization, but Cassandra would rather blame the recent excitement. "I can't believe I was so stupid. Of all the ridiculous things to do."

"I'm terribly sorry. I should have kept an eye on the time."

"It's not your fault. Anyone would think I didn't want to go home." Cassandra realized that she was furious enough to quarrel with Harry in order to relieve the tension, and she didn't want to do that. "Why don't you light a fire in the drawing room while I clean up here? We'll just have to be more careful tomorrow."

They hardly spoke that afternoon, but sat together reading. Cassandra fought the temptation to work further on the calculations. She knew from experience that at this point she'd only make mistakes. Instead, she read Sir

Humphry's *Chemical Agriculture* without understanding a word of it.

Another meal, this time of ham and eggs, marked the end of the long afternoon and the start of an indeterminable evening. They went to bed early, and the next morning Cassandra dressed in her sweat pants and lab coat, and used Aunt Tavie's cloak for warmth. They both went out with the sextant at eleven o'clock, and as soon as Harry had taken the necessary sightings, they hurried to the laboratory and did the final calculations, speaking only of the work.

Once they were finished, Harry gathered up all their notes. They had decided it would be safest if he burned them as soon as she left. If she took them with her, someone at the Center might find them; and if Harry kept them, there was a chance that they might be preserved among his family papers and discovered later on. It was a minuscule risk, but one neither was prepared to take.

He had only to arrange things so that the current in his wire would be reversed and carefully charge the battery he and Cassandra had made with the correct voltage. They planned for her to leave at four o'clock. It was fifteen minutes before that hour when he stopped fiddling with the equipment and came to stand next to her.

"I cannot tell you, Cassandra, how much I have enjoyed having you stay with us." He sighed. "That sounds so conventional, and this is a most unconventional situation. One might draw comparisons between your circumstances and those of a person about to embark on a voyage of immigration, but while it is unlikely that an immigrant's friends will ever see him again, it is certain that we shall not meet again. I am sorry that I was so ungracious that evening when we discussed how I would go on after you left. I am very, very grateful for all you have taught me."

"Harry, you sound as though I was dying. All that is happening is that I am going home, and we'll each live out the rest of our lives. It was by the merest chance that we ever met. I only wish that I could stay long enough to make sure that they catch Job, but I'm sure that Edmund is safe, and if I don't go now, I'll never go. I mean," she added hastily, afraid to think about what she really meant, "that there will always be something happening that I want to see the ending of, and the sooner I go, the less danger to you. If I'm not here, no one can hear my lunatic ideas."

Harry bowed. "It has been an honour to know you."

Cassandra hugged him, hard. "Thanks for everything. I'm going to miss you, and Aunt Tavie, and Edmund and Anna and Tom, and everyone. I'm almost glad I came, and not just because of everything we learnt about the nature of time."

Harry returned her embrace, and blushed slightly as she kissed him on the cheek. "I'd better take my place."

The last few minutes had all the awkwardness of an airport farewell, as the travelers and well-wishers stand about, waiting for the flight to be called. There was nothing to say. Cassandra stood in the correct place, clenching her hands, and Harry stared at his watch, holding the connecting wires a fraction of an inch apart.

"Good-bye," he called.

There was a loud discharge . . .

= 17 =

. . . AND CASSANDRA STOOD exactly where she had stood that spring morning before she'd first been transtemporalized. Dr. Jenkins was still talking to Brad and Janet Font, though she seemed to have missed a few words of his speech.

"As you can see, our equipment is not very spectacular, although it weighs over a ton. All the action takes place inside, at the subatomic level. Once we've begun a run, it spits out an electron every thirty-nine and one half seconds for twenty-four hours."

"Could this machine leak radiation?" Brad Font asked dourly.

Dr. Jenkins chewed on his lip for a moment. Cassandra knew that he was only trying to formulate an answer that a layman could understand, but it did look as though he was trying to be evasive. "In short, no," he said. "We work with a very, very, very tiny amount of material. In fact, we shield it to keep background radiation outside."

"But you don't try to keep the radiation it produces from harming people," Brad Font said stubbornly.

Dr. Jenkins had very little tolerance for what he called no-nuke-nuts. "This accelerator is neither a power plant nor a bomb. It does not produce radiation."

"Could it explode?"

Dr. Jenkins lost patience. "No. Categorically and emphatically, it could not. Ah, Cass, there you are, I thought you had slipped out. Take Mr. and Mrs. Font upstairs for some coffee before they leave."

Cassandra stepped forward, swallowing hard. The room seemed overheated and she felt a little faint. "I am Dr. Brown. How do you do, Mrs. Font, Mr. Font. I would be delighted. Please follow me."

"You sound like an American, Ms. Brown, a Yankee," said Brad as they went up the metal staircase and into the hall. Cassandra remembered Harry telling her that it had been built in the reign of Queen Anne.

"I'm from Boston."

"Janet and me, we're from Virginia, but my ancestors came from this part of England. They were horse breeders in Virginia before the War Between the States."

Cassandra felt it might not be tactful to ask what they did after the war. She took them into the lounge. In Harry's time this had been the drawing room, and it gave her a start to see an ugly mustard-colored armchair in the very place where the setee had stood. That morning, more than two hundred and seventy years ago, she had slept there.

She poured coffee for all three of them, left Janet to put in milk and sugar for herself and her husband, and sat in the window seat. "Is this your first visit to England?" she asked Janet.

Her husband replied for her. "It may not be just a visit. Why don't you tell Ms. Brown all about it. I want to talk to that Dr. Jenkins some more. No offense," he added as he opened the door, "but I don't think your boss is playing straight with me, lady. There's something going on here."

It seemed Cassandra was fated never to be addressed as "Dr." by members of the Font family. Brad Font may have learned to say "Ms." but he didn't seem to have much respect for scientists, female or otherwise.

"I have a home office, Dr. Brown," Janet was saying. "For years I've studied genealogy and made up family trees for people. When I got engaged to Brad a couple of years ago, I decided to investigate his family. His mother's family, at least, is one of the oldest in Virginia, and you'd never think that no one had studied them before.

"Well, I traced his father's family back to 1816 when a Thomas Bestor bought some land not far from Richmond."

Steady, steady, Cassandra told herself. Thomas is a common name; and even if it is the same Thomas, however could it affect you? After all, Will did say that Brad Font thought he was the baron.

"Then it got very exciting, because Brad's great-uncle had some old letters which had belonged to Thomas. He was an officer in the English army, and some of the letters were about that. I traced his regiment, and when I wrote to them, they gave me all sorts of information about him. So I used that and started writing to vicars—that's what they call their ministers here—who are always so impressed by my research that they look things up for me in their parish records. Thomas, it turns out, was related to the family which had owned this building. It used to be their house. And they were lords.

"As soon as I found that out, I wrote to the British embassy in Washington, and they began to look into it, to see if there was any property which really belonged to Brad—he's in the direct line of descent, oldest sons all the way."

"Then how is his last name Font?"

"Thomas's eldest son used the name Font. Thomas's last name used to be Grange; I don't know why he changed it in the first place."

Then you don't know much about the family, Cassandra thought jealously, or you'd know that Aunt Tavie adopted Tom. She guessed that his son had used the name out of snobbery; it probably sounded better to be related to a baron than to a mere baronet. Did Janet Font expect to become a baroness? Cassandra knew that titles could not pass through the female line, and Thomas's mother, not his father, had been a Font.

"I understand that the title is extinct," Cassandra said,

fishing to see if Janet would reveal an ambition to be Lady Font.

"Well, honey, that's what the British embassy people told us. The last baron was killed in a duel, and his heir was just a little kid who died of smallpox. I already knew about him. The vicar at a place called Bristix Minor." She pronounced it "Bry Stick." "Isn't that a real British name for you—sent me a copy of a page where his death was written down. But just before we left home, Brad got this letter from this man with something called the College of Heralds, and he said that there was some old correspondence about inheriting the title, and hinted that there was some way Brad could do it after all. But Brad doesn't care about that. He just wants to be sure he can get the house, and that way, if you are doing anyting that's bad for the environment, well, he can make sure you're real careful."

Shut us down, more likely, Cassandra thought. I expect he'd take any stray money that was lying around with the name Font on it, too, if they twisted his arm. "We don't do anything that could have an environmental impact," she said.

"Well, honey, that's what Brad's going to find out."

"You'll have to excuse me," Cassandra said, "I have work to do."

"It's been a pleasure talking to you."

"It's been most interesting," Cassandra replied, and quickly left the room.

She asked a graduate student to talk to Janet, since the Center's policy did not allow visitors to remain unescorted at any time, then went and locked herself in one of the lavatories, the only place where she could be sure of a few moments' privacy. It was a large room—Cassandra now knew that it had been Mrs. Drinkwater's linen room. The large window, where Martha had often sat sewing, had frosted glass in it. There was a toilet and sink at one end and a wooden armchair at the other. Cassandra recognized it as one that had stood in Harry's library. She sat down on it and burst into tears.

She had no way of knowing if the last baron had been Harry, or the heir Edmund, and she hadn't wanted to find out by asking Janet. If she'd cried in front of her, it would have been impossible to explain. Intellectually she knew that the second she'd left 1815 everyone there had been dead for centuries, but emotionally she felt as if she had killed them. It was so easy to think that if she returned, she'd bring them back to life, but she knew that was a fallacy.

Eventually she calmed down enough to return to work. Not surprisingly, she felt as if she'd been away for a month, and it took her some time to pick up the threads. At lunchtime Will gave her back her watch.

"Your hair looks nice," he told her. "I've only just noticed that you've had it cut."

"I had it done over the weekend," she snapped.

"Touchy, touchy, aren't we," he said good-humouredly. "I was just going to say that it suits you."

"Thanks," Cassandra said, sorry that she had snapped at him. It wasn't his fault.

Cassandra went home promptly at five. She took a long bath, with plenty of hot water and bubble bath. Her small flat seemed very empty. It was funny how she kept thinking of things to tell Anna and Harry. She opened a tin of soup and one of rice pudding for her supper, and went straight to bed, where she read *Persuasion*.

"Dr. Brown, oh Dr. Brown," the receptionist called as Cassandra walked into the Center the next morning. "Look what has come for you, hand-delivered just now." She handed Cassandra a thick envelope.

"I thank you, Miss Baker," Cassandra said, not knowing that the reception thought Cassandra was making fun of her.

The return address was "The Bank of England," and

Cassandra took the letter straight to her desk and opened it, still wearing her coat. Inside there were two other envelopes, both with her name, Cassandra Brown, Ph.D., typed on them. One was marked, "Please read this first." Cassandra tore it open.

> Dear Madam,
> I have the honour of forwarding to you a letter which was entrusted to us some years ago, with instructions that it be delivered to you on or after this date.
>
> I remain, etc.,
> E. Samuels,
> Director

The other envelope contained an old piece of paper, folded and sealed with red wax. It bore the words, "Mrs. C. Brown, Font Hall, Leigh Font, near London." The handwriting was unfamiliar, but the letter could have only come from Harry.

He had had such faith in the Bank of England, justified faith, since they had found her despite the outdated address, and sent the letter to her with a note that suggested it was the most ordinary thing in the world. The seal did not appear to have been tampered with, and she thought of all the people who must have handled it over the years and never once given way to the temptation to read it.

She opened it slowly, unable to imagine what could have prompted him to write to her.

> Dearest Cassandra,
> You would, I know, forgive my writing these few words, for they seem to violate my promise never to mention certain matters. [The ink was fainter at the end of the phrase, then darker, again, after he had dipped his pen.] But since you will never read these words, they can not offend you. These days, I often wonder if I imagined

your presence, for there are none here with whom I can speak of you as I wish to.

I lie in Anna's house, but she is with her husband in France. Poor, wretched Anna; the news of my death will add little to the grief she feels now. Tom set sail before this whole wretched business began.

I feel quite strong some days, and those times in particular I wish you were with me, to talk of old times, and *new*, but I fear that the infection has a fatal grip. My fondest hope now is that my prayers are answered, and you returned to your own place, have found not only honours in your scholastic endeavours, but a man worthy of your hand and heart and, with him, domestic bliss.

It is my fancy that you will read these words, and remember me kindly.

Then, in the same hand which had addressed the letter, were written the words,

"Madam, I visited my nefew in his last illness, and, delearious, he spoke of you, and his wish to send this paper, kept under his matress, to you. While I have no confidince in his feavered sugestion that you were taken to the future and there reside in his house, I shall undertake to forfill his last wish.

Octavia, Lady Bestor
March 19, 1816

P.S. My perls are not recovered.

Cassandra found a large manila envelope, carefully put all the papers and envelopes into it, put the folder into her backpack, and ran down the row of cubicles and into Dr. Jenkins's office.

He was talking on the phone to someone, but she went right up to his desk and, as soon as he hung up, said, "Do you have Janet Font's phone number?"

"They're staying at some hotel. Miss Baker knows where. Why do you want to know?"

"I need to ask her something—and I'm taking the day off. I have heartache, headburn, I mean a headache."

"If you're going shopping with her—" Dr. Jenkins started to say, but Cassandra shut the door while he was still speaking.

Miss Baker said that she could not remember the name of the hotel where the Fonts were staying, but after Cassandra showed no sign of accepting that answer, she gave her the telephone directory, and Cassandra stood in the hall, phoning the local hotels rather than wasting time by going back to her desk.

"How is your heart?" Dr. Jenkins called to her as he passed by.

Breaking, thought Cassandra as she dialed yet another number.

By the time she reached Janet, Cassandra had regained a little self-control. "Hello, Mrs. Font, this is Cassandra Brown. I was sorry to have to rush off yesterday, I was so interested in your research, but I'm afraid that I needed to do something in the lab just then. I was hoping we could meet for an early lunch, and you could tell me more."

"Well, honey, I'd love to. I'll just check with Brad."

Cassandra heard her put the phone down. She hadn't thought of that complication. Brad Font would probably want to talk about the Center's work, and she knew that in her present state she couldn't cope with fielding his questions while trying to get the answers she wanted from Janet.

"Honey, that will be great. Brad's going to have lunch with someone from the council, something about city planning, to see if the zoning permits the Center—" She broke off, and Cassandra could hear her muffled voice saying, "Oh, sorry, Brad, but I don't think she'll figure out what you're doing."

"I'm back. Where would you like to go?"

Cassandra named a small Indian restaurant which generally did little business at lunch time and rang off.

At home she changed out of her turquoise sweat pants and her M.I.T. sweatshirt into a blouse and skirt, and put the kettle on. Then she sat down and reread Harry's letter.

Infection suggested an injury—she didn't think the word was used then to indicate a disease—and infection could follow a gunshot wound. She thought that duels were fought with swords, but blood poisoning could result from any septic cut.

Why was Anna grieving, grieving so deeply that Harry's death would add little to her sorrow? Had the child who died of smallpox been Edmund? She recalled that Janet had said he died at Bristix Minor, the village where Author Font's father lived. Or perhaps he'd just been buried there.

And who was Anna's husband? When Cassandra had been transtemporalized, Anna had still been swearing perpetual widowhood. Who had caused her to change her mind so quickly? She must have married fairly soon after Cassandra left. And had Harry married Laura and left her a young widow?

It was only ten o'clock, and by the time she left for the restaurant at half past eleven, knowing she would arrive twenty minutes early, Cassandra had painted twenty or thirty alternative scenes in her mind, each more horrible than the last.

Janet was twenty minutes late arriving at the restaurant, but proved very willing to talk about genealogy. Unfortunately, she knew that she had a captive audience, and saving the best for last, she first told Cassandra about her own family in great detail. Cassandra asked about the Fonts, and Janet said that the history of the Coppersmith family was necessary background in understanding the Fonts' saga, since she learned her research techniques tracing the Coopersmiths.

Finally Janet started talking about the Fonts, and Cassandra got some answers to her questions. The little heir who died of smallpox had been called Edmund Font and had died early in 1816, when he was only three years old. He had been staying with some relatives called Charles and Verity Font. Cassandra recognized the names from Aunt Seppie's recitations of relations. They were the parents of awful Cousin Arthur.

"What about the duel?"

"Well, I don't know what it was about, but this baron shot it out with some other guy. The baron missed, and got wounded, and died months later. People seem to think it had something to do with the duel, so I guess he just took a long time to die. They didn't have penicillin in those days. I guess it must have been a real mess. Why, honey, I didn't realize you were so squeamish."

"I'm fine." Cassandra wrapped her hands around her teacup to warm them, then pressed her fingers against her temples. "Was he married?"

"Yeah. That's a weird thing. His wife had some daughters with real funny names: Henrietta, Octavia, and Tamsen. I couldn't find much out about them, but it looks like they were born after he died, so I guess they were triplets, or else they let her pretend they were his kids. They were called Font, and I can't find a record of her marrying again. I think having triplets back then would kill you."

"Maybe she married her brother-in-law," Cassandra said ingenuously, trying to show that she knew nothing about the Fonts. "That way her children would have still been called Font."

"She couldn't have done that. Harry Font's brother was already dead, and besides, way back then they had this old law that said if your brother died, you couldn't marry his widow. They had one for women, too, about not marrying your brother-in-law. I know all about it, because one of my ancestors was one of the first people to do it after World War I when they changed the law."

"Have you tried looking in the records in St. Anne's Church?"

"Would you believe it? The parish house, where they used to keep the old records, got bombed in the war, and everything was destroyed." Janet sounded personally affronted.

"Are you sure that Harry died?"

"Harry?"

"Harry Font, the last baron."

"Honey, have I got evidence! There was stuff in the newspapers, because people weren't supposed to fight duels. The other guy had to go to France. And I got letters from Harry's relatives to Thomas in America. You know, he's buried in that lab of yours. It used to be a church. They'd just take up one of the stones in the floor, and stick them in. Why, you really are sick."

"No, no," said Cassandra. She wanted more information, but the morbid idea that she'd been walking on Harry's grave for months before she even knew him made her feel faint. "Tell me more about his family. I guess the heir was his son?" She hoped that she could turn the conversation from Edmund to his mother, and thus learn who Anna's second husband was, but Janet was already calling for the bill.

Janet insisted on paying for the lunch and drove her home. Cassandra had no chance to ask any questions because Janet told her frankly that she was nervous about driving on the wrong side of the road and would prefer silence.

Cassandra came home to a horrible smell of heated metal and a ruined kettle. She hadn't even heard it boiling before she left, and it must have been dry by then.

She washed her face in hot water—grateful that all one had to do was turn a tap—changed back into her sweats, and sat down with a sheet of paper, trying to work out what had happened. She knew that the grief she felt for Harry's and Edmund's deaths was irrational, but she felt it very strongly and was trying to deal with it the only way she knew, by treating the deaths as a problem to be solved.

Why was Edmund with Arthur's parents when he died? Why had Harry fought a duel?

It was after midnight when Cassandra fell asleep on the couch, worn out with crying and frustration. She dreamt of Aunt Tavie. They were in the lab, and the old lady was cutting Cassandra's hair, saying, "This is the only way to prevent smallpox, you know. This, and wearing pearls."

Cassandra woke with a start, put on her high-tops, grabbed her coat and keys, and ran to the Center. As she expected it was empty. There was little for the staff to do while the accelerator was running. Next week, when this run was over, the staff would be working overtime to analyze the results and publish a report as soon as possible.

Cassandra went to her terminal and started to design a security program that would take a hacker a couple of weeks to get through, a program to protect the one she'd write next: a program based on the calculations she and Harry had done. She was working against time. If Brad Font had his way, the Center might not be running the accelerator in the fall, when the next series of experiments was scheduled. She had a week in which to return to 1815 and prevent Arthur from murdering Edmund.

There was, of course, no guarantee that she would be able to return to Harry's time. It was necessary to have the 4-D accelerator running, and for there to be a current in Harry's wire. It would be relatively easy for her to alter the accelerator so that it could send her back to 1815, but she would transtemporalize only if Harry had his wire connected. She could not return at the very moment she left, for the current would have just been discharged. Her return to her own time had been thirty-nine and a half seconds after she had left.

She could always arrive before her first visit, but things would be so difficult once she arrived that she decided to try to be carried back the very next time Harry charged his wire—the next time after four o'clock on Christmas day, 1815, and accept the possibility that he might never use it again. He had once told her that he couldn't face continuing his scientific investigations now that he knew so much. If that were so, she would have to settle for arriving at a time before her first visit.

She knew that some people would argue that by preventing Edmund's death, she would change history, but she had discovered nothing to suggest that the Conservation of Reality theory was unsound, and her experience of spending several weeks in 1815 and returning to her own time to find nothing changed was strong support.

The week passed in a blur. Cassandra went to the Center each evening after six o'clock, and spent the night programming and inputting data, leaving at seven to avoid being seen by anyone arriving early. She went home, called in to tell Miss Baker that she still had the flu, took a nap, then worked on debugging her program.

She barely had time to finish, but at eight o'clock on Friday morning she printed out the tables which would let her do the calculations in minutes and, barely able to control her delight, used the tables to find out what she needed to do to arrive as soon as possible after she had left Harry in 1815.

Then she went into the heart of London where she visited a theatrical costumer and a coin shop. On the way back home she stopped at an ironmonger's, where she bought a wicker shopping basket and a very ordinary-looking metal water bottle, and at a supermarket, where she bought an unsliced loaf of bread and some cheese. She was afraid that anything else would attract too much attention when she traveled in Regency London. Finally she visited one of the shops at the Leighs, a clothing store which catered to women with a sense of the dramatic, where she bought a hooded black cloak.

Once back in her flat, she wrote a letter of resignation to Dr. Jenkins and a letter to her landlady asking her to have her clothes packed and sent care of M.I.T. She enclosed a check for one hundred pounds, and very much doubted that the landlady would do anything but try to sell her possessions secondhand.

This did not distress her, for she only wanted to make sure that no one reported her missing. If her landlady sold her things, she would not want the police involved. Cassandra left both letters on the mantlepiece, where they would be found if something happened to her in 1815 and she did not return. She also made sure that she had her passport with her. If she wanted to make people think that she had returned to America, it wouldn't do to leave it behind.

Her understanding of transtemporalization was not yet sophisticated enough to let her know what would happen to the present day if she did not return, but it seemed impossible that time would stand still forever.

By ten o'clock that night Cassandra was back at the Center. She logged on the computer and implemented her masterpiece of a program. It would slightly alter the timing on the 4-D accelerator, making it look as if there had been an error in the original program. It would also go deep into the archives, removing any trace of her recent programs, including itself, then crash the computer. They would be able to replace all the files from the archive, but the crash would remove all trace of her meddling.

She changed into her Regency costume—correct, she was told, in all details, including the shoes, although they had not been able to provide her with stays, and dropped her other clothes into the incinerator. Clutching the basket containing her food, a heavy woolen cloak over her arm, her watch, and two pounds in coins minted before 1816 in her reticule, she stepped into the alcove behind the 4-D accelerator . . .

18

. . . AND HEARD THE accustomed loud blast, and Harry saying, "What the devil! Cassandra?"

"Who else. Harry, what is the date?"

"January 17—1816. Do you realize that you might have been yourself from before the last time your were here?"

"Don't be a fool," she said sharply, worried that she had come too late to save Edmund and, at the same time, relieved that Harry was all right. "If I'd already been here last time, I would have known what was going on."

"Of course. I must say that I'm glad to see you. Do step out of the niche, you can't be very comfortable. Are you planning to make regular journeys."

"No," Cassandra replied, coming forward and putting her basket on the table.

"Oh," said Harry, disappointment in his voice.

"I've come here for a very important reason. Little Edmund is in grave danger. Where is he? Is he all right."

"He is with his mother, and perfectly all right."

"In France?"

"In London, of course. She has gone back to her own house, though."

"So they caught Job."

"No, I am afraid that he is still at large, but it seems unlikely that he would return after all this time. You must come upstairs and have some breakfast whilst you tell me everything. I'm delighted to see you again. Oh, no, you'll have to stay here, because the Drinkwaters are back, and I told them you had returned to London."

"With the family jewels, no doubt?"

"No, I could not bear for them to think ill of you, so I merely said that you were going to visit friends. Let me fetch you a glass of wine."

He brought down a tray with glasses and some little plain cakes. He poured them each a glass, and raised his, saying, "A glass of wine with you, madam."

Cassandra used to think this custom a little ridiculous, but now she did not even notice.

"Now, Harry," she said, "some of this is going to sound fantastic," and proceeded to tell him an edited version of Janet Font's story. She did not mention the duel, but concentrated on her suspicion that Arthur had taken—or would take—Edmund to his parents' house and kill him. "There was something odd about Arthur all long. He'd been getting information about your family. He knew my name before he first called on Anna, and there was the strange way he stopped you from going to his father."

"Mr. Font died two days after Christmas," Harry said. "I never did see him."

"I don't see what he stood to gain from killing Edmund. Could he be pathologically jealous of your family?"

"If Edmund were to die—God forbid it—Arthur would be my heir."

Cassandra now knew with whom Harry had fought the duel—but was it at his instigation or Arthur's?

"Promise me you won't challenge him to a duel over this."

"I am not a complete idiot, Cassandra."

"I am most gratified to hear it." She smiled. "Oh, Harry, it is nice to see you. But we must go to London and keep a careful eye on Edmund. Perhaps Arthur has him kidnapped. He was getting very friendly with Anna. You don't think she'd take Edmund and go visit him in Bristix Minor?"

"I can't see her intruding on Mrs. Font. It is not as if she knew her. But you are right. It is very odd that Edmund should be there and that the cause of death be given as smallpox. I shall bring you some breakfast, then get you upstairs somehow and onto the road. I can pick you up in the curricle and we'll drive to London. You can stay with Aunt Tavie. I'm sure she'll be pleased to see you."

"I brought food with me," Cassandra said. "I thought you might have gone back to London and I'd have to make my own way there but what about Drinkwater? Won't he need the horses?"

"I only left him with them so that he could take the wagonette at Christmas—and because they're not exactly high steppers. I hope you won't mind being seen behind them, but it will be faster than the stagecoach, and by the time we've driven to the mail coach, we could be halfway to town."

By midmorning they were on the road. The day was fairly mild, and Cassandra, remembering her wretched journey from London, was thankful. The journey was not comfortable, for the carriage jolted and she had Harry's valise under her feet. It might have made a comfortable footstool for a shorter woman, but she was nearly as tall as he was. Fortunately Harry wore his sword, or she'd have had to hold it as well as her basket in her lap.

"Have you been at Font Hall ever since I left?"

"I went back to London the next day. But Anna's house was full of Captain Tom's army, and I didn't feel like imposing on any of the relatives. Tom offered to let me stay in his rooms since he was staying with Cousin Sarah—Aunt Sophie's daughter—to keep a close eye on Edmund, but I didn't feel I was being any use there, and we thought Job might come creeping back to Font Hall, so I was here again by the new year.

"You know, you put Anna in quite a pother. She won't

tell me what you did, but she was quite insulted. Could you have said something she misunderstood?"

"I did. In my time, there is nothing wrong with a man marrying his brother's widow, and so I asked Anna if she'd ever thought about marrying you."

"Actually—" Harry began.

"Just speculation—I had no reason to think she ever had," Cassandra said quickly, hoping to avoid embarrassing Harry.

"I did think of asking her, once. A long time ago, before she met Edmund. I fell in love with her at first sight, like a great many young men did. I was all ready to be noble, and wait years in silence until she was old enough. I was a bit put out when Edmund proposed the evening he met her. After a while I realized that while I was very fond of Anna, we'd have never suited. I fell in love with a pink-and-white doll—she could have had the character of a murderess, I'd have worshipped her. Edmund saw and loved the girl under the pretty mask. I think Tom understands her the same way. I have hopes that he will bring her up to the mark."

"So that is why you were always asking me about him!" For some reason Cassandra felt very relieved.

"And I shall be married in May," Harry said. "The engagement will be announced next month, on Miss Larchmont's birthday."

"Oh. Do you think Anna could be persuaded to forgive me?" Cassandra asked, before realizing how rude it sounded. "I'm sorry. I meant to say that I wish you joy."

"I thank you. And Cassandra, I'm sure that if you wanted to—oh, never mind."

But Cassandra was sure that he was going to say something about her getting married, too. She was sick and tired of all this talk about weddings. "What were you working on when I arrived? I was afraid that you'd sworn off electricity for ever."

"I had, until yesterday. It seemed too ungentlemanly to

use the knowledge you had given me to complete my investigation. But last night I read *Chemical Agriculture* again, and was intrigued by Sir Humphry's experiment of using positively charged water to encourage the sprouting of corn. I thought I'd turn my efforts in that direction."

"I know almost nothing about plants," Cassandra said. "In graduate school I wanted to take a course in hydroponics, growing plants without soil, but I could never fit it in."

Harry took her to Aunt Tavie's house, where they found the old lady alone, except for Tom. She was delighted to see them, and shocked Harry by asking Cassandra as soon as they were shown into her presence if she was expecting a child.

"Of course not," Cassandra said, amused by the expression on Harry's face and Tom's sudden interest in the Crown Derby figurines on the mantelpiece.

"Then why have you left your stays off?"

"I forgot them at Anna's."

"Forgot them, she forgot them!" Aunt Tavie was overcome by laughter. When she finally stopped laughing, she ordered tea. "Your aunt Seppie's gone out, so I have the drawing room to myself. She only goes to christenings and funerals, you know, but Mrs. Frances Clutterbuck was delivered of twin boys, alike as two peas in a pod, or so they say, and Seppie had to go look at them."

"Aunt Tavie!" Tom said. "You know that's not true. She goes out every bit as much as you do."

"Only when the weather is fine," retorted the old lady.

As Harry had predicted, she professed herself delighted at the prospect of a visit from Cassandra. "I shall send Culpepper for your stays directly. Tom, ring the bell for me. You and Harry shall dine here, if you're not engaged, and we'll go to the theatre afterwards."

Cassandra had hoped to see Edmund that afternoon, and make her peace with Anna, as well as make plans for dealing with Arthur. Harry, who knew this, suggested that Cassandra might be too tired after the long drive.

"Pooh," said Aunt Tavie, "she's no bread-and-butter miss. But if you are overcome, take yourself off to Tom's and leave us alone. It will be time to dress in an hour, so make sure you're not late getting back."

No one gainsaid Aunt Tavie. Culpepper fetched not only Cassandra's stays, but also the other things she had left at the house in George Street. The green silk gown was sponged and pressed so that Cassandra could wear it that evening.

They dined quickly, for Aunt Tavie would not hear of the dinner hour being moved up, but liked to arrive early at the theatre so that she could watch everyone else come in. They set off in her equipage, with a footman sitting on the box to take charge of Aunt Tavie's footstool and cushions and bring up refreshments in the interval.

Cassandra found the evening at the theatre an immense irritation. The only time the audience did not chatter was during the singing of "God Save the King." The play was *Pericles*, reworked to include Hamlet's famous soliloquy and the sword fight from *Romeo and Juliet*, and after the first act, there was a series of vignettes illustrating the virtues and vices. The actors overplayed their parts, declaiming and gesturing. Of course, they had to speak loudly to be heard over the noise of the crowd.

During the interval, the footman brought them wine and lobster patties. Footmen arrived from other boxes with notes, and Aunt Tavie became the center of a court of elderly gentlemen.

"Would you care to take a turn around the lobby with me?" Harry asked. Cassandra gratefully accepted, thinking that anything would be better than remaining in the crowded box.

The press of people downstairs was fierce. Through the crowd Cassandra caught a glimpse of Arthur Font and drew Harry's attention to him. As they fought their way through the crowd, she saw that Anna, dressed in a dark blue gown, stood next to him, and tried to pull Harry away. Cassandra did not want to confront Anna, for the first time since their misunderstanding, in public, but it was too late. She saw Arthur bend close to Anna and say something quietly to her. Anna nodded and moved away from him, toward the staircase.

Arthur hurried to them. "Mrs. Brown," he said in a loud voice. "I hear you are just returned from the farm."

Harry's hand on her arm tightened. Cassandra said, "No, I have been visiting a friend."

"A gentleman friend, no doubt."

Cassandra realized that she was being insulted and said, "Excuse me" as she turned away.

Arthur was not willing to let the conversation end. "I see, Lord Font, that you have your father's taste in women. You'll never know whose bed—."

"Sir, apologize at once," said Harry. "Mrs. Brown has done nothing to deserve your insinuations."

"And Lady Font?" said Arthur.

"Apologize."

"Why?"

"Then you will hear from me in the morning," Harry said. He turned to one of the many people watching them. "Mr. Tinsdale, would you be so kind as to escort Mrs. Brown to Lady Bestor, and ask my cousin Lieutenant Bestor to join me here."

"Good God, sir," said Mr. Tinsdale, "you don't mean to fight him. He's a crack shot, and you can't see to shoot straight at fifty paces, even with the your spectacles. You challenged him. He can name the weapon."

Cassandra realized that a duel had been arranged, even if no one had literally thrown down a gauntlet. Arthur, a self-satisfied smirk on his face, had already turned away.

"Surely," she said, in a loud carrying voice, "a *gentleman* such as Mr. Font would never take such advantage in this sort of matter."

Arthur turned and bowed to her. "For a *lady* such as you, Mrs. Brown, I shall settle this matter of honour in a way no one could object to."

"Tinsdale," Harry begged, "take her away."

Mr. Tinsdale obliged. "Not really done," he told her as they climbed the stairs, "for a female to interfere. And Arthur Font's handy with a blade, too."

"You think he'll fight with a sword, then."

"Bound to," Mr. Tinsdale said gloomily.

Ill news travels on wings. By the time they reached Aunt Tavie's box, she and Tom had already heard. Aunt Tavie had dismissed her admirers and Tom was about to go down and join Harry.

"This," Aunt Tavie hissed at Cassandra, "is what comes of not wearing your stays."

"What?" Cassandra was completely puzzled.

"He did say you looked as if you'd visited the farm."

"So?"

"It's an expression, girl. When an unmarried lady finds herself increasing and goes to the country, the gossips say that she was sent to the farm."

"I don't think Arthur knew anything about my stays. He just wanted to pick a quarrel."

"Well, I thought he was sniffing around Anna. Had no idea he was hanging after you."

"He's not. Lady Bestor, could we please go home? Arthur Font is trying to murder Harry and little Edmund so that he may inherit the title, and without your help there is nothing I can do to prevent it."

Aunt Tavie held out her hand so that Cassandra could help her to her feet. "Send James for the carriage, Mrs. Brown. I daresay you are speaking rubbish, but even so, it will be a deal more entertaining than this farce."

As soon as they were in the carriage, Aunt Tavie began to fire questions at Cassandra, who was hard put to answer them without giving away too much. When they were settled in Aunt Tavie's drawing room, she said, "I have no doubt that you are right, Mrs. Brown, for I never liked Charles, and I could not abide Miss Verity. Miss Falsehood, they should have christened her. But there is nothing you can do to prevent the duel."

"Isn't there some way to stop it?"

"Only if Arthur Font apologizes, and we both know he'll never do that. Or you could report the duel, if we could find out where it was being fought. That would delay it for a day or two. But Harry would never forgive you for that."

"As long as he isn't killed!"

"Mrs. Brown, if he does not feel you respect him, he might as well be dead—for all the good it will do you. So, you look surprised. Well, either you are an excellent actress, or you don't know your own heart. You have done all you can for him. I am sure that you shamed Arthur Font into naming swords.

"I shall call on Anna in the morning, and tell her that Edmund is to be brought here. After all, Harry is the child's guardian, and can decide where the boy is to stay."

"But if Harry dies—"

"Then he is dead, Mrs. Brown," Aunt Tavie said sternly, but Cassandra noticed that her eyes were moist. "I am not going to sit here talking nonsense all night. I am for bed, and you are advised to do the same."

But Cassandra sat alone downstairs, refusing to believe that there was nothing she could do, and racking her brain. Obviously, asking Harry not to fight would do no good whatsoever, and using legal means to prevent the duel would only postpone it. Well, that would give her a little more time to think. She was about to ring for a servant to send for the watch when the door opened, and the footman announced that Lieutenant Bestor was without.

"Please send him in."

"Harry sent me, Mrs. Brown. He's staying in my rooms, with Miller to look after him."

"Will he fight tomorrow?"

"The next day. I'll take his note to Font tomorrow

morning and meet with his seconds to arrange the place and time, and for a surgeon. Harry is very anxious that you do not blame yourself in any way, and sent me to see if there was anything you need."

"Nothing, thank you, nothing you could do."

Tom sat silently with her for a moment, then stood to take his leave.

"Wait," cried Cassandra, for she had just remembered Aunt Tavie's friend Helena, who had gone to watch her husband duel. If there was nothing she could do to prevent it, at least she could be there. "Where will it be held?"

"Mrs. Brown, I hope you aren't thinking of doing anything foolish."

"No, I just want to be able to think of him. Who will the physician be?"

"I shall ask Dr. Witten, and I'll make sure he follows your instructions, Mrs. Brown—although Arthur Font will be his patient," Tom said encouraging.

"Dr. Witten. Of course."

Cassandra knew she had not the slightest chance of passing herself off as a page, but she could dress as a well-muffled, middle-aged physician. She'd have to go see Dr. Witten first thing in the morning and persuade him to let a colleague take his place.

She was at the house in George Street before eight o'clock. A harried-looking James opened the door. "Mrs. Brown," he said, "we did not expect you. I mean, Mrs. Font is not in."

Cassandra supposed she had been foolish to expect welcome there. "I only want Dr. Witten's address. I thought that since he'd come here several times . . ."

"I wouldn't know, ma'am," replied James, and shut the door in her face.

Cassandra walked slowly away, trying to remember if she had ever known Tom's address. When she reached Manchester Square, she heard hurrying footsteps behind her and turned to see Peters following her. "Beg pardon, ma'am, but Mr. James told us belowstairs what you were after. I do hope, if I may make so bold, you are not ill."

"No, Peters, thank you. Do you know where Dr. Witten lives."

"Yes, ma'am. If you please, ma'am, I could show you the way, but he don't take on folk in a regular way, I bin told."

"I just need to ask him something."

"Could I call you a hackney, ma'am?"

Cassandra considered her small store of coins and the expenses that her masquerade might call for. "Better not, I think. If you could just give me directions, I'll be fine."

"I'm not going to let a lady go into that part of town alone," Peters said firmly. "I'll just follow behind, ma'am."

Cassandra insisted that he walk next to her so that they could talk. "How is Jemmy?"

"Mending well, thank you, ma'am. He'll be swinging hisself round on a wooden pin and a pair of sticks soon, and he'll have another peg leg when he's healed. We'll be on our way soon, for Lieutenant Bestor has found a glass-maker to take him as a 'prentice."

Dr. Witten lived at one end of a narrow street that stank dreadfully of fish. A woman, whom Peters pointed out as the doctor's landlady, sat on the doorstep, a child at her breast and another hanging on to her skirts.

"We're looking for Dr. Witten," Cassandra said to her.

"Hello, me old salt," she greeted Peters. "You go right on up. I'm not lugging these two up the stairs."

"Do you come here a lot?" Cassandra asked as they climbed the narrow stair.

"Only once, ma'am."

"That woman seems to know you."

"No, she just can spot a tar."

"Why didn't she speak to me?"

"You're a lady, ma'am, she wouldn't know what to say to you."

Dr. Witten answered the door, and stood staring at

them. "You shouldn't have come here, Mrs. Brown. I can't ask you in."

Cassandra elbowed past him before she realized that he might mean that he had a woman with him. However, his room, which contained little besides an unmade bed, a table, and a chair, was empty.

"Peters, could you wait outside?"

"Of course, ma'am." He pushed Dr. Witten into the room and closed the door behind him.

"I suppose, Mrs. Brown, that you've come to ask me to intercede with Lord Font."

"So Tom's been here. Good. I've come to ask you something else. Did you agree to go to the duel?"

"I was trying to decide what to do. Frankly, Mrs. Brown, I want never to see another injured man again, but Lieutenant Bestor, at great personal risk, once prevented my wagon from being captured. I suppose that sounds a small thing to you, Mrs. Brown, but without it I would have had little with which to treat the wounded."

Cassandra was trying to see if Dr. Witten was drunk or not. There was a half-empty gin bottle on the table, next to a piece of closely written paper and a couple of pennies. Two glasses stood on the windowsill, with a jug and a bowl. He was not drinking now, but he stood stiffly and spoke slowly.

"May I sit down?"

"Please, forgive me, Mrs. Brown. I am afraid that I have nothing to offer you." He sounded flustered.

Cassandra sat down on the chair. "Dr. Witten, I imagined, from various things which I was told about, that you would not wish to be present at the duel, yet might hesitate to say so for fear of putting Lieutenant Bestor, who is very busy right now, to further trouble. I have an uncle, a Dr. Brown"—Cassandra paused for a moment, cursing herself for not having used a different name—"who often involves himself in affairs of honour. If you cared to write him a note, and you may use my name, asking him to take your place, I would be most happy to take it to him. You might want to write a letter to Lieutenant Bestor, saying that you have asked Dr. Brown to take your place. I would be happy to deliver both notes."

"Lieutenant Bestor would not be pleased at your involvement, Mrs. Brown."

"Then do not mention me in your letter to him, and Peters can deliver it."

"I ought not to, Mrs. Brown; if they duel with swords, I could manage."

"They will use guns." Cassandra had no hesitation in lying.

"I cannot write. I have no ink."

"Peters can buy some."

The sailor was despatched with some of Cassandra's money to buy ink, paper, and a quill. Dr. Witten, with an exaggerated sense of nicety, waited on the stairs for his return.

Cassandra sat in the small dark room, a little angry at Tom. How could he leave his friend, a man who worshiped him, to live in poverty, alone save for the bottle?

"Well," said Peters as they came out of the alley, the two letters in Cassandra's pocket. "I'll be off to uncle's now. You'd better give me a pound."

"A pound for delivering a letter! I don't want you to take that one, either," said Cassandra, not surprised that he'd overheard the conversation.

"Yes, ma'am, but unless you've got some gent's slops put by, someone'll have to get them for you."

"Whatever are you talking about?"

"I know your plan, ma'am. You'll go as that sawbones, and throw yourself between them at the last minute. I saw a play like that, only the lady was dressed like a soldier."

"Actually," said Cassandra, relieved to find an unexpected ally, "I was going to do just that."

"I don't hold with these gentlemen taking shots at each

other," Peters said righteously. "They ought to fight it out with the fist, man to man."

Now that Peters was part of the scheme, Cassandra opened the letter to Dr. Brown. As she'd expected, the time and place of the duel were given. Peters walked with her almost to Aunt Tavie's house, then they parted. He promised to have a suit of gentlemen's clothing delivered to her in a hackney early the next morning. Cassandra would be waiting to take the bundle inside. She would order the hackney to wait, change into the clothes, then ride in the hackney to the site of the duel.

Aunt Seppie was in when Cassandra returned and invited her to join her for a nuncheon. Aunt Tavie, she learned, had gone out to see Anna just after ten, and had not yet returned. Cassandra waited for her in the drawing room. As the afternoon drew on, there were more and more callers.

Tom came to assure her yet again that Harry would be fine. "I left him at Boodles, playing whist, and arguing about the Corn Laws. Such a laugh, there he and old Larchmont sit, neither of them knowing."

"Knowing what?"

"Oh, knowing a thing about corn, Mrs. Brown."

"I just thought of something. Is it really all right for Harry to fight a duel over one woman while engaged to another."

"Not exactly, but then he's not engaged anymore."

"Not because of the duel?"

"Pretty little Laura Eliot put an end to the betrothal."

"Laura Eliot?"

"She's not wed yet—she will be. James Eliot is taking her to his mother, the elder Mrs. Eliot. Her parents think she's visiting her sister, the younger Mrs. Eliot. After this there'll be nothing for her father to do but let her marry as soon as the banns are read, so long as she sticks to her guns and refuses to do anything else. She won't back down, not with Eliot beside her. She wrote a very affecting letter, come last night, begging his forgiveness, and asked him not to call James Eliot out since it seems the young man was not aware of her engagement."

"How does Harry feel?"

"Doesn't know yet. I wouldn't be such a fool as to tell him at a time like this."

"You read his letter."

"Of course," Tom said, "what else would I do, when on the night a duel's declared a letter comes from his intended with 'very private' written on it? But I know you'll not tell anyone else, Mrs. Brown."

Cassandra had until dinner to absorb that news. In the middle of the meal a footman whispered that Lady Bestor had returned, and wanted to see Cassandra in her bedchamber directly.

Aunt Tavie was propped up on her bed, looking pale and worried. "Anna, that damned fool, married Arthur by special license this morning. I'd forgotten that fool Ponddabble had a son who was the dean of York. They were married at noon, but she'd left the house when I arrived, and since she'd not told the servants of her plans I had to cool my heels for a good three hours. Then in comes Madam without her little boy, and her husband forbids her to see me and won't tell me where the child is. Those fool solicitors won't do anything until Harry complains."

"Then we have to send for Harry."

"Sit down, child, and listen to me. Harry will fight Arthur Font, for your sake and his mother's sake. As a man of honour he has no choice. From all you've told me, if he can kill him, it will be a good thing. If we trouble him with *anything*, it may distract him, and he could be killed. I saw Edmund in the nursery, when I first arrived. Arthur has a duel to fight tomorrow. He won't be taking the boy anywhere."

"But you said he wasn't with Anna."

"He wasn't. And that is the first time I've ever seen her without him. Now let me rest."

"Lady Bestor," Cassandra said rather guiltily, for she had never seen Aunt Tavie looking so tired and worn, and the old lady obviously wanted to be left in peace, "I'll go directly, but I need to do something in the kitchen—"

"Culpepper, take Mrs. Brown to the kitchen and tell the cook that he is to follow her orders. Good night, Mrs. Brown!"

"Good night, Lady Bestor. Thank you."

Under the puzzled eyes of the cook and the footman, who slept on the kitchen table and could not go to bed until Cassandra left the kitchen, she boiled strips of old sheeting, made packets so that the bandages were completely folded inside another piece of cloth, inexpertly ironed each packet dry, then poured more boiling water into bottles she had sterilized with heat. She finally packed everything into a large hamper, added a bottle of gin, and took the basket upstairs with her. She knew that the servants would gossip, but the news could hardly travel to Harry in the few hours left till dawn. She set the alarm on her watch and went to bed, where she slept fitfully.

19

Harry paced across the long shadows cast on Hampstead Heath by the rising sun, his feet making sharp sounds on the hoarfrost. He was dressed completely in black, even his neckcloth and gloves were black, for it did not do to give one's opponent an obvious target. He wondered, not for the first time, how he came to be there. He opposed dueling as a matter of principle: it was obvious that a man superior in intellect and morality could be overcome by a fellow larger than he.

Furthermore, as a man who firmly believed in the necessity of law, Harry had never expected to find himself deliberately breaking it. Nor did he see how the fact that a lady's name had been bandied about by a scoundrel could be changed by the villain's death. His mother had always said that if a lady's honour were fought over, it was obvious that she had none, or else she would not have put herself in the position where her reputation could be called into question.

But his mother had never been faced by a man who planned to use the illegal institution of the duel to commit murder. Harry knew that he could have let Arthur Font slander Cassandra and his mother without saying a word. But if that means had failed, Arthur doubtless would have found some other way to provoke him, or concocted another scheme to cause his death. If Cassandra had not spoken—and received another vicious insult for it—it would have been murder. Harry was certain that with his poor eyesight Arthur would have been a mere blur at the fifty paces called for when dueling with pistols. But now there was a chance that when Arthur arrived in a few moments, he would name swords as his weapon of choice.

Tom patted his arm encouragingly. "I could do with a chop. Shall we go down to The Green Man for a bite after this?"

"Yes, if you like. Tom, would you do something for me, if I don't come through?"

"Come, come, Harry. This is hardly a duel to the death."

"I think it may well be. I want you to promise to take care of Cassandra, see she gets back to Font Hall. She'll have a rather odd request to make of you once she's there, but please tell her I said she could rely on you to see her all the way home, and do whatever she asked."

"Your ghost? I thought so! I would be delighted to assist Mrs. Brown, you know that."

"My ghost?" Harry was surprised at Tom's macabre words. Until now his cousin had been a pillar of encouragement and strength.

"Well, that's what she is, old man. Look at her. Obviously intelligent, but no idea of how to go on. All that rigmarole when Jemmy was cut. Knowledge from beyond the grave. Of course I'll see she comes to no harm."

"I left some cash for you to give her in case you have to stay in London a few days. And Edmund will get the estate, of course. Poor Anna. After all her work. I told you that I've named you executor, didn't I? And Miss Larchmont. I hope she doesn't marry Ponsonby after this."

"Harry, stop talking fustian. It's Arthur who needs to worry about his will. Trotter," he called to one of his brother officers, a veteran of many duels who was serving as the other of Harry's seconds. "Come and tell Harry a joke. I'm going to see who's in that hackney. I daresay it's Witten and I'll need to pay the driver."

Harry watched as the driver gave a note to Tom, then

Harry turned away, trying to find humour in Trotter's off-colour jests. If only Arthur would arrive.

Arthur arrived very near the appointed hour. He was driven in a phaeton by one of his seconds, a tall heavy man. The other, a shorter man, rode beside them. All three were in evening dress, giving the impression that Arthur hadn't even bothered to sleep before coming to fight.

As custom demanded, the seconds tried to effect a last-minute reconciliation, but Arthur would not apologize for his remarks. The tall second brought over a sword case, and as Harry tried the balance of one of the sabers he felt some of his confidence return. He handed Tom his coat and gloves and took his place opposite Arthur.

A fight for one's life was no place to try a fast lunge to take one's opponent off guard. One might learn in a most unpleasant manner that he was a better swordsman than anticipated. Harry and Arthur circled each other, feinting and parrying several times before Arthur's blade flashed neatly through Harry's guard and scratched Harry's arm despite his quick backward leap. As Harry had expected, Arthur made no effort to end the duel, even though blood had been spilt, and therefore, honour satisfied.

He was pleased to see, however, that Arthur was not playing with him, but fighting hard. He pressed his own attack, and Arthur, surprised at Harry's ferocity, stepped back and tripped over a tussock of grass.

Harry stepped away from him and lowered his blade. He watched Arthur lie there for a few seconds, breathing deeply. Behind him his seconds conferred briefly and the shorter one moved towards the horse. After brandy, Harry thought, then Arthur was on his feet again. He did not seem to be hurt, for he rushed at Harry without warning and in a manner not approved in the *code duello*.

Harry sidestepped him and let him go rushing past. "If you wish to fight, Mr. Font, stand still, and fight like a man," he called, rather pleased with his coolness. Trotter would no doubt also approve.

After that Arthur regained control of his temper, and Harry again found himself well matched, but he was slowly able to maneuver the fight a quarter of a turn so that the sun, which had been on his left, now shone directly in Arthur's face. The pace of the fight began to tell on Arthur, and Harry judged the time was ready to strike.

But then Arthur slipped and fell again, deliberately, thought Harry, so that he might gain a few moments' respite. He took his time in getting to his feet.

The delay gave Harry time to think. The thought of killing a man in cold blood was repulsive. Arthur had not actually harmed Edmund yet—and unless Harry was dead, Arthur had little reason to kill Edmund, as Harry might at any time marry and father a son, who would replace any heir presumptive. True, he believed that Arthur was conspiring against his family, but he had no proof. One of the greatest strengths of British Common Law was the assumption that all men were innocent until proven guilty. If Harry took justice into his own hands and presumed to execute Arthur, would that not make him a murderer?

By now Arthur was up again and lunging towards Harry. In a flash, Harry decided to disarm Arthur and then extract from him a promise—one which would be as binding as solicitors could make it—that he would quit the country and never trouble Harry's family again.

Harry's first attempt failed, and now Arthur knew that Harry did not wish to kill him. This gave Arthur a great advantage. Harry was forced to scratch his face to show that he meant business. His knee was beginning to ache, and his wrist and shoulder were sore. In practise he would still be fresh, but the effort of fighting for his life was taking its toll.

The pace of the fight slowed now, as they circled each other again, looking for an advantage. Harry made feints of several disarming thrusts, trying to see which Arthur was familiar with. With a quick series of cuts and thrusts as a distraction, he prepared to disarm Arthur.

Then came the cry, "The watch, the watch!"

Harry and Arthur both drew back and turned to look at the screen of trees which separated them from the road. One of Arthur's seconds came galloping along, screaming at the top of his lungs.

Over that noise came Trotter's bellow, "What a damn blasted shabby trick."

Tom and Arthur's other second ran forward. As Tom took Harry's arm to pull him away, Arthur made a last, cowardly effort, and thrust his saber at Harry's chest. Tom wrenched the saber from Arthur's hand and threw it to the ground. Then he dragged Harry towards the hackney where the physician waited and flung him inside. A pair of slim hands grabbed him and pushed him flat on the seat.

His shirt was torn open, and a familiar voice said, "Damn, damn, damn."

Cassandra had barely been able to watch the duel. She had tried regarding it as a fencing match, but as soon as Harry was bloodied, she'd had to give up the pretence. The duel bore little resemblance to fencing, for the men were using sabers and slashed instead of using just the points. The savagery with which the two men attacked each other made the comparison even more farfetched. So she stood next to the carriage and watched the men's feet as they circled and lunged, but she knew that if Harry fell, she'd be running to his side at once.

Then there was a shout of "The watch, the watch!"

Tom threw off his greatcoat, revealing a black coat and breeches like Harry's. He ran forward, and as he reached his cousin, she saw Arthur slash him fiercely. She started forward, but Trotter grabbed her arm.

"You can treat him in the carriage, sir," he said, and opened the door.

With an effort Cassandra fought the impulse to rush to Harry. She would do more good by waiting here for him.

The few seconds it took Tom to help him to the carriage seemed an age.

Trotter gathered the strewn clothing and took it to Tom's curricle, where he calmly drew out a sketchbook. Meanwhile, Arthur's tall second helped him into the phaeton and they drove away.

Finally Tom boosted Harry into the carriage. She grabbed him by the front of his shirt and thrust him down on the seat, trying to pull his shirt open to see how badly he was hurt.

"Damn, damn, damn," she muttered, terrified he would be too badly injured for her to help.

"Really, Cassandra," he said, "it is enough that I find you embroiled in this affair. Must you swear as well?"

The carriage lurched, and she nearly fell on top of him. It took a moment for them to straighten themselves out. Cassandra was trying to keep her weight off him, and he was, she eventually realized, trying to sit up and help her to do the same.

"I suppose that you are not too badly hurt if you can be so pompous," she said with relief when they were sitting next to each other. She had to cling to the strap to keep from falling again as the hackney jogged over the uneven ground. "I thought you were going to be killed. There is blood all over your chest."

"Well, I was not killed. I must say, you make a most convincing man. Though I am not sure that it was necessary to cut your hair. It makes your neck seem so long. I don't like it."

Cassandra yanked off her hat, and her hair tumbled down. "There. Now, I would like you to be quiet, please, and take your shirt off." They had reached the smoother road, and the carriage slowed.

Harry opened the window and looked out, craning his neck to look up and down the road. "No pursuit, it seems."

"I can't see Arthur coming after you. Now, take your shirt off."

"Cassandra! I'm not that badly hurt. You won't be able to see anything. It's too dim in here."

She smiled. "It won't be anything I haven't seen before."

Harry said nothing.

"Well, don't blame me if you bleed to death."

The carriage slowed, then halted. "Put your hat on!" Harry cried. "And behave like a man."

"What's happening?" She found her hat on the floor and tucked her hair under it again.

"I think we are about to be taken up by the watch. I'll try to have them release you."

The driver opened the trap in the roof and called down, "Which way, sir?"

"Is there anyone after us?"

"No, sir, which way, sir?" the driver repeated impatiently.

"Oh, Inns of Court—" Harry began.

"No, Anna's house. We need to reach Edmund, and I never told you, Anna married Arthur. Or do you want to go to a doctor?"

"Good God," said Harry, without apology, and gave the driver directions to George Street. "I don't need a physician."

Cassandra quickly told him about Aunt Tavie's visit. "Now are you in danger of being arrested? I thought it was only illegal to be caught dueling."

"In theory, I could be taken up. But since the only witness who was not also involved is the driver, and he isn't exactly innocent of wrongdoing, I don't think it's likely that charges will be pressed."

Cassandra was full of questions, but she decided they could wait until things were over—whatever that comforting phrase might indicate—and turned her mind to the matter at hand.

"You can't go around looking like that. You'd better take off your shirt—what's left of it—and let me try to clean you up a bit and bandage you." As she spoke, she began to unbutton Harry's shirt, and this time he let her help him out of it.

The sword cut on his arm looked to Cassandra's untrained eye deep enough to need stiches. She washed it with the water she had brought with her and the gin, then made a pad of cloths and bound it tightly in place. Blood seeped through to stain the dressing. The slash on his chest was nearly eight inches long, but not very deep. She washed it as well, put strips of cloth along it, and wound his torso with the rest of the bandages. She wished that she had brought more with her, for the binding looked as if it might slip.

Harry was silent while she worked, moving when she asked him to and holding the ends of the wrappings. When she finished, he took the bottle of gin from her lap and drank half of what was left in it. He was shivering, despite the sweat on his face.

"You'd better have another drink," said Cassandra, tearing the unbloodied sleeve off his shirt and wetting it with water, "because as soon as I've cleaned off your face, I'm going to take off my clothes."

"Not much of a jest," he muttered.

"You're freezing. I can give you my shirt and coat and keep the greatcoat," she said, wiping the blood off his face.

"I'll be all right," he protested.

"You can't walk into someone's house half-naked. You'll need something to cover yourself, and if I give you my overcoat, people will have a pretty good idea I'm a woman." Cassandra said firmly. "Just close your eyes."

It was difficult to undress without brushing against him in the small jolting carriage, but Harry kept his eyes firmly closed, breathing through his teeth. Cassandra wondered how badly his injuries hurt him. She knew from experience that alcohol on a paper cut stung; the gin she so liberally anointed him with must have burned.

The shabby shirt and coat that Peters had found her

were a little snug on Harry. She tried to wrap her scarf around his neck, but he took it from her and did it himself.

"It is fortunate, Cassandra, that you are a tall woman. I ought to be cross with you for coming to the duel—it was very dangerous—but I am glad to see you. It is a strange feeling, to fight for one's life."

Cassandra slipped her hand into his, and he held it tightly. "Do you have any idea what we should do at Anna's?" she asked.

"I am still Edmund's guardian," said Harry. "I shall take him to Aunt Tavie's, for the time being, and then to Font Hall."

"But can't Anna just take her son back?"

"No. If I don't want my ward to live with her husband, there is nothing she can do about it. I wish I knew what possessed her to marry Arthur."

"Do you think she knew about the duel?"

"I do not see how she could not."

When they pulled up at the house, the driver opened the trap and said, "You wouldn't like me to mention the fact that yer ruined me hinterior wi' yer blood, would you, sir?"

With a sigh, Harry dug into his pocket and handed him several notes.

James, when he answered the door, was not inclined to be friendly, but Cassandra and Harry pushed by him, and Cassandra ran upstairs to Anna's room, leaving Harry to make up some sort of explanation for James.

Anna screamed when Cassandra entered her room. Cassandra could hardly blame her. What else did a lady do when a strange man rushed into her bedchamber?

"It's me! Cassandra!"

"So it is," Anna said. She was dressed, although it was early in the day for her to be up, and was clutching one of Edmund's little coats. "Why on earth are you dressed like that?"

"I went to see Harry fight Arthur."

"Oh, the wretch," moaned Anna. "First he steals my son, and then he lies to me."

"Where is Edmund?"

"Arthur sent him to his mother, Mrs. Charles Font, and he sent him all alone with one of his footmen. He wouldn't even let Hester go. He said that we were to follow today, but that he did not want him in the house last night. But Harry—is he?"

"No, and neither is your husband."

"Oh, Cassandra, do not reproach me. I did it only to save Harry. Arthur swore he would not fight if I married him. Oh, I was such a fool."

"Anna, Harry is downstairs. Come with me, so we'll only have to explain everything once. Have your chaise sent round. We are going to get Edmund."

"I shall be ready at once," Anna said, almost running to the door.

"And I need a shirt—and Harry a coat," Cassandra called after her.

She wasn't about to go back into skirts for the rescue. Cassandra was given one of James's shirts, and Walter's greatcoat fit Harry well enough. He also borrowed a neckcloth. They stood agitatedly in the hall, waiting for Anna's carriage.

"I do not think you should come, Sister Anna," Harry said firmly. "What should happen if your h—if Arthur were to return."

"I don't see why I should obey him," Anna said. "He married me under false pretences. I wish to go to my son."

"But it might be dangerous," Harry said foolishly, and Cassandra knew that they had lost the battle. Once they had explained what he meant to Anna, nothing short of locking her up would have kept her from travelling with them.

"Anna *should* come," Cassandra said firmly, to save the time the argument would take. "What about Tom?"

"I'll send a message."

The streets were beginning to be crowded now, and as they crept through the traffic, Anna sat silently. Cassandra considered, and rejected, asking Harry if they should call in the police or bring a lawyer. He knew the legal system of 1816 better than she, and had not mentioned either.

Harry was careful explaining the whole story to Anna, beginning with Cassandra's first suspicion of Arthur, her return to the future, and the events since she had come back to 1816.

"I never, never should have listened to him. Oh, Harry, what can I do? What if he has killed my baby?"

"Why ever did you marry him?" Harry asked.

"He promised not to fight you if she did," Cassandra said.

"He first asked me because of little Edmund, he said that he needed a father, and I told him that while . . . Edmund . . . forgiveness . . ." Anna's words were rendered inaudible by sobs.

"Anna," said Harry testily, "I do not mean to be unkind, but I feel a trifle less than quite the thing, and I have no idea what you are talking about. Could you try to be clearer?"

Anna blew her nose. "Before Edmund sailed, I found I was going to have a child, and when I told him, I said that if the child were a boy, he might be the next Lord Font—I didn't mean anything by it, but Edmund rightly reproached me for wishing ill fortune on Harry, and I am afraid that I quarrelled with him. I never forgave myself. And now I have placed his only child in danger. I should never have confided in Mr. Font, but he assured me that he wanted only to help little Edmund. I thought he was acting so to atone for his father's dastardly behaviour, and so when he asked me to marry him, I told him everything, then explained that while I now felt that I should remarry and that I would always hold him in high esteem"—her voice grew hard—"I did not feel that we would suit. And he said that he only hoped that we would still be friends. I even stopped wearing white at his suggestion and went out in the evening."

She began to cry again, and Cassandra tried to comfort her. A number of things were clearer now. Anna had sworn perpetual widowhood from a misplaced sense of guilt. Her insistence that Harry marry sprang from the same source; the words whispered by Peters must have been a message of forgiveness.

20

Cassandra was beginning to think that life in the 1800s consisted of nothing but unending carriage journeys. They changed horses twice. Harry grew paler, but steadfastly refused to lie across one of the seats.

"I should have brought my sword," he muttered at one point.

They had long since exhausted all conversation, and Anna seemed to be praying. It was nearly dark when they finally drew up at the park gates.

"They did well enough without Ponddabble's money," Harry remarked.

"I think the late Mr. Font provided beef for the Navy," Anna remarked.

The lodge door opened as the gatekeeper hurried out. From inside the cottage came a child's voice screaming, "No, no, no."

Anna struggled with the handle on the door. "It is little Edmund," she cried, leapt out, not waiting for the step to be let down, and ran through the gates. Cassandra and Harry hurried after her.

The lodge's door opened into the kitchen. Inside, huddled on stools around a tiny fire of pine cones and sticks, sat five small children, holding chipped bowls full of what looked like bread and water. A girl of sixteen or so, large with child, knelt next to Edmund, trying to persuade him to eat.

"Oh, Mama," he cried when he saw Anna. His bowl fell

to the floor as he ran to her. "I am so glad you came. This horrid woman"—he pointed to the gatekeeper, who had come in after them and closed the door to keep in the heat—"says that she is my mama, and that I am to stay here. It is a very boring game. They call me Teddy, and they won't give me any milk with my bread. Oh, good evening, Uncle Harry. I am very glad to see you and Mrs. Brown."

Harry turned on the gatekeeper. "Well, what it the meaning of this?"

"I don't know, sir. I don't know." She faltered, then gathered her courage. "But I don't know you. Dick, you run up the house."

The eldest of the children, a boy of seven or eight, got to his feet, but Harry stood firmly in front of the door. "Sit down. I am Lord Font. The child you kidnapped is my nephew. That is a hanging offence."

"No, Ma, I'll go," the pregnant girl declared.

"Never, Lucy, it would kill me to see you in the workhouse!"

"What are you talking about?" asked Harry. "No one has said anything about the workhouse."

"Me name is Lucy, Lucy Winters, me lord, and me mother is Mrs. Herrick. Me da and Sam, me husband, and me little sister died of a fever this summer, so I came back home. And with no men, there weren't no money, so when Mrs. Font says we can live in the lodge and keep the gate, we was very grateful, for she even gave me a place in the kitchen, and with me wages, we buy food. Then yesterday, she says that I be too big to do me work, and that I'm turned away, unless we take this little boy in."

Mrs. Herrick took up the story. "Without Lucy's earnings, we'd all starve, me and my children. I could never keep her and the baby, too. But Mrs. Font said she'd give us extra, as long as Teddy grew up thinking he was mine."

"Brother Harry," Anna began, "this is intolerable—"

"No."

"But—"

"No. This woman would have kept your child from you for ever."

"Harry, I feel that she is as much a victim of Mr. Font's villainy as I."

"I am not going to cart four children about the countryside, not to mention their mother and sister."

"No one is asking you to," Anna said with dignity. "Mrs. Herrick, my brother-in-law is going to give you some money. In a day or two, his solicitor will call upon you, and arrangements will be made to take care of your family until your daughter can work again. Thank you for taking care of my child. Good night."

Hand in hand with her son, Anna left the cottage. Harry handed Mrs. Herrick some money, cut short her thanks, and took Cassandra's arm. As they left the lodge, he was leaning on her slightly. "I believe the only thing that saved those two women from Anna's just wrath is the fact that they are both widows."

"Can Mrs. Font really do that? Just fire the girl and let that family starve at her gates."

"I fear so."

He sounded so weary that Cassandra did not take him to task for it as she had done for other social injustices. "Can you afford to support them?"

"Anna is able to, if she wishes, or if Arthur will let her. I could do something for them until Lucy is able to work again."

Edmund, a carriage rug wrapped over his shabby clothes, related his adventures in great, but incoherent, detail as they went slowly down the lane. Cassandra was worried that Mrs. Font might attempt some sort of retribution against the Herrick family before the solicitor came to their aid. Her fretting was interrupted by the sound of galloping hooves.

"What sort of a fool would be riding like that at night!?" Harry exclaimed.

"Hello, hello, is that you, Daniels?" called a familiar voice.

"Uncle Tom, Uncle Tom!" Edmund crowed delightedly.

Daniels stopped the carriage, and after a moment Tom opened the door and pulled himself in.

"I've been shouting after every driver since I left London," he remarked. "Glad to see you looking so well, Harry. Ah, Anna, I was looking for you. Your servants told me that you eloped with Dr. Brown."

"She is Mrs. Brown," Anna protested.

"She turned up in place of your physician," Harry added.

"It was bad enough that you married Font—but now I find you running away with a woman. Anna, this is the outside of enough. You are going to marry me next. Would you like me for your papa?" he asked Edmund.

"Above all things."

"But I am married to Arthur Font."

"Oh," Tom said airily, "that need no longer concern you. I'm going to ride to the next inn and bespeak two rooms and dinner. I'll tell you everything there."

As he had promised, Tom was waiting for them in a warm, well-lit private parlour. There was a hot punch, and the landlord promised to send up a meal directly. When everyone was seated and sipping punch, he said, "This morning, after Harry and Mrs. Brown made their escape, I left Trotter sitting in a hired chaise, drawing the tree line—he's a tolerable sketcher—found him invaluable in the campaign. Well, I rode for a half hour, and realized that if the watch had come, they'd not mistake me for Harry, so I stopped playing decoy and went back to Trotter, who said he'd seen no one. Font had played us for the fool.

"I went back to town, to your house, Anna, where I learnt that Harry had walked in on his own two feet, so I knew he couldn't be hurt too badly. I also learnt that you'd eloped with Harry's help."

"I never said anything about eloping," Harry protested, "just that it was necessary for Anna to come with Dr. Brown."

"Well, the servants drew their own conclusions. When I learnt that Font had sent Edmund to his mother, I had a fair idea of where you'd be heading. By the by, where did you find him?"

Anna quickly told the story. She seemed remarkably calm and unshaken now that her son was with her again.

"James also told me," Tom continued, "that Font himself had been in only long enough to find out that you'd left before him. Drove himself off in his phaeton—with a well-muffled tiger on the step. I caught up with him six miles out of London. He'd turned the phaeton. Broke the tiger's neck—our old impatient biblical friend."

Cassandra nodded. There was no need to frighten Edmund by mentioning Job's name.

"Font had impaled himself on one of the shattered shafts and was confessing all he was worth to the local vicar. I arrived just in time for the last act. He admitted he'd forced you to call him out, hoping to kill you. Tried to put a period to our little lad's life once, with a little help. Oh, Anna, I know where your jewels are hid. Now, Arthur planned to have our lad grow up in ignorance of his true identity and falsify his death."

"However did he plan to keep the truth from me?" asked Anna.

"I don't think he did. Font thought that threats to the child's safety would prevent you from telling anyone what you knew about the duel and about his other irregular activities."

"Uncle Tom," Edmund interrupted. He was sitting on his mother's lap, drinking hot milk laced with honey and nutmeg.

"Yes."

"What I would like to know is, are you my papa yet?"

"That is rather up to your mother."

"Well, is he, Mama?"

"He will be, little Edmund, very soon."

Harry stood. "Let me drink a toast to the bride," he said, and collapsed without further ceremony.

The local apothecary was called. He said dryly that men who managed to cut themselves so badly practising swordplay and then did not eat all day were prone to fainting. He sewed up the gash in Harry's arm, and recommended that he spend the next day in bed.

That night Cassandra learnt that when one shares a bed with a three-year-old and his mother, one can expect battered ribs and a sleepless night. When she took her place at breakfast the next morning, she was pleased to see Harry there, looking considerably better than she felt.

"Good morning, Dr. Brown," he called to her.

"I thought you were to stay in bed today," she replied.

"I feel entirely better, and I did not want to waste any time."

"Are you in that much of a hurry to leave? Edmund is still asleep."

"I meant of the time you are here. Now that Edmund is safe, and Arthur dead—or as good as—you have nothing to keep you here."

"Anna asked me to come to her wedding. She is thinking of getting married in six weeks. I thought I should stay that long."

"And then I suppose you'll go home again."

"I don't know what I'd find if I did. I was awake most of last night, thinking about everything that has happened, and I found two interesting discrepancies in Janet's story." She paused while the waiter brought her a cup of coffee. "One is easily resolved. You remember that the first Font Janet found a record of in Virginia was the eldest son of a Thomas Bestor, who used the name Font. I think that was Edmund. He was really Thomas' stepson. So, historically, Tom and Anna were married. But Janet also told me that she had seen a record of Edmund's death. I suppose that

Anna and Tom might have found Edmund after Arthur had the false death recorded."

"Aunt Tavie has property in Virginia. Maybe Tom and Anna will settle there one day. What is the other contradiction?"

"Not only did you die in a duel in 1816, but you also survived to father three children. Since I find the idea of posthumous triplets farfetched, I can't reconcile the two stories."

"When you first arrived, Cassandra, you suggested that time could be split and two separate histories result. Perhaps that is what happened, and your actions here have mended the break."

"Perhaps. I don't like thinking about it; it gives me the shivers."

"Then shall I tell you my plans for Font Hall instead? I am not the only one who spent the night thinking. The garden is five acres of wasted land—I thought I could do experimental agriculture. Not on so a grand scale as Mr. Coke, but I could develop ways to improve smaller plots. That could make a substantial difference to some of the country people."

"Why not set up a market garden while you're at it," Cassandra said excitedly. "Grow table vegetables—asparagus and so on. Sell the produce in London. You could turn the greenhouses into hothouses, and grow orchids. Anna's sailors could come to work for you. I don't think they'll ever find jobs in London. And you can use the fountains as a basis for irrigation—cut down on the time spent watering the plants."

"Yes—and we could plant fruit trees along the south wall. My father tried some once, but they didn't flourish. Perhaps there was something lacking in the soil. We'd need a lot of men to break up the garden before we could really start. Perhaps I could hire a company of ancient Britons for the summer?"

"What is that?"

"Welshman. They come out of the hills in bands seeking employment. They have a horse between them, and take turns riding it without a saddle or bridle. Some say they whisper to the animal in their own tongue. Often there is but a man among them who knows English."

Harry reached across the table to take her hand, then drew back. "I can't be seen in a coaching inn pouring my heart out to a man. I did want to say, Cassandra, that were we both of your time or mine, I would have hoped things could be very different between us."

Cassandra knew what he was asking. It would mean giving up her career—but she had already made that decision. She would be giving up certain freedoms, certain privileges. And while she did not expect that Harry would demand total obedience, she would always know she was dependent on his generosity. But Harry was an honourable man. He would never begrudge her that, or hold it over her.

"Since we can travel between time, Harry there is no reason why one of us cannot choose to live in the other's time." She felt too shy to be more direct.

"From what you have told me of your age, I do not think that I could just arrive there. I happen to think that the advancement we hope for has not arrived by your time, and that we now have a more civilized manner of living than you will, but think of all that you would have to give up. The advances in medicine, the comforts of your homes—"

"Harry, modern medicine did not save my parents. I could have a child here who would live to be as old as Aunt Tavie, and a child in the twentieth century who could be killed in a traffic accident. As for the comforts of home, the only thing I would ask for is warmed bedrooms and more hot water. But we could make a few adjustments at Font Hall."

"Cassandra, you are everything a man would wish for,

but I am not free." The anguish in Harry's voice was palpable. "We cannot—'

"Laura Larchmont!"

"Yes, and because of her, there are certain constraints on my tongue—"

"But Harry, Tom told me before the duel she ran away with James Eliot. I told him while we were dancing that he and he alone could save her from Ponsonby, and he took me at my word. I never thought then that you would ask her to marry you."

"I only did it because I knew that you'd go home, and I would never find someone like you. Since you were so concerned for her, I thought it would please you. Look, Cassandra, I can't go down on one knee, not in the middle of the public room of a coaching inn, and certainly not while you are still in male attire. If you're sure you don't mind staying here with me . . . ?"

Cassandra nodded.

"I love you. Could I ask you to do me the honour of agreeing to become Lady Font?"

Cassandra didn't have to consider her reply. "With all my heart."

If you would like to receive details of other Walker Regency Romances, send for your free subscription to our Walker Regency Newsletter, *The Season*.

Regency Editor
Walker and Company
720 Fifth Avenue
New York, NY 10019

821.914 FAR 2010   262943

Farley, Paul
The Atlantic tunnel

JUN 09 2010

DATE DUE

Mesquite Public Library

000262943M

THE MIND

Asleep, the organs form a line to see
the mind. The liver won't stand for much more,
so the mind issues a warning in the form
of a sad dream that will haunt it through the day.

The kidneys do their double-entry audit,
the same old calculations: the mind has heard it
ten thousand times, but feigns interest and calm.
This number crunching can't do any harm.

The spleen reminds the mind that in the death
it will stay open longest of them all,
remaining at its post, admitting cells
to a party gone cold, past each lung's last breath,

beyond the heart's much vaunted in-and-out.
But the mind reminds the spleen *glorified pump*
is out-of-line; that it must learn to let
go of the heart's cruel *overrated sump*.

Let go. Forgive. Fall into line. Move on.
The mind repeats itself. When all is said
and done, as the last gland shuffles out at dawn,
tired, the mind comes to the bit it dreads.

away, and which of us could say:
To morrow do thy worst, for I have liv'd to day . . .
    Quinoline Yellow, Beta-carotene,
Allura Red, Riboflavin, Tartrazine,
you took us out of time and gave us power
to hype the moment, dye the day, and rob the hour.

at depths where light isn't supposed to go.
But too much blue is bad: it suffocates
    the senses to spend all your time
    in this sliver of the spectrum;
  and blue is precincts of celestial fate,
the concrete present flooded by eternal weight.

    Adding a yellow wrapper to
      the sheet of blue
creates a green which covers everything,
    a thousand years of growth at once,
  our steady state, if given half a chance,
      and you can hear birds sing.
    Empire of moss and long barrow,
    each doorway is an earth entrance
    to *long ago* and *ever since*,
a source, Eurydice's hatch, a mammal burrow
    that slows the eye and leads us down
    into a sump where we could drown
  happily, in a medium we've never known:
  the future yet to rain, the past long flown.
But winter comes back harder, flesh falls from the bones

    of trees whose flooded nests hang plain,
    this novelty of looking drained

But this is now, or rather, then. The gold
is taken from a toffee penny and held
   over the eyes: gold cellophane
   that makes a legend of the rain,
   a sheet so small being beaten out
by greedy vision until the whole estate
turns lustrous from the eye's electroplate.

Blue next, from a coconut macaroon,
      the day-for-night
      filter you might
   look through to turn a sun into a moon.
That dog's a Quink hound now; the swing park is a ruin;
   the shrubs outside The Highwayman
   scratch up against the galleon
   pub-sign that's swinging in a wind
   straight out of Queen Anne's England,
and there's a general deepening, a thousand shades
   cast by the washing on the lines
that tacks hard like a navy in full sail.

      Lee, Wrangler, Fruit of the Loom
      restored to virginal denim,
      and midges in a street lamp's glow
      are swirling like marine snow

QUALITY STREET

How many other kids would turn
    themselves into a camera
replete with scrims and gels and tints
    to see the world in new colours?
Soul billows through net curtains.
    A glutton takes his favourite seat
and sets to working through a tin of Quality Street.

The wrapper of a strawberry cream
    unpeels a vivid red to dye
the evening bloody monochrome.
    Under a pre-Cambrian sky
the scale of blood and blood-shadow has made
    an ancient fortress of the maisonettes;
a dog crossing the square is flayed
    alive, leaves bloody tracks
and looks back with a blood-bright eye
    before it finds a bin-shed door
and roots the opened guts of bin liners,
    all in the light of a great fire,
and when our sun becomes a swollen core
there will be other evenings like this to endure.

MOLES

Within sight of the blue of the sky,
with meadow scents and the song of birds
as the gradient slackened, he looked back to find
more emptiness than he thought earth held.

In this version of the myth
we leave him there, helpless and blind,
skimming for worms in the topsoil, cursed
with shovels that can't even hold a lyre.

THE POWER

Forget all of that end-of-the-pier
palm-reading stuff. Picture a seaside town
in your head. Start from its salt-wrack-rotten smells
and raise the lid of the world to change the light,
then go as far as you want: the ornament
of a promenade, the brilliant greys of gulls,
the weak grip of a crane in the arcades
you've built, ballrooms to come alive at night,
then a million-starling roost, the opulent
crumbling like cake icing ...
                              Now, bring it down
in the kind of fire that flows along ceilings,
that knows the spectral blues, that always starts
in donut fryers or boardwalk kindling
in the dead hour before dawn, that leaves pilings
marooned by mindless tides, that sends a plume
of black smoke high enough to stain the halls
of clouds. Now look around your tiny room
and tell me that you haven't got the power.

ODOMETER

Whatever way the tale is told—

—it always ends with a new owner
screwing open the odometer
all keen for winding back the clock
and finding there a folded note
which reads: *Oh no. Please. Not again.*
Or something else along those lines.

The surgeon lifts a heart from ice.
In the heat of his hands it begins to purr
like a bat being brought from a house at dusk,
and the way I always tell it, whoever
receives the heart feels ten years younger.
They only remember a blinding light

and a joke they must have heard when they were under.

Now I'm a balloon by Odilon Redon.
And now my chute snags up on power-lines.
If we looked outside, eyeballs might block the sun.

Even above the lake isles of Lough Gill,
Adlestrop's dismantled barrow, a hill
on the road north of Poughkeepsie, there are eyes

now all the world's a drop zone of the mind.

GOOGLE EARTH

Now I'm a hand setting the globe to spin,
finding a country, starting to zoom in
now I'm an eye. Now I'm a meteorite.

The scars of business corridors, the white
clay works, national parkland, estuaries.
A refinery built from Camemberts and Bries!

Now I'm a hand again, steadying my fall,
steering by starlight on the ground, black holes
of reservoirs, flight paths of major roads.

Now I'm an eye and there are never clouds
because the west wind of the Internet
blows silently down lost bus routes, birth streets,

the school roof still in bad need of repair,
the swing park all deserted at this hour,
which is no-hour. Now I'm the midnight sun

lighting the places where we've been and gone.
The ground comes up. A field sharpens to grain.
The trees screw into leaf. Now I'm a drop of rain.

CYAN

I'm one of those model men
in barbershop or unisex
salon windows. I've held my breath
here, like this, for decades.

O distant youth, O brilliantine,
I saw myself the other day
across the street in running time:
gabardined, red-faced, gone grey.

The cow's-lick and the kiss curl.
I'm holding out. I'm blue in the face.
Telstar still orbits the earth.
We don't like what you've done to the place.

NEW POEMS

DORMOUSE STRONGHOLD

Over a hundred years we've fortified
our range; at the last count just thirty miles
from where we escaped The Collections: while the mink
and grey squirrel are coming soon to a place
near you (if they're not there already) you'll find
us keeping ourselves to ourselves, only breeding if
the beech harvest is good, sleeping the northern
winters off, bingeing through good autumns.

Think of me as everymouse, whom the Romans ate
and the raindrop coshed, as I climbed and sprung the stalk
in fields where ploughs turn up pieces of pot;
Rome fell, but here my radius reaches out
to Luton, Leighton Buzzard, the green on the map,
the blur in the wing mirror, the hills from a train;
a conquest of the back gardens slow as money
taking root, as it does. I've noticed of late

the arrival of the dormouse box, and I'll take
to this like a stockade. So civilized.
Crawling out under a sky brilliant with stars
a few degrees out of whack, full of dead gods
and symbols I'll outlive, I feel a rush
pass through me, tip to tail, like the express
heading north, for what lies ahead, for whatever's past.
Before the night's hard work, I allow myself that.

THE WESTBOURNE

AT SLOANE SQUARE

You again! Of all the bomb-scarred stonework
and air vents underfoot I knew by heart.
You, still going strong in your black pipe
above the passengers and mice-live tracks.
You, flowing through eighteenth-century parkscape
into an ironclad late-Victorian night.

Pissed and standing on the eastbound platform
I was a tin soldier who'd fallen in-
to London's storm drain, sent spinning around
the Circle Line long after closing time,
and all along I've carried these trapped sounds
I hear again and recognise deep down.

How many miles of shit have you crawled through
since we last met? I'd do it all again.
We've less choice than we think, the likes of you and me.
Blind water, borne along or bearing through,
escaping in a hurry for open sea.
To think we start as innocent as rain.

PAPERBOY AND AIR RIFLE

A little hunter, I could have shouldered a gun
in the Highlands or Apennines. I would have loved
a wax jacket with a poacher's pocket sewn in,
but at Gerrard's Lane, where I reached the furthest point

and letterbox from the newsagent, where the fields
began, I took wood micks, shebbies, spadgers;
would have taken game if there'd been any to take;
would have knocked a partridge from the head of her brood,

I was that mean. I was doing all right at school,
shining in English composition, my similes
like my reading age running on ahead of the class:
The instant noodles hang from the end of my fork

like a Portuguese man-o'-war. But I lived for the light nights
walking home on my own, all the papers delivered, a bird
in the bag. I've never been happier than the time
I got a goldfinch, looked it over in my hand—

just a line of blood between the mandibles—
and, taking the shortcut through a thistle field,
a summer's worth of goldfinches, the rest of his charm,
flew with me, a little ahead of me, from crown to crown.

AN ORRERY OF HATS

Everything in this display is moving
        and circling nearest to its sun are snoods
only meant to last a shift—they take
        hours to orbit. The party crowns
which see the light of day just once a year
        are meteoric, but if we stand well back
there are outer planets in the wings, top hats
        moving into a comet's night—we'll not
be seeing much more of them in our lifetimes
        though their sheen will come around again to grace
the evenings—and bonnets of beaverskin
        have reached the boreal brim; a naval rating's
peaked affair still has the salt-stained band
        from the night the ship went down with all hands,
sinking to the bottom of the clock;
        and look how many feathered confections float
as satellites that send no signal back,
        an entire species lost to a brief craze.
Passing through a belt of baseball caps, it's good
        to think of all the checks and tweeds sent up
as objects in a deep-space probe, and hope
        that, on a night no one will live to see,
a deerstalker on its lonely course
        could provide the only clue to who we were
in some far corner of the universe.

THE SCARECROW WEARS A WIRE

The scarecrow wears a wire in the top field.
At sundown, the audiophilic farmer
who bugged his pasture unpicks the concealed
mics from its lapels. He's by the fire

later, listening back to the great day,
though to the untrained ear there's nothing much
doing: a booming breeze, a wasp or bee
trying its empty button-hole, a stitch

of wrensong now and then. But he listens late
and nods off to the creak of the spinal pole
and the rumble of his tractor pulling beets
in the bottom field, which cuts out. In a while

somebody will approach over ploughed earth
in caked Frankenstein boots. There'll be a noise
of tearing, and he'll flap awake by a hearth
grown cold, waking the house with broken cries.

is banging from His sealed-up chimney breast),
ammonia, wire wool, black residue
on the brain pan, the upright honky-tonk
of metals cooling down when morning comes.

A GOD

A god who checks you've turned the oven off
in some unnumbered radio galaxy
never sleeps or swerves from His one duty.
You never know: in the middle of the night
you could be up putting a pizza in,
and what does He care? It's the Middle Ages

where He lives. Watching over your stove
beats anything closer to hand: in two places
at once, He'd rather listen to the ticks
of the oven preheating than sit through jousts
or another spit roast. He enjoys the rings
glowing concentrically in your dark kitchen;

planetary, He thinks. Music of the spheres.
Hell, in His pianoless world, what He'd give
to stand before it like an instrument
and set its greasy dials for the hearts of suns,
careful not to raise the number of the beast
on its console—that would be a mistake—

but play all night bathed in its infra-reds;
electric music (the god of hearth

THE HERON

One of the most begrudging avian take-offs
is the heron's *fucking hell, all right, all right,
I'll go the garage for your flaming fags*
cranky departure, though once they're up
their flight can be extravagant. I watched
one big spender climb the thermal staircase,
a calorific waterspout of frogs
and sticklebacks, the undercarriage down
and trailing. Seen from antiquity
you gain the Icarus thing; seen from my childhood
that cursing man sets out for Superkings,
though the heron cares for neither as it struggles
into its wings then soars sunwards and throws
its huge overcoat across the earth.

WINTER GAMES

Very comfortable in that skeleton
the commentator says during one run.

This is sport stripped down to the bare bones,
as democratic as a childhood tea tray,

familiar as a frost fair out of Breughel.
Almost faster than the camera's pan.

Thousandths of a second separate
world-record holders from the also-rans.

The women achieve the same speeds as the men,
very comfortable in their skeletons.

WHITEBEAM

The sixty-miles-per-hour plants, the growth
that lines the summer corridors of sight
along our major roads, the overlooked
backdrop to "Preston, 37 miles."
Speed-camera foliage; the white flowers
of Mays and Junes, the scarlet fruits of autumn
lay wasted in the getting from A to B.
Hymn to forward-thinking planting schemes,
though some seem in two minds: the greenwood leaves
are white-furred, have a downy underside
as if the heartwood knew in its heart of hearts
the days among beech and oak would lead to these
single file times, these hard postings,
and civilized itself with handkerchiefs.

MONGREL

When she dreams, kicking on the kitchen floor
or whining softly to herself in the shade,
it could be she's an Airedale again
aloof with strangers at a gate in Bradford;
a Border terrier, worrying no-man's-lands
between counties; ragging a rat from her jaws,
the legend of some overrun mill town;
or a toy breed, even, scooped into gloved hands.
Then she bares her teeth, as if to say it goes
much further back than that, and checks the start
of something cute on my part, who can't know
what pulls the leashes of her sinews taut,
nor understand the huge thing that pursues
her through the dark and deep world outside ours.

Their low puns and their proverbs used to coat
     your tongue, but now you pity them at windows
ghostly in plasma light, smoking in door-
     ways, scraping back long bolts, checking locks
half cut on supermarket shiraz or
     sauvignon blanc before turning in. They watch
the clock. Sometimes a boss will tap his watch
     and shake his head, slowly. Poor bastards. Coats
never visit theatre cloakrooms; angry razor
     -burn blooms in call centres without windows
where Post-its stick like shit to shoes. They'd lock
     horns with the likes of you. Get back indoors
where razors glide, where windows hiss tight shut,
     where watches flow, where coats dream on their pegs
and doors lock with a satisfying click.

PHILISTINES

They enter here and leave here through the big doors
    and pass by, unnoticed, though if you watch
any city street your eyes can learn to lock
    on to them. Follow the money. Find your big coat
and get outside: all this looking out the window
    puts daylight between things. Keen as a razor
you see them now: fuzzy-edged, in need of razors
    or loaded down with bags, slamming the doors
of taxis; stood in pairs at shop windows
    absorbed in a new season, keeping watch
from bus shelters, nodding to iPods, coats
    stinking with rain. A mechanism locks
them outside Wittgenstein and Kant and Locke,
    outside *The Rights of Man* or Occam's razor;
prevents them slipping Arnold in their coats
    or hearing what's beyond the Frostian door;
admiring *Las Meninas* or *The Night Watch*,
    or writing sestinas in Word for Windows.
Do they see a world we miss, squeegeeing our windows
    or cutting keys to fit our abstract locks?
When she tweezers up the mainspring of a watch
    does it feel like giving birth? When he strops razors
or applies gloss to a freshly sanded door,
    what riptides flood the arm with every stroke and coat?

a sun like blood. Next thing, I'm waving *Goodbye!*
to the hydrogen atom as the seas boil dry,
        which is no way to live. So I take shelter
in the moment's coral, careful not to look
        into the whirlpool of the conference clock.

FILLER

This doodle darkening my delegate pack
        on the sixth day of a seven-day conference
is keeping me from screaming. I have this knack
        for honeycombing out the present. Once
I didn't, and the world would turn to filler.
            Not hardnosed economics, like the soldier
            being sent up to the front, or why our butcher
saw fit to scoop sawdust into his mince.

Neither makeweight nor object from the past
        sticking it out from surplus-to-requirements
to value; time sanctifying waste.
        Not superstitious acres farmers grant
            to their crop devil, or a brewer's angels' share.
For me, none of this was strictly filler.
            I saw the use in test-cards and screen-savers.
        Even *Farley, get in goal!* bore fruitful stints.

But never listening to Horace, nor my mother,
eternity turned everything to filler,
our landscapes ground in time to a fine powder,
the bones of Stone Age man, readers and writers,
        the great iron ships, the balance sheets, the sales spikes,
            the last plant standing ancient history,

reminding blood. And anyone who heaves
their own will know, the law of gravity
can pull it back to weight and worthlessness.
Between our little lives and the great work
there is bad blood, pent up, an ancient feud.
You'll understand if anybody will.
    But don't come back. If you can stand it, stay
dead with the dead. The dead have their own tasks.
But help me, in your own time, in your own way,
as far-off things can help us: deep within.

let go. Any infant's finger-grip will prove
how holding on comes easy. We must unlearn it.

    You're not still here? Still hiding in some corner?
Nothing you didn't know already, I learned it
mostly from you. You seemed to pass through days
wide open, opposite to shade. First light
on Green Lanes. Love is walking home alone
and art is one long runner, an escape
in nothing like real time: both courses meet
and this is where you live, an attitude
that will outlast the big dune shifts, the minor
aftershocks. You'd already withdrawn
beyond us all, slipped out the back, split early
before the slow dance and the house lights up,
into the ashen dawn of your sixth decade,
leaving the customary great unfinished
poem: the one that has to stay unfinished.
    If you are still here, moving through the darkness,
if my voice has found a sympathetic resonance
and solid things are stirred on shallow sound waves,
then hear me out, and help me out. It's easy
to slip and lose our balance, and it's *back
to your post and look busy and here's your desk.*
One day, just sat there staring at my hands,
a pulsing in their vein-work broke a spell
just for a dreamlike moment. It happens: blood

of rain feeding a puddle on the platform
from one cracked pane a hundred feet above me—
then I don't want to know. I'd sooner warm
to a galaxy of pigeon shit than dwell
on ideas of angels crying in anger.
    All this suffering has lasted far too long,
we can't bear it: it's grown too big to handle,
a generator of mechanical love
which runs itself and barks up trade and makes
a profit out of showing us our loss.
Who really has a right to their possessions?
And how can any of us hold on to things
that cannot hold their own selves; who can catch
themselves whole, as they glance past their reflections?
That childhood trick is gone. No more than divers
can grasp the light that leads them onto wrecks,
nor any of the bright groupers or wrasse
survive the sudden bends back to the surface,
the tonnes of air; so we can't call back one
who, unaware of us now, moves along
a narrow beam of single thought and faith
that keeps the great night out, that sees him safest:
unless we have a calling to do wrong.
    Because this is wrong, if anything is wrong:
not to unlock the freedom of a love
with all the inner freedom we can summon.
In love, you only need respect one truth:

the same old world, even as each distant landslide
re-writes the coves and inlets of its shores.)
    And so you died and were put out to sea
from a neuro ward early on a Thursday evening,
lights coming on as nurses snipped you free
of oxygen mask, wires, indwelling needles,
the night schools silent for summer re-opening,
their door bolts scraping through old ruts and puddles.

    Once there'd have been a right to-do: coloraturas
on wax cylinders; daguerreotypes; death masks,
where now we all observe small silences
or fail to rise to feature desks' requests.
The high styles have all gone or been disowned.
Could this be why you've come back: to flesh out
the bone-clack of lament? Can you hear me?
I'd like to spray my voice out like a mist net
over the slivers of your death, and rag
my range—from shout to whisper—down to tatters
so all my words would have to go round bare-arsed
and shivering in the snarls of that torn voice.
Lament never being enough, I'll point the finger:
no one person withdrew you from your tasks
(and anyway, he's everywhere and nowhere)
but I accuse him: you know who you are.
    Whenever, walking through the day, I'm mugged
by some transporting detail—say the sound

itself through halls of everything you'd thought,
a slow stain on a scan but from the ground
perfect cathedrals, chambers of errors.
Trouble was, such sightseeing leads down slipways
that take you into Time, and Time is long,
and Time runs down, and Time slams all the doors,
and Time is like a medium's lapse in recall . . .
    Your leaving as the days began to shorten
has left me wondering if the hours you spent
back here sent leader shoots, mycelial
pathways into your futures, as we all
could go so many ways each given moment.
And if one message came back through the drowned
Bronx subways, or the scorched earth of North London,
meaning you knew, or knew as threads in soil
weave through the dark, build instinct in the hope
of being heard before the nights draw in.
    (Nothing. No spinal shiver. No failing light
the moment you sat bold upright in bed
and called out, isolated as a sea stack.
No boom of blood like waves crashing inside
a cellar. All the skilled, frantic attentions
around you didn't register. As wars
and weather systems do their worst, as seabirds
must wheel now at the world's edge, others sleep.
Until bad news comes falling from the heights
of column inch or midnight call, we walk

you find a place of pure aphelion.
You let the night get in; invited it.
Just shadow by shadow at first, as bar room smoke
entered the exoskeleton of your coat
and found a home there with the poisonous looks
and sly remarks absorbed, the ones you never
reflected back, with interest. Lifting it
onto its peg, I have you frisk its warmth
and deep inside its bottomless pockets
winkle what feel like seeds along its hems.
Gallstones, fulgurites—but still you pick the fluff
from them like ancient mints and are surprised,
alone there at the end of some lost night,
to find some trace of sweetness has survived.
Inside your senses you were sweet enough.

  Time to lament. Your cometary blood
lost track; the circuit broke; how could it know
its point-of-no-return was being crossed?
A stanza-break can stand between two seasons
but blood is curious and your blood rushed
amazed into a room it never knew,
escaping from its greater circulation.
This party was worth crashing. If you could
you'd always stuff your pockets, weigh up ashtrays,
and stretch the hospitality to its limits;
your blood was no different. Ill-bred, it flung

they've every right to step out from the shadows
and harden once more in our field of vision.
    Slip into an element more visible
as someone moving through the dark will trip
a lamp sensor outside and flood the garden
with halogen, a false dawn for the rose
and December moth, which comes to light—but real
enough for a few seconds—so a shade
can stand before us plain as day, even though
we know its sun lies deep in the horizon.

    It takes a while to grasp but I think I know
the worst: sometimes I have you waking up
inside a funhouse room, the ceiling trying
to rain above the mosh-pit of your bed,
and as the paper peels in long sad scrolls,
you inch your way as firemen feel ahead
using their knuckles down a smoke-filled hall
(because a hand that feels its way palmwards,
if shocked, can trip and grab live wiring),
finding a snow globe boiled dry, a mirror
blackened and cracked, the brickwork kiln-hot,
and sometimes pass, eyes streaming, into chambers
of utter loss, carbon-encrusted dark
like houses where the roof has gone, from childhood,
abandoned to what wind blows through. In short

of mirrors, and we were taken for a ride
as willing passengers along a strong-line
not found on Beck's map or The Great Bear,
barely skimming the surface, then rattling down
to coalmine depths. Dropping your knife or fork
you'd frown skywards as if the object fell
from some great height. It had: Washington Square
in the rain, where you'd watched Robert Lowell's quart
of liquor shatter when his brown bag broke
and he looked up to heaven or low cloud.
To prove there was a downside to each joke
the ground gives way if someone tries this now.
    It seems there was a world before I knew you,
a world I was at large in, but back then
its plate glass and its mirrors just confused
or startled me with angry slaps of sun.
You showed me how to move about this stage,
so why now are you banging into things
and throwing your weight around? Did you leave clues
strewn like flowers up to your final afternoon?
Should I have seen or read an evil omen,
in a house whose front and back doors had blown open,
an unexpected bar of small-hours birdsong,
or breaking news of flash floods through a village?
    Slip into the light. See if I'm afraid
to look you in the face. When the dead return

a city just a few shades out of whack
from this, built in its shadows of slant rain?
   Then I'll enter into it: I'll climb its stairwells,
its steps that won't add up; I'll stand for hours
and learn to make myself invisible
as its buskers do; I'll walk from north to south
approaching all its Big Issue vendors
on their blind sides; I'll mark the surfaces
where women straighten hair and fix their lipstick,
sift through an Oxfam shop's doorway moraine;
paused on the threshold of a tattoo parlour
I'll be in two minds—neither one thing nor the other—
and down one street I'll find a taxidermist
who deals in urban fauna, mesmerized
by a fox's backward glance, a pigeon's arabesque,
a feral cat's gelled hackles. This city casts
strange shadows and is full of trapped light, closed
out back in meat safes, stockrooms, nurseries,
the curtained blood glow of insomniacs,
of penlights shone into a captive's mouth,
of hands placed over torches deep inside
a cave system, of faces turned to masks.
I'll leave before that moment loved by guides
the world under: *Now turn your torches off*.
   If there was one thing you knew inside out
it was illusionism, the ticket hall

their minds, and can arrange a late-night visit
for an audience of one; others go looking
and tune in to a mighty passing trade;
and the medium of the page is close to hand,
but until the words choose me I'm left with things
going bump: and these all say you want back in.
The opposite—again—of birds that board
a tube carriage for crumbs, but just as afraid
on the journey between stops. Is this what friends
are for: to say the door is always open?
Heart on the latch, I lie awake and listen.
Classic haunts demand some bricks and mortar
and yours are London stock. Their soot-caked yellow
constructs a meeting place on every corner
and draughty rooms you read your poems in,
though the herringbone tweed you wore each winter
disturbs the steady signal of the pointing
so sightings have been abundant—across streets
I've watched you blur into shopfronts and windows—
and now even the tolling of a skip
being filled, or a door slam in the downstairs flat
are noises off, a loud prompt from the wings;
they run a thumbnail down the cellophane
sleep wraps me in, and strip it. So. What's up?
    Instead of begging at the station mouth
are you trying to press the all-zones travel pass
of night into my palm? Should I explore

REQUIEM FOR A FRIEND

AFTER RAINER MARIA RILKE

My dead are doing fine and are at home
wandering off the street into a night class
or half-lit drinking school among their own,
glad to be out of it. But since you've gone
on ahead—forgive the spatial shorthand,
it's all that works in this world—I've been troubled
by little things: a polystyrene cup
edging across a table on the train
like contact at a séance; a squirrel who stops
and eyes me sadly through the kitchen window;
opposites of portents, things that have me stand
to damp a past soon as I feel it build.
      This is a worry. I never had you down
as someone who'd stray back, being the sort
on even terms with the dead, and never one
for doing things by half; lighting your breath
on overproof rum, and other party tricks
for sure, but mostly your approach to the art
convinced me that you'd fit right in "out there";
so why is it when a radiator knocks
I think of you as frightened? They say Death
requires that those left behind secure

JOHNNY THUNDERS SAID

You can't put your arms around a memory.
The skin you scuffed climbing the black railings
of school, the fingertips that learned to grip
the pen, the lips that took that first kiss
are gone, my friend. Nothing has stayed the same.
The brain? A stockpot full of fats and proteins
topped up over a fire stoked and tended
a few decades. Only the bones endure,
stilt-walking through a warm blizzard of flesh,
making sure the whole thing hangs together,
our lifetimes clinging on as snow will lag
bare branches, magnifying them mindlessly.
Dear heart, you've put a brave face on it, but know
exactly where the hugs and handshakes go.

TRAMP IN FLAMES

Some similes act like heat shields for re-entry
to reality: a tramp in flames on the floor.
We can say *Flame on!* to invoke the Human Torch
from the Fantastic Four. We can switch to art
and imagine Dalí at this latitude
doing CCTV surrealism.
We could compare him to a protest monk
sat up the way he is. We could force the lock
of memory: at the crematorium
my uncle said the burning bodies rose
like Draculas from their boxes.
                                      But his layers
burn brightly, and the salts locked in his hems
give off the colours of a Roman candle,
and the smell is like a foot-and-mouth pyre
in the middle of the city he was born in,
and the bin bags melt and fuse him to the pavement
and a pool forms like the way he wet himself
sat on the school floor forty years before,
and then the hand goes up. *The hand goes up.*

DUEL

Split pistols on a woodchip wall a decade,
faked alloys, brandished, facing one another
above a brick fireplace (another bullshitter—

ersatz and cold). These two bisected bastards
were only half there, but they stared me down.
The horse brasses and Spanish fans were harmless

but guns form in the womb. If my dad was out,
bored, I'd take up arms and clasp each half
together, then I'd pick a photograph

along the mantelpiece, and draw a bead
between the eyes of some ancestral second;
or (this was harder) turn the pistol on

myself. I'd hold its shape along the midline
by sucking the muzzle—it tasted of television—
and use my thumbs to blow my fucking brains out.

and those particles—smaller than rods and cones—that escape
the filters and treatment plant won't register
in any sense. And so my ripples
head for God-knows-where
as light strengthens by increment
and a tree falls in the woods and no one hears,
though I can't swear to any of this: I wasn't here.

Someone else packed up in a hurry, walked back
up a slope, bastard tricky with roots, came to
the quiet road in the green shade
that leads round the lake;
passed a city's coat of arms
and some Latin he couldn't read, looked out
from a wall across a body of water at chest height

and gasped at the thought of the pressure, the pounds-per-brick,
and felt alone up there then, and wanted to drive
far away from those high offices,
from the danger signs
where water stands in the hills
with the eyes, from the man-made distances
that have haunted his ears; from the paranoia of pines.

and miles of hedgerow. A Water Board van snakes its way
  silently northwards up the A591
    along the opposite bank,
     and it's getting light
    so I step back into the trees
   not wanting to be seen by anyone.
In this poem disguised as a meditation on water

it's now as good a time as any to tell you, reader,
  how I've driven up to this spot in a hire car
   and stand at the water's edge
    drawn by a keen sense
   of civic duty: I plan to break
  the great stillness and surface of this lake-
cum-reservoir by peeing quietly into the supply

and no harm will come to anything or anyone. Consider
  this: no shoal will surface out of sync
   like driftwood; no citizens
    will draw a cold draught
   of LSD, or run a hot bath
  of nerve agent in two days' time. This act
is so small it will only really occur in the mind's eye

are favourites too. Wind from out of nowhere disturbs
the signal. Some of these trees are mobile masts
disguised as trees, I'm told, and this
lake a reservoir
disguised as a lake. It looks
the part all right; in fact, has already starred
in films as body double to Como and Geneva

though it knows it's an offcomer, a baby in glacial terms,
and nothing much has pooled and stuck. There's no
host of golden daffodils, no
Bluebird going down
in black-and-white to rise
again in colour, no Post Office Tower
leant like a dipstick to illustrate its unnatural fathoms,

just those rumours that seem to follow reservoirs around:
a drowned village, church bells on rough nights,
the souls who stood their ground
calling from the depths,
that kind of thing. Then a blackbird
breaks cover, and its cries manage to sound
genuinely bereft for lost acres of thicket and undergrowth

and-burdock. You could walk: no Roman would have given
a second thought to the hike, no Romantic neither.
But this is water's pause for reflection.
This is its downtime.
Water seeking asylum
lying low for a while, taking a chance
to gather its thoughts. Years ago, in the Liverpool aquarium,

I read how the lungfish would dig into the parched
riverbed, curl into a ball, secrete
mucus, and generally do
what it needed to
to weather a spell between
broad sheets of sudden rainfall that fell
weeks or months or years apart, wrapped up in itself;

though there was no word next to the tank on how water too
needs to introspect, to find some high cistern
or a road's camber after a storm
that can hold a moon;
those baths you see in fields
plumbed into whitethorn, where the Green Man
might take his watery ablutions before going to ground

and gravity holds open the door onto a man-made dark,
   culverts at first, and then the all-enclosing
      mysteries of pipe-work;
      a gentle incline
   and two-miles-per-hour
   average flow through the fell, blind
though sometimes proud when bridging a beck or ghyll

aloofly, sealed in concrete, on official council business.
   Two miles per hour; a hundred miles,
      so by my reckoning it'll take
         just over two days:
      if there was anybody else
   up here with me I'd suggest "Pooh sticks"
played out on a glacial, OS Pathfinder scale

or introduce those bright dyes I've seen used in the field
   in this very catchment area, turning streams
      a turbulent day-glo in a matter
         of stop-watched minutes;
      then catch a train or bus in my own time
   down to the city, and wait in the Albert Square
for the fountain to run orangeade, cream soda or dandelion-

when all at once it's before me, a great glassy sheet,
  dark trees and hillsides held upside down
   in starlight: I've found Manchester
    at source, in the blues
    of a bathymetric map, in the clean
   and still repose before the nightmare of taps
  and kettles. I scoop a cold handful up to my mouth

and taste the great nothing that comes before pipes
 pass on their trace of lead, before fonts
  leech their peck of limestone,
   before public baths
  annihilate with chlorine.
 The mind, honeycombed with aqueducts,
laps on the walls of Nineveh or Imperial Rome

but this is where it begins, if we can describe
 water in such terms, with middles and ends.
  I can hear the sluices—sound
   carries at this hour—
  and the start of the journey
 down, to the distant city, a steady roar
acting as water's own bar pilot, river guide, exit sign

CIVIC

Somebody should write on the paranoia of pines
I wonder, making my way down to the shore
of the reservoir in the dark,
  ignoring the signs
  which warn of deep water;
there's a spring underfoot made up
of a billion needles and cones that carpet the floor

and a criss-cross of roots that keep the earth in its place
and so the water clear: I've read the reports
of the city engineers, done my homework,
  and move through the woods
  warily, the canopy high above
whispering, watching (though I'm about as far
from another human being as it's possible to get here,

from our cities where you're never more than a few feet
from a rat; where cameras comb the streets
all hours), looking over my shoulder
  and seeing myself
  like that footage of Sasquatch;
or the private eye in *Chinatown*, hired
in a drought to find out what's happened to all the water

AS THE CROW FLIES

Became an idea, a pure abstraction,
all black vector, a distance in air miles;
Watling Street on the wing, a one-track mind
hell bent against a white, wintering sky.

One by one the shopkeepers will shut
their doors for good. A newsagent will draw
the line at buttered steps. The final straw
will fill the fields beyond. Now live in it.

BRUTALIST

Try living in one. Hang washing out to dry
and break its clean lines with your duds and smalls.
Spray tribal names across its subway walls
and crack its flagstones so the weeds can try

their damnedest. That's the way. Fly-tip the lives
you led, out past its edge, on the back field;
sideboards and mangles made sense in the peeled
spud light of the old house but the knives

are out for them now. This cellarless, unatticked
place will shake the rentman off, will throw
open its arms and welcome the White Arrow
delivery fleet which brings the things on tick

from the slush piles of the seasonal catalogues.
The quilt boxes will take up residence
on the tops of white wardrobes, an ambulance
raise blinds, a whole geography of dogs

will make their presence felt. And once a year
on Le Corbusier's birthday, the sun will set
bang on the pre-ordained exact spot
and that is why we put that slab just there.

THE NEWSAGENT

My clock has gone although the sun has yet to take the sky.
I thought I was the first to see the snow, but his old eyes
have marked it all before I catch him in his column of light:
a rolled up metal shutter-blind, a paper bale held tight

between his knees so he can bring his blade up through the twine,
and through his little sacrifice he frees the day's headlines:
its strikes and wars, the weather's big seize up, runs on the pound.
One final star still burns above my head without a sound

as I set off. The dark country I grew up in has gone.
Ten thousand unseen dawns will settle softly on this one.
But with the streets all hushed I take the papers on my round
into the gathering blue, wearing my luminous armband.

where mineral Liverpool goes wouldn't believe
what hit it: all that sandstone out to sea
or meshed into the quarters of Cologne.

I've felt it a few times when I've gone home,
if anything, more often now I'm old,
and the gaps between get shorter all the time.

LIVERPOOL DISAPPEARS FOR A BILLIONTH OF A SECOND

Shorter than the blink inside a blink
the National Grid will sometimes make, when you'll
turn to a room and say: Was that just me?

People sitting down for dinner don't feel
their chairs taken away/put back again
much faster than that trick with tablecloths.

A train entering the Olive Mount cutting
shudders, but not a single passenger
complains when it pulls in almost on time.

The birds feel it, though, and if you see
starlings in shoal, seagulls abandoning
cathedral ledges, or a mob of pigeons

lifting from a square as at gunfire
be warned, it may be happening, but then
those sensitive to bat-squeak in the backs

of necks, who claim to hear the distant roar
of comets on the turn—these may well smile
at a world restored, in one piece; though each place

of finding out for ourselves what death smelt like.
Long afternoons. Lying on our backs watching clouds
with the slow Doppler of a plane being bowed across the sky.
Give us back the giant day. Give us back what's ours.

THE LAPSE

When the cutting edge was a sleight, a trick of time,
we blinked our way through *Jason and the Argonauts*,
thrilled by the stop-motion universe,
its brazen Talos grinding like a Dock Road crane,
and the Hydra's teeth sown into studio soil
by Harryhausen, who got between the frames
like a man who comes in bone dry from a downpour
by stopping the world and snapping out a path
through glassy rods right up to his front door.

Something as simple as Edgerton's milk splash
stilled to an ivory coronet would do it,
keep us quiet for hours as we learned to understand
the howling gale we stood in. Chilled to the core
we gasped as Ursula Andress stepped up from the flame
and the unseen British Pathé make-up department
took down her face, applying gravity with a trowel.
And I'd have to say something was taken from us.

On the dead sheep's seconds-long journey to nothing
with maggots working like a ball of fire,
every now and then a long bone settled awkwardly
like a break in continuity. Like an afternoon

THE FRONT

It stood firm for a fortnight, a cloud coast
that marked the front. All along the west
it towered; a full pan from north to south
held it in view. We watched it from the beach
each day for signs of movement. It didn't budge.
I thought of a tidal wave, freeze-framed,
but didn't say. Somebody on the third night
described it as a parting of the Red Sea
and then I couldn't help but squint for seals
or fish caught in its watery updraft,
but saw nothing. At certain times of day
you would have sworn you looked upon a land mass
with terns and gannets nested in its darkness.
Once, it grew the grey lip of a carrier deck.
Sunsets came a few degrees early
and, backlit, it glowed like something molten,
the birds heading for home crossing its lid
like car adverts with the sound turned down.
A two-week high of learning to live with it,
of tuning in to paperbacks and rock pools;
the way the thrill of snow-capped peaks in summer
will slowly thaw, become invisible
and be just there: so it was with the front.
On the last day we woke to rain as thick
as diesel slicking the windows, all the shadows
scattered, the light turned low. We were inside it.

FROM

TRAMP IN FLAMES

2006

which took me in had shallow seas like milk
beneath it, all the time, a nourishment
tapped into after rain-dark sandstone hours.
And whether this lies in my bones, or is heaven sent,
my mind, idle, at rest, always goes there.

suspension in the fluids before Truth
and Faith and Valour is strangely comforting.

    And so I'd wipe my slate and sink to sleep
each night by carefully imagining
a chalkscape. I see no reason to keep
to this story of me writing from a room
in childhood: over thirty million years
of mindless building work and one mad zoom
at the end, a couple of decades here and there
will make so little difference as to mean
sweet nothing. And I have lived on chalk for a year
at the end of the millennium: summer storms
stacked up over the Channel, the West Pier
still in its slow collapsing fade, great swarms
of birds like northern lights in negative
trawling for home, that bookshop's big window
with millions of closed pages on the move,
all intricate, unreadable, vast and slow.

    Sea walls, water levels, old horizons . . .
Is there some vestige of a memory
which makes me feel nostalgic for the Downs
and Weald before I'd been there? Did I see
beyond the bright green hills, the washed blue skies
of books, the solving undercoat of chalk
as paradise? This picture book disguise

these maps that haven't seen service outdoors
have place names stepping out beyond the shelve
of beaches, into the blue, like little piers,
and on the spoiler of a Brighton train
I hurl in sped-up footage for this coast,
from the clinker of Victoria, through the grain
of fifty miles of bramble, to the last
great buffers, with the sea at the end of the road,
where "Brighton" is the word "Britain" switched on,
every day is Whit Monday and I'm a Mod
being baton-charged along the shingle. Then

    putting out the light, my fringed lampshade
leaves the after-image of a jellyfish,
and I'm plunged into a warm sea without words,
and let the prehistorical saline wash
the wounds clean. After all this rushing about
my frame of reference is barely a film
a molecule thick, picked up by slant sunlight.
The Chalk-hill blues flittering between Latin names
are doing so on an eternity's skin,
a mass, unnumbered burial at sea,
a steady marine snowfall; skeletons
of creatures off the end of a pin, algae
who had their lives to lead as we do now.
The surface scratched, the bone pile underneath
revealed, you'd think might lead to nightmares, though

I'm writing this for you in one of their flyleaves,
the only kid around here who believes
these full-colour illustrations of the South.
Bright red post vans climbing from village mists,
look-outs calculating the curve of the earth
from cliff-tops, spying as a clipper's masts
sail beyond the publisher's remit: *What to Look For in Spring*
means what grows in, or turns up on, British soil.
I've scoured the days and never found a thing
but read these books in bed and pray it's all
happening elsewhere. Did those illustrators
have any idea that they inspired
such devotions in the North? Am I a traitor
for harbouring such thoughts? Either way, I've wired
a landscape up: the picture books have brought
the same faithful construction work to mind,
the sunken lanes, dusty and white, have caught
their corridors of day-heat; rivers wind
their way slowly to sea, rivers with names
from maps—Adur, Arun—which I can stock
and fringe carefully with other names which come
from the Observer's books. I know it like
the scaled down universe of the hobbyist
who walks giant-like between papier-mâché hills;
as intimately as a shower or sea mist
will feel its way inland. I dwell in details
and learn how words can be things in themselves:

CHALK: AN EPISTLE

    I'm writing from a box bedroom of childhood,
breeze-blocked on some lost night. If I wrote "Rain
moving in from the west" or "Irish Sea: good"
you'd catch my damp drift, could easily clone
the sea wall I slept next to, the escarpment
wind that rakes the landing, lifting up
the letterbox. Ideas become fitments
and before you know there is a northern landscape
and me inside a lit window within it,
cosily setting down this black wet idyll,
the whole thing up and running in a minute,
a second. Let me stop you in the middle:

    I'm only interested in chalk. I've had enough
of what surrounds me. If this is to work
imagine how, today, I've pulled the legs off
creatures, spat and been spat on, got kicks
from setting fire to things, and in the cruel light
of my imagination and a bedside
lamp, I've opened up a book to write
myself out of the day, dusting its blackboards
down. So, clean and blank, I start again
using my library of Ladybirds.

FROM

FIELD

RECORDINGS

2009

the Portaloos of vulcanologists;
spend Surtsian nights far from the red-shift
of streetlight, knowing it still exists

on the edge of memory. The cameras
have gone. I used to kid myself on cold
evenings walking home from school, and wonder
in the quiet after such a difficult birth;
the cries of seabirds leaving me old
beyond my years in the youngest place on earth.

SURTSEY

Someday I'll make the trip via Icelandair
then boat to Surtsey, to stake a claim
on an island that was still active the year
I was born; a toe-hold in the North Atlantic
being photographed from planes for future terms
in distant Comprehensives. I could walk

that same dark coastline we watched thrown up
in Geography; its lava lakes, lagoons
and fountains cooled to a concrete townscape;
could spread a palm against its walls and floors
like kids who climbed the apron to feel the screen
for warmth; could catch that same trace of sulphur

we caught on a Widnes wind; could carry the words
we learned then—*magma, pumice, rivulet*—
back to source, and see how well the birds
have done since a pair of gulls in sixty-eight;
or how a cruciform of sea rocket
has bloomed beyond the classroom's colour plates

and flourished like the grasses in the play-scheme.
I'd find what else its first habitants have left:
a breeze-block ruin some scientist called home;

AN INTERIOR

They ask why I still bother coming back.
London must be great this time of year.
I'm not listening. My eyes have found
the draining-board, its dull mineral shine,
the spice rack, still exactly how I left it,
knives, a Vermeer vinyl table-mat.
How many hours did I spend watching
the woman pouring milk into a bowl
that never fills? I never tired of it.
Vision persists, doesn't admit the breaks
the artist must have taken, leg-stretching
alongside a canal twitching with sky
not unlike the leaden one outside;
or just leant on the door jamb, looking out
onto a courtyard, smoking a pipe
before going in, to sleep on his excitement.

GIBRALTAR

It suits me down to the ground, the idea
of living on that rock, where the grey Atlantic
meets the Med, and the streets all wind down
to the sea; where they keep a decent Guinness
and the pubs are open all day. Who would I be?

I'd be an ex-pat, a career criminal
doing time in the sun before admitting
there's nowhere left to run; I'd be a waster
selling timeshare; but mostly I would be

a twitcher, living for the spring and autumn,
when all the birds of Europe are on the move,
and we could be the stillness in the heart of
all things, me and the rock, watching the swallows
bound for where the sex-lines terminate.

with a man stood shivering at a thousand feet.
My speech is still a thorny, north-west stew;
I walk along each public right-of-way
a trespasser; there is no single view
worth taking; rootless man, still clinging on
to some idea of truth, some ideal state
just round the next bend, found out today
he's bound towards a republic of thorns,

the flag it flies: straining, grey polythene;
its rhyme and scheme, the way it founds a voice;
its bird-life, clinging to an older way;
the way it soldiers on and knows its place.
The wind picked up. And so I left the thorn
abiding there, and dropped onto the green
and soft floor of an easygoing valley,
imagining I could start from scratch again.

But finding such an image of myself
in such an unlikely place
left little room for blame, and the sap
soon dropped. Surprising myself, I said to his face:
"The two of us both wanted the same thing
once. Many's the time we've taken off
out of the hardness, going way past our stop
into the sticks and breaking into song

as townee dreck tend to when on the move,
littering the sides of public roads.
It's happened here before: a girl from Manchester
left proof, a few sorry words
at the door of a two hundred years old journal;
or the discharged soldier, still seen from a grove
of 'thick hawthorn,' in verse, not far from here.
Though by and large they've become invisible."

The teenage me kept shtumm, inscrutable
and bush-like again on these matters,
and a softness rose in me thinking of him
failing to make his mark, and all the others
who grew up in those unraked Zen gardens
among the bonsai thorn, the babble
of television on in the daytime;
and if this were a vision, then here it ends

Remember me? I know I'm looking rough.
It's me, you silly cunt: you if you'd stayed
back there until the bulldozers moved in.
I'm everything you might've but never made
of yourself, a man stripped to his fighting weight.
I'm what you like to think you've shaken off,
though every place you've ever been since then
has seen something of me along the way.

Even here—walking in the English Lakes!—
they'll meet the prickly pear, the spiky fucker
beneath the surface, as you see me here.
The years have been cruel to you, old mucker;
turned you shite-soft, your sharp edges to mush.
See how I've still got everything it takes
to hang on, while you've drank a lake of beer
and toked so much you could turn into a bush!

All his soft tissues eaten away.
I wanted to point the finger, to blame someone,
to turn this bush into a voodoo doll
reversed out; so I could impale Lubetkin
and Luftwaffe; the faceless councilors
and aldermen who gave the nod one day
decades ago; all those I thought accountable
dangling in an aquatint by Goya.

I could spike pages from that world up like receipts:
The Observer's Book of Birds' Eggs,
the Edge westerns, Ed McBain and Sven Hassel,
the works of Herbert (Frank and James), *Street Drugs*,
The Joy of Sex I doubt anyone shared,
Papillon, with its butterfly-and-rusty-padlock conceit,
the Pan Book of Horror series, the Bible,
Valley of the Dolls and *The Thorn Birds*.

I could get my wires crossed and hear my mother
whacking the ganglion that grew in her wrist
with our bible, the Freemans catalogue
or the phone book, whichever was heaviest;
could hear the air-brakes of buses bound for town,
the grudging *all rights* between two shift workers
below my window, the barking of great-grand-dogs,
and a voice I'm sure was my own:

by now, the bush had started to look
like a sprinter coming out of the blocks
or as if it were about to jump
like an angry hill god, or a Jack-from-a-box.
The blood must have drained from my face: body-clock
and mountain time seemed to be stuck,
bringing another world to life and I felt a lump
harden in my throat as the bush spoke:

there'd be a snowfall of bright feathers
as if angels were having a pillow-fight.
Branches fork and meet, twist and snarl
the way fiction and fact collude and clot,
drawing blood and attention.
I follow one. It leads to my grandfather,
who lived just long enough to see us go decimal
and move out twenty stops to "that midden,"

only here he's a soldier again on the Western Front
caught on one inch of the millions of kilometers of wire
that coiled through his stories: Arras, Amiens,
Ypres. A teenage Volunteer
feeling the wind turning volte-face,
and from across the salient
the first whiff of phosgene.
He pisses on a handkerchief and covers his face

and I lose his features to the twisting thorn,
mediaeval in its methods of war
and the best defence for a sleeping Ladybird princess.
I helped build such a zareba
myself once; wove thistle, bramble and nettle
to fortify and hold on to a back-field den,
to keep out the shite-hawks of Halewood, Speke and Widnes.
Helix of carpet-tacks, staples and BCG needles

they planted thorn in the Groves and Brows and Folds
we moved out to in 1971
and it thrived, above and beyond
the caged saplings, the windbreaks of pine,
old beech shedding its mast onto concrete
and dying slowly in streetlight. Its stranglehold
was absolute and everywhere you'd find
great brakes and stands of it.

I look back on that time as into a thorn bush:
never some easy flashback,
more a tangle to be handled with due care.
Speared among the larder of the shrike
I imagined the wrappers of extant/extinct brands,
unspooled cassette tape, a cash-till cartouche,
all snagged on the hardy perennial of my childhood years.
I moved in with my hands

past a house sparrow—a *spadger*—airlifted up
from some lowland estate
by the butcher-bird, which brought to mind
some early lore: when budgies headed straight
from their cages for open windows, to fly
out into that world, they'd manage one aerial lap
before the scrambled spadgers found
their range and locked on. From a slate-grey sky

THORNS

I saw it all sharply again at a thousand feet,
above the tree-line, my eye being drawn
away from The Lion and the Lamb, coming to rest
on the solitary black mass of a thorn
growing out of grey rock;
or my ear was led by the song-flight
of a shrike on its way to the nest:
either way I was hooked.

It looked like a mould of the veins of the heart,
a fright-wig, a land-mine under a dugout
stilled by a shutter, depending on where I stood;
it was crooked at an angle, set
firm as if in the face of a gale
even on the calmest day, in one mind, alert
should one of those "worst blizzards
in living memory" come over the hill.

A bush fitted with its own weapon system.
I approached it the way you would
a Burryman, his arms outstretched for a burr-hug,
or a porcupine ready to draw blood.
The biblical ur-plant, twisted to its core,
knotted and fibrous, each wizened stem
carrying code out to its furthest twig.
I'd seen the like of all of this before:

MONKFISH

Fishmongers, with an eye on trade,
will usually take the head
clean off, and offer up the tail
on slopes of oily piste instead.

A waste. Eyes that have known a dark
so absolute deserve this kind
of afterlife in ours; to look
upon this kingdom of the blind.

Memento mori in Waitrose.
A skull dropped in my parka hood
by John the Grave, who terrorized
the Liverpool of my childhood.

NEGATIVES

Years after the chemist we hold them aloft
to see if all is right in that other world:
this sliver of a snowy strand at midnight,
its rocky outcrop molten in dark sea,
and in its lee an aunt emerging from
a black beach-towel, pupal and six years old

again. Your mother builds an ice-palace
and stares back radiantly as if her soul
is burning to escape; everyone frames
an inner light, even the men who've found
a half-decent alehouse and stand soot-faced
at a long bar of porcelain and glass,
glamorous in silver tuxedos.

We have to handle negatives carefully
the envelopes say as we slide them back
in paper frosted up like lounge-bar glass,
like ice knocked from a pond, the middle key
we sometimes find unchanged and by itself
on hot afternoons; that has no negative.

PETER AND THE DYKE

He's in there still, with Johnny Appleseed,
with all the frogs and sleeping princesses
but won't budge. I've tempted him with liquorice,
with pipe tobacco and Dutch magazines.
This is dedication, a child's endurance.
Outside, the longshore drift of my late teens
and pull of every tide that's turned since
are as nothing to his freezing fingertip.

decaying by the minute, gaining a power
to divert and transfix: before you know it
you're marrying the voices of childhood
(whose faces you forget) off to initials
and streets, streets where the rain gurgled from gutters
to grids you knew like birdsong, back-entries
which gave back a clean, metallic footfall,
or that kippered damp between the weighted doors
of phone-boxes, their cracked vanity mirrors
and punished books, like this one . . . Time passes
in the fluid, eddying way that those absorbed
in words enjoy, until something rouses you—
that irruption into the old phone-box
back there, say; a tea-ring, or a number
circled in pen that tears the register
right down the middle like mail-order muscle—
and brings the afternoon back, those curtains,
a plane going over and the grainy silence
of an empty room. Singular and plural,
they lie there blank as any tabula rasa,
but can yield up multitudes. Out-of-work actors,
sometimes we find ourselves sitting on boxes
reading from the phone book, to nobody.

PHONE BOOKS

You find them in the dark of meter cupboards,
in kitchen drawers, part of the scenery
left over from the last lot, like the sliver
of soap on the enamel, the flowery curtains.
They belong there, in the receding spaces
where somebody has turned from their unpacking,
looking to change the locks, to phone a curry
or just to thumb-flick through the Residential,
accepting its counsel of proportion
and scale: a city reduced to these pages.
A book you open somewhere in the middle
like cities themselves, like books of poetry.
Soon, this aerial photograph of print
has shape and contour—terraces of Smith
and Green, abutments of Honeycombe
and Read (see also Reed or Reid), exotica
in the columns of Q and X and Z—an atlas
drained of its delicate colours that offers up
the chance to find how many of our namesakes
are locked into its sequences, these districts.
Older editions, the ones that wandered
up into lofts, or down to sheds they share
with mildew and a Lucozade bottle
of weedkiller, the codes all changed, the numbers

RELIC

One's a crown, two's a crown,
three, four, five distal occlusal,
six distal occlusal, seven occlusal.
Upper left: one mesial incisal,
two mesial incisal, three's a crown,
four, five is absent, space closed.
Six occlusal, seven occlusal, eight.
Lower left: one's a crown, two mesial,
three, four occlusal, five is absent,
space closed. Six occlusal, seven occlusal,
eight is absent. Right: one, two, three,
four distal occlusal, five's a buckle,
six and seven are absent, space closed.

THE BARBER'S LULL

Unwinding from my crown, a weather system
of hair, anticyclonic since a birthroom
howl of laughter at the dark Mohican
I was issued with. I've watched him work his way

clockwise about the cow's-licks and the split-ends
of my youth, and now can feel him closing in
as he does around the ears; sense his scissors'
ticking screw-pin, granular snicks.

We go eyeball to eyeball for the fringe:
he wins, then takes a step back, has a look
at his work, then looks again in the big mirror
at the two of us, looking; and though my mind

is elsewhere—underground in fact, picturing
my long bones set like jewels into a pad
of grave-hair—I sanction him, the first word
that's passed between us since I took his chair.

He's been doing me so long it's all unspoken.
I watch a nod begin in the nape mirror,
then step outside the ring of my own making
and sweep aside such thoughts, until the next time.

UMBRELLA

I'm looking for a classical umbrella,
the kind Freud dreamt of, newly evolved
from walking-stick, before it lost its ferrule
or gained a fancy telescopic action.

I'm not interested in going so far back
as parasol or bondgrace, or lurching
sideways into Crusoe's skin and bones
contraption, or the lean-tos of antiquity.

No. I want the deeper, bat-wing pitch
that swarms and darkens streets in rainy footage;
a stick with weight and heft—hickory perhaps—
that lightens when its canopy is raised,

cut from a cloth that blocks out light as sure
as camera capes or courthouse head-blankets;
that, taut, could envelop the listener's head
and amplify the racket from a cloudburst.

Eight spokes, the heavens carved up into zones.
Italian work, the black Strad of umbrellas.
I'm still looking, soaked to the skin outside
an importer of handmade fetish wear.

THE SEA IN THE

SEVENTEENTH CENTURY

God's foot upon the treadle of the loom,
the sea goes about its business.
The photogenic reefs of the Pacific
can build for an eternity before
the cameras come, the kelp-forested shelves
of cooler waters absorb the wrecks
that scour their beds, a hint of the drift-net.
Ocean life goes on as usual, though.
A pulsing, absolute state of affairs
where all our yesteryears go through the lives
we might still live. It's boring in a way,
like heaven. Good Friday, 1649:
the first elvers have gained the estuaries
of Europe; a generation of spider crabs
are wiped out by a crustacean virus;
box jellyfish are deserting the shores
of a yet-to-be-uncovered continent.
You'd almost think, nature being nature,
there would be some excitement at the trace
of poison from the Severn; at one part
night soil to the billionth of Thames:
that sightings of the brass-helmeted diver
would start a murmuring that God is dead.

DIARY MOON

You are the plainest moon. Forget all others:
shivering in pools, or spoken to when drunk,
that great Romantic gaze of youth; shed all
sonatas, harvests, Junes, and think instead
of how your phases turn here in a diary:
stripped of sunlight, surface noise and seas
you move unnoticed through the months, a bare limn
achieving ink blackness, emptying again.

You who turned inside the week-to-view
my father carried round each year, past crosses
that symbolized pay days, final demands;
in girlfriends', where red novae marked the dates
they were "due on," and I shouldn't've been looking;
who even showed in weighty Filofaxes,
peeping through the clouds of missed appointments,
arrivals and departures, names and numbers.

On nights like these, which of us needs reminding
to set an eel-trap, open up the bomb doors
or sail out of the harbour on a spring-tide?
What sway do you hold over our affairs?
Although for some you're all that's there, printed
across the white weeks until New Year;
moving towards windows that will not frame us,
into the evenings of our sons and daughters.

A TUNNEL

A tunnel, unexpected. The carriage lights
we didn't notice weren't on prove their point
and a summer's day is cancelled out, its greens
and scattered blue, forgotten in an instant

that lasts the width of a down, level to level,
a blink in London to Brighton in Four Minutes
that dampens mobiles—conversations end
mid-sentence, before speakers can say

". . . a tunnel"—and the train fills with the sound
of itself, the rattle of rolling stock amplified,
and in the windows' flue a tool-shed scent,
metal on metal, a points-flash photograph,

and inside all of this a thought is clattering
in a skull inside the train inside the tunnel
inside great folds of time, like a cube of chalk
in a puncture-repair tin at a roadside

on a summer day like the one we'll re-enter
at any moment, please, at any moment.
Voices are waiting at the other end
to pick up where we left off. "It was a tunnel . . ."

FOR THE HOUSE SPARROW,

IN DECLINE

Your numbers fall and it's tempting to think
you're deserting our suburbs and estates
like your cousins at Pompeii; that when you return
to bathe in dust and build your nests again
in a roofless world where no one hears your cheeps,
only a starling's modem mimicry
will remind you of how you once supplied
the incidental music of our lives.

JOSEPH BEUYS

To write about elemental things, to render
the world in its simpler smells and shapes and textures,
to describe how tallow collects under the finger-

nails, how felt feels against bare skin
is not, I repeat, not an option
having lived several times removed from the world as itself,

although it can do no harm to imagine
myself as the stricken airman
carted indoors by the local women

who'd take it in turns attending to the matter
of rubbing in the Stork SB and Flora,
the Golden Churn and I Can't Believe It's Not Butter.

ESTABLISHING SHOT

It might as well come here as anywhere.
Pick any card: street lamps, tall leylandii,
rotated ryegrass in available light.
A long, slow take. Half-closing day. No one
playing out. A goal-mouth chalked on brick
is a frame within a frame just for a moment
before the artless pan resumes: bollards
and gutter-grass; and those who've just dipped in
expecting wide-screen, a lone rider
descending from high plains; the sans serifs
of Hollywood, strong language from the outset
or a director's trademark opening
will want their money back. We may as well
admit this is THE END too, while we're here.

and declared, "Looks like you've done this all your life, girl . . .":
so a chance remark in the light of forty years back
lives on in other minds, and you had so much to tell

which makes this silence harder. I can stand here and say
anything fluently now, to a woman in a wheelchair
who read to me, who took time out of those days

that must have contained so many things—newspaper
under a maiden strung with drip-drying nappies,
kindling in the grate, buttery fire-lighters—

and even though this stranger knows the little good
it does, talking into the wind; that his words are gone
before you know it; that you hear only collapsed chords,

I'll tell you how corncrakes have been heard again
out on the Isle of Man; how it's being said
that salmon are jumping the Howley Weir above Warrington;

that the grey river recalls each note and will reel them off
like verb forms taught by rote. The river remembers
its whiting, fluke and mackerel well enough

and their counterpoint that sounds in the shell of our ears
and moves in from the west, that peak and trough
and roil of surf which is our cantus firmus.

I'm listening under a pram's hood; against the sea wall
a wind whips up your hair, a bottle blonde
I must have tugged a thousand times but can't recall;

gulls blur; the superstructures of Laird's stand
over the water, the brake is fast against the pram-wheel,
a curlicue of smoke rises, and for a split-second

I guess what story you were reading there. She knows,
looking up from her picture book microcopy,
caught in a long vowel sound. Though the shutter was slow

the grey river hides its tons of cadmium and mercury.
The arteries harden and little by little the flow
stops. Oxygen-sensitive memory.

They say the deepest strata are slowest to fade,
so maybe you wander somewhere earlier, lost
in that job straight out of school, still learning to thread

the bobbin and foot, the samplers you ran off, the tests:
like a fern in a split coal, cracked open like code,
so the light of old afternoons can shine out of the past

and who knows what survives us. On that first five o'clock
in the machine-shop—the air revved up, a smell
of lint and sweat—the supervisor raised your work

THE LANDING STAGE

I've got this noise in my head: background or bedrock
is the best I can do for now. I've brought you here
to see if any of this might do the trick

like the tape of a favourite song or voice, familiar
and played in the hope the sleeper will awake
from a spell. I haven't been back here for years

and it takes a while to realize we're afloat;
the gangway down to the landing stage is steep
at low tide. I'm hoping the river's moods and play of light

might kindle a sentence, or raise you from the deep
and empty stare that gives nothing back. I've brought
you to this exact spot, better to make the leap.

You know those hostages blindfolded in a boot
who memorize each bump in the road, the scent of tarmac
where a road opens up; who retrace their lost route

through its peals and toll-gates? This is how I get it back:
in pieces, the tang of a dream you can't forget
so carry around all day. Some proof: in this photograph

DEAD FISH

Remember how they made us play Dead Fish?
If it rained, the dinner-ladies kept us in
and we cleared the canteen of its chairs and tables.
Have you forgotten how we lay so still?
The smell of old varnish, salt on the parquet,
or how the first five minutes were the easiest?
You'd find an attitude that you were sure
could last until the bell. Foetal, recovery:
each had his favourite. I'd strike a simple
flat-on-back, arms-by-my-sides figure
and concentrate.
                Some fell asleep,
easy after seconds of tapioca,
and this proved fatal. Sleep is seldom still.
Others could last as long as pins and needles
allowed, or until they couldn't frame
the energies of being six years old:
some thought would find its way into a limb
and give the game away. But you were good,
so good you always won, so never saw
this lunch-time slaughter of the innocents
from where we sat out on the bean-bagged margin.
Dead fish in uniform, oblivious
to dinner-ladies' sticks poking their ribs,
still wash up on my mind's floor when it rains
in school hours. Blink if you remember this.

THE AGES

The trees lay down their seam of coal as thin
as hammered gold leaf all afternoon
when a child is called in from the Iron Age war
he's been waging with the next street; road-works reach
the water table by teatime then knock off
for the day; late sun catches the last post
being emptied from an Edwardian pillar box,
warms the sleeping sandstone in its vertical dream;
there is a low Vent-Axian hum round the backs
of buildings, the usual insect holocaust
on filaments and coils; that hardening of the heart
that steals up on us like an early frost.

The ages, coming thick and fast tonight.
I caught one on my bedroom ceiling: the globe
of a paper light-shade caught in headlights
was a Golden Age symbol of truth and reason;
then a cold planet again. I yawn and fear the dark
like any good caveman. The buzzing that disturbs
my sleep might be a moth, or just the Creation
doing its thing on the skyline. I lie awake
in the blue chill, listening to the last teenagers
passing the house, their cries in the ever-after.

COD

Those deep-sea fish had claims upon our souls.
What held the sense of mystery in our lives
like dark Good Fridays? Sometimes, if the rain
had slickened the streets into a Stanhope Forbes
and turned sandstone to pewter; if the forecast
gave more rain from the west for days on end
and warnings to the various fishing grounds,
we'd feel them close, a nuzzling all around,
the brush of barbels on causeways and piers,
their sea lanes washing into B-roads;
and, huddling in around our radios,
we'd trawl the bandwidths for a sign that soon
the sheet of cloud would break, the fish recede
back to the ocean cold from whence they came.

BIG SAFE THEMES

You can look all you like but the big safe themes are there
all around, forestalling what you were going to say.
A robust description of a cedarwood cigar box
has grown so big it could now contain Cuba and history.

No refuge in things. They stand at one or two removes
from the big themes; so any warm-weather fruit might bring
visiting times and the loved one we begged not to leave
as soon as you sniff at the rind or spit out a pip.

You can start with a washer, a throat lozenge, a mouse-mat
and watch them move in like the weather. Trying to be brave
ends in tears: I've seen the big safe themes walk all over
incest and morris dancing in their ten-league boots.

Why resist anyway? Bend with the big safe themes.
Let them do what they will and admit that the road you walk
again and again—right down to its screw-thread of blood
in a quivering phlegm—is becoming your big safe theme.

THE READING HOUR

Placed under house arrest: a sentence long
as the Arctic tern's yearly flight, a straight ray
of arrowed light that left the sonorous
blues of an ocean trench and climbed
above sea-level, through giant sequoia,
Manhattan skyline, high as Everest
and cruising airliner. Let me play out
(he'd pray each evening, hearing the cries
of other kids) and live life in the quick
of bin-sheds and off-licences, moment
to moment; please abandon all hopes
for me, before the autumn term and rain
clear the streets; leave London's Underground
pressed in end-papers, and let me travel
no further than yourselves, my only pens
chained to post-office counters, or dangling
on string next to tomorrow's meeting-card.

11TH FEBRUARY 1963

The worst winter for decades. In the freeze
some things get lost and I'm not even born,
but think until you're many Februaries
deep in thought with me and find London
on that day as held inside a glacier;
a fissure where two postal districts touch,
its people caught mid-floe, at furniture,
the contents of their stomachs, a stopped watch.
At these pressures the distance has collapsed:
the studio clock winds up over Primrose Hill,
or the poet and her sleeping children crossed
the mile to Abbey Road. This milk bottle
might hold what John'll drink for one last take;
that she'll leave out for when the children wake.

set for dinner are tinkling at a bend,
a carriage full of ghosts taking their places.

Now drink to slow outskirts, the colour wheels
of fifty years collected in windows;
to worlds of interiors, to credit deals
with nothing to pay until next year, postcodes
where water hardens, then softens, where rows
of streetlights become the dominant motif
as day drains, and I see myself transposed
into the dark, lifting my glass. Belief

is one thing, though the dead have none of it.
What would they make of me? This pinot noir
on my expenses, time enough to write
this on a Virgin antimacassar—
the miles of feint, the months of Sunday school,
the gallons of free milk, all led to here:
an empty dining-car, a single fool
reflected endlessly on the night air.

FROM A WEEKEND FIRST

One for the money. Arrangements in green and grey
from the window of an empty dining-car.
No takers for this Burgundy today
apart from me. I'll raise a weighted stem
to my homeland scattering by, be grateful for
these easy-on-the-eye, Army & Navy
surplus camouflage colours that seem
to mask all trace of life and industry;

a draft for the hidden dead, our forefathers,
the landfills of the mind where they turned in
with the plush and orange peel of yesteryear,
used up and entertained and put to bed
at last; to this view where everything seems to turn
on the middle distance. Crematoria, multiplex
way stations in the form of big sheds
that house their promises of goods and sex;

to the promise of a university town,
its spires and playing fields. No border guards
will board at this station, no shakedown
relieve me of papers or contraband:
this is *England*. Nobody will pull the cord
on these thoughts, though the cutlery and glasses

FROM

THE ICE AGE

2002

NORTH ATLANTIC CORRIDOR

Halfway, it's noisier than you'd expect.
A wind-up gramophone is playing Caruso
in a U-boat underneath a convoy lane,
whose crew can testify to whale song,

and most have heard the eel and salmon pass
on moonlit nights, when the click of binary
cabling the ocean floor is deafening,
and the elements compete above the swell

where the tern's wave-top flight path intersects
with ragtime from a glittering liner,
where woodworm in the Old World's darkwood hold
meets the tongues of RKO and MGM

and there's no peace, even at altitude:
halfway between London and New York
an in-flight movie can't make up its mind:
A Matter of Life and Death / Stairway to Heaven.

FROM

FIELD RECORDINGS

2009

listening to far-off sirens
and the sound of my breathing. He was stretching,
getting used to the name they'd given him.
It grew, until one night in September
we ran low on smokes. You sent me to the garage.
I walked down that road with the trees
heavy and still. Hardly a whisper. Turned
past the all-nighter and kept on walking.

STRAY

Whatever brought me to the gutter
had something to do with this:
a tree-lined journey to the shop for booze,
paracetamol and papers
where I came across his name
on a photocopied flyer
tacked to the bark of every other trunk.
I soon got to know his sooty coat,
reflective collar. So tenderly written
I half-expected a *Last seen wearing* . . .

Someone had added *Try the Peking Garden*
in shaky freehand. There was a reward
so I started to keep an eye out.
When you asked me what I was thinking
staring through a cloud of midges
those evenings we sat outside drinking
it was usually to do with him—
slowly turning to mulch in deep thicket;
eaten alive by pit bulls;
or his carbon copy, given to a child

who thought him lost to the night.
We'd take in the chairs. I'd sit in the window

The door shuts soft. The rain has turned to ice.
She lifts the arm out of infinity
in Huyton, and in Skem and Speke and Stockie
née Cantril Farm, so good they named it twice.

THE SLEEP OF ESTATES

In living rooms where fathers sprawl, still clothed,
the bumpy core beyond Sinatra's voice
beats inside a radiogram, a pulse
deep under. There's rain on the windows.

The last buses have left their termini,
each destination cranked to a blank stare.
The grilles that scented underpass and square
have wound down now after the final fry.

The hour belongs to slamming taxi doors,
the clack of heels and laughter in the night;
while mothers wait for clubs to empty out
and faulty street lighting blinks out a Morse

that no bare-legged curfew breaker reads.
Young addresses dream of being listed,
double-glazed, damp-coursed, sandblasted,
and rid of roosting seabirds. Overhead

the air is rich with night-time radio,
with baby-listeners, and coded words
that leak from patrol cars and amateurs
across backlanes where cab drivers won't go.

I ease myself back down among the wreck's
ice-dusted cache—the dials the crew misread,
the Bopper's dice and Ritchie's crucifix—
and wait for history.

NOT FADE AWAY

A cornfield deep in drifts. I walked an hour
without moving. The outskirts of a town
that felt, with all its ploughed streets and neon,
like stepping from a page. I found a bar
and tried to force a boilermaker down.
The barman asked if I was twenty-one.

You don't crawl free from crashes every day.
In celebration of that windchilled night
I've pissed the intervening years away
in dark corners, doorways, and come so far
from all those screaming girls, the cold limelight
winks back faint as a star.

No one believes the bore who doesn't wash
or listens to the stories he lets slip
while stoking the jukebox. Nobody looks
twice at the guy being given the bum's rush;
my legend melts down to a tiny blip,
a half-tone dot on album sleeves, in books.

I retrace my own trail and wipe it dead.
The scene is how I left it. Carefully

this future in the late schedules, where I
can't sleep, and watch your flight from the big screen;
on the other side of drink and wondering why,
the zany, household-name years in between?

KEITH CHEGWIN AS FLEANCE

The next rung up from extra and dogsbody
and all the cliches are true—days waiting for
enough light, learning card games, penny-ante,
while fog rolls off the sea, a camera
gets moisture in its gate, and Roman Polanski
curses the day he chose Snowdonia.

He picked you for your hair to play this role:
a look had reached Bootle from Altamont
that year. You wouldn't say you sold your soul
but learned your line inside a beating tent
by candlelight, the shingle dark as coal
behind each wave, and its slight restatement.

"A tale told by an idiot . . ." "Not your turn,
but perhaps, with time and practice . . . ," the Pole starts.
Who's to say, behind the accent and that grin,
what designs you had on playing a greater part?
The crew get ready while the stars go in.
You speak the words you'd written on your heart

just as the long-awaited sunrise fires
the sky a blueish pink. Who could have seen

THE LAMP

AT SEA, DECEMBER 29, 1849

Aboard, at home again, this book closes.
No written record of that westbound voyage
survives. I have you travelling with the sun
and mangy Irish packets, dreaming up
your story. Five weeks berthed alone, below
the waterline, immersed in printed matter
from Holborn, Charing Cross Road, and the Strand.
Was it like this? The artificial glow
of sperm oil lit those words across the miles
of ocean swells. Having the presence of mind,
you saw yourself, a reader in the dark,
dependant on the whale's "sweet grass butter."
The lamp hung true despite the pitch and roll.
You had the shortest chapter by landfall.

DOCUMENTARIST

It's clear I love the footage of the past:
its herring catches, silvery flinders
that flap in unimagined elements,
the miner's face that bares bright teeth and eyes
to camera, the skies scribbled and crossed
by a century's dust. A cold, unglamorous

photography no starlet or leading man
could feel at home for long in. Peeling walls,
five to a bed ... See how they're smiling still
from deep inside their mould-invaded tins—
a porterage through equatorial damp,
incisors flared. Look back into this lens

beyond the here-and-now, to darkened rooms:
the future screens its ideas of us,
to rows that multiply back endlessly.
Smile, as they file out to a world
of worked-out seams, depopulated seas,
the ancient shock of daylight still playing.

"CREAM"

If Melville and Hawthorne had taken the same drugs
what would they have made of the counting-houses
all suddenly full of lasers and bass drums
that pummel the sternum and stop down the iris?

What would they have made of this light show's finale
unexposed, as they were, even to the flashbulb,
or amplified breakbeats through 20 K sound rigs
and scantily clad boys and girls going apeshit?

Unaccustomed, as they were, to front-of-house etiquette
how would they get past the private security
decked out in cummerbunds, high hats, fob watches
(hands swapped like compasses turned in a thunderstorm)?

How would they get past the offers for "love doves"
or know how to dance in the amorphous mass
that's peaking as one to the sum total effect,
without any handbags to act as a focus?

RETROSPECTIVE

1. *Stubs.* 1989, aluminium, wood, glass, stainless steel, monitors, betting slips, cigarettes (smoked), silkscreen reproduction of the bay filly *Molly Longlegs*

2. *Sisyphus.* 1990, 30° inclined escalator (set to descend), tank, aerator, water, any anadromous fish of the Salmonidae family

3. *Odds.* 1992, refrigerated vitrium, fluorescent light, the artist's semen (note: at temperatures of −2° to −4°C, this is malleable as putty)

4. *The Optic Nerve Is a Lazy River.* 1993, telescope (8-inch reflector, altazimuth mounting), perspex, Mersey Yellow Pages (on microfiche)

5. *Waveform.* 1995 (lost), franking machine, sealed air Jiffy, brace of Manx kippers, first class postage within mainland UK

WITHOUT POTATOES

> Without potatoes we would be like loose threads on a loom, for potatoes are what bind life together. AMARAYAN PROVERB

We took spud guns onto the terraces,
Threw King Edwards spiked with razor blades.
Ate chips salted and vinegared,
Burnt our cheeks on the polished nickel, waiting.

We danced the mashed pah-tay-tah;
Wrestled with earthy sackfuls
Dropped from chutes on childhood errands;
Watched the roasty fall from ubiquity
On Sundays centered round gas ovens
To french fries, Spud-U-Like and waffles.

I miss the simple pleasures—of rinsing
A tuber under a cold tap; of coiling the peelings
Into a bucket; of gouging the eyes out.
I never thought I'd come to say such things.

that is all song, all talk, all colour, mixed.
Before that whistle bursts a hole and brings
the air rushing back in with arc lighting,
calls for owners of the double parked,

the last verse of "You'll Never Walk Alone"
(never . . . *the sweet silver song of a lark*)
listen, to where the shore meets the salt water;
a million tiny licking, chopping sounds:

the dead, the never-born, the locked-out souls
are scratching on the thin shell we have grown
around ourselves. Listen. The afternoon
is dark already, and there is a moon.

by hooters or sirens. Like early audiences
we have left the street to its own devices
to watch the flicking shadow of itself
onscreen, the purring spool somehow apart

from all of this. It leaves the one-way system
and finds less work to do outside of town:
a rookery, light aircraft, and the wind
banging gates or moaning through the lines.

(How still without birdsong. It still guts me
to think of all the havoc wreaked each spring
we combed the hedges outside our estate
and stole the still-warm clutches from each nest;

all that music, blown and set in file
on sawdust in a two-pound biscuit tin,
displayed to rivals in attack formation,
a 4–3–3 of fowls and passerines.)

Sooner or later silence reaches the coast
and stops just short of getting its feet wet.
There's something of the Ice Age to all this.
The only sound's the white noise of the sea

A MINUTE'S SILENCE

The singing stops. Each player finds his spot
around the ten-yard circle that until
tonight seemed redundant, there just for show.
The PA asks us to observe the hush.

We find we're standing in a groundsman's shoes,
the quiet he must be familiar with
while squeaking chalk-paste up the grassy touch,
or overseeing a private ritual

and scattering the last mortal remains
of a diehard fan beneath each home-end stanchion.
No one keeps a count or checks their watch
so space is opened up. It seems to last

a small eternity—the happy hour
that stretches to three, the toast, the final spin.
I observe the silence sneak through turnstiles
and catch on quick—a bar muffles its pumps;

in function rooms, a wedding reception
freezes still as its own photograph;
an awful bagwash winds down mid-cycle—
a Saturday gridlocked, unaccompanied

MONOPOLY

We sat like slum landlords around the board
buying each other out with fake banknotes,
until we lost more than we could afford,
or ever hope to pay back. Now our seats
are empty—one by one we left the game
to play for real, at first completely lost
in this other world, its building sites, its rain;
but slowly learned the rules or made our own,
stayed out of jail and kept our noses clean.
And now there's only me—sole freeholder
of every empty office space in town,
and from the quayside I can count the cost
each low tide brings—the skeletons and rust
of boats, cars, hats, boots, iron, a terrier.

DEPENDANTS

How good we are for each other, walking through
a land of silence and darkness. You
open doors for me, I answer the phone for you.

I play jungle loud. You read with the light on.
Beautiful. The curve of your cheekbone,
explosive vowels, exact use of cologne.

What are you thinking? I ask in a language of touch
unique to us. You tap my palm *nothing much*.
At stations we compete senses, see which

comes first—light in the tunnel, whiplash down the rail.
I kick your shins when we go out for meals.
You dab my lips. I finger yours like Braille.

see how a spoonful won't let go of its past,
what the tin calls back to the mean of its lip
as you pour its contents over yourself

and smear it into every orifice.
You're history now, a captive explorer
staked out for the insects; you're tarred
and feel its caul harden. The restorer
will tap your details back out of the dark:
close-in work with a toffee hammer.

TREACLE

Funny to think you can still buy it now,
a throwback, like shoe polish or the sardine key.
When you lever the lid it opens with a sigh
and you're face-to-face with history.
By that I mean the unstable pitch black
you're careful not to spill, like mercury

that doesn't give any reflection back,
that gets between the cracks of everything
and holds together the sandstone and bricks
of our museums and art galleries;
and though those selfsame buildings stand
hosed clean now of all their gunk and soot,

feel the weight of this tin in your hand,
read its endorsement from one Abram Lyle
"Out of the strong came forth sweetness"
below the weird logo of bees in swarm
like a halo over the lion carcass.
Breathe its scent, something lost from our streets

like horseshit or coalsmoke; its base note
a building block as biblical as honey,
the last dregs of an empire's dark sump;

AQUARIUS

More fool you who believe in the end of decades.
The seventies live on in top-floor flats
you can't see in for overgrown pot plants;
where someone struggles to crack a dial-band set
and Che stares down onto an unmade bed.

Letters pile up, shoring the front door
like a drift. Mung shoots replenish themselves
and the tap water's good for ages yet.
They never leave the room or check the view.
The neighbours wonder, as they come and go,

at such bad taste in music and curtains;
but eventually come to admire such cool retro.
Behind closed doors there is low talk of scurvy
as they carve a dice from the dwindling oatcake
cast years ago inside a chest of drawers.

After they tune out their hair will grow, for a while,
and the plants will still pull to the sun, until
the soil cracks and dries. Then, and only then,
will the old decade die, and your amazing nineties
shed its light; its seen-it-all-before light.

ERA

Hide some under the carpet, line a drawer
so they will know about us, who we were
and what we did on one day years ago,
our births and deaths, our sales and tide tables.
Make a mental note of sizes no one
has seen or heard of, before it's too late—
Colombier, Imperial, Elephant—
and though the forests exhale a long sigh
of relief, what hope is there for this page
you're reading now? Cash in your mattressed wads:
they cease to be tender as of midnight.

all happened in the air above a mall.
Each edifice, each gargoyle and grotesque
is gone. The earliest thing I remember:
as our van dropped a gear up Brownlow Hill
I looked back at the panes of distemper
that sealed a world. We reached our overspill,
and this is where our stories overlap.
The coming of the cradle and sheet glass
was squeezing out the ladder and the slap
of leather into suds, and less and less
work came through the door. And anyway
you were getting too old for scaling heights.
Now, when I change a bulb or queue to pay
at fairs, or when I'm checking in for flights,
I feel our difference bit down to the quick.
There are no guidebooks to that town you knew
and this attempt to build it, brick by brick,
descends the page. I'll hold the foot for you.

the arse-flap of their overalls turn brown.
As a rule, he writes, *your sense of angle
becomes acute at height.* A diagram
he's thumbnailed shows a drop through a triangle
if you miscalculated by a gram.
Sometimes, his senses still blunted from booze,
he'd drop his squeegee, watch it fall to earth
and cling on to the grim hypotenuse
of his own making for all he was worth.
He seems to have enjoyed working that hour
*the low sun caught the glass and raised the ante
on every aerial, flue and cooling tower,
and gilded the lofts, the rooftop shanty
town, when everything was full of itself,
and for a while even the Latin plaques
ignited with the glow of squandered wealth.
At times like these I see what our world lacks,
the light of heaven on what we've produced*
and here some words lost where his biro bled
then *clouds of dark birds zero in to roost.*
There's IOUs and debtors marked in red
and some description of the things he saw
beyond the pane—a hard-lit typing pool,
a room of faces on some vanished floor
closed off and absolute like a fixed rule.
His story of the boy butting a wall,
the secretary crying at her desk,

LAWS OF GRAVITY

FOR JULIAN TURNER

I found a guidebook to the port he knew
intimately—its guano-coated ledges,
its weathervanes, his bird's-eye river view
of liner funnels, coal sloops and dredgers.
It helped me gain a foothold—how he felt
a hundred rungs above a fifties street,
and whether, being so high, he ever dwelt
on suicide, or flummoxed his feet
to last night's dance steps, still fresh in his head.
It's all here in his ledger's marginalia:
how he fell up the dark stairwell to bed
and projected right through to Australia;
and said a prayer for rainfall every night
so he could skip his first hungovered round.
The dates he's noted *chamois frozen tight
into bucket*. When he left the ground
a sense of purpose overtook and let
a different set of laws come into play:
like muezzins who ascend a minaret
to call the faithful of a town to pray.
Take one step at a time. Never look down.
He'd seen the hardest cases freeze halfway,

A THOUSAND HOURS

There were false starts, but life, for me, really
began the night he unplugged the telly
and snuffed the pilot light. As last-man-out
he worked right through to dawn, between the street
and this bedroom, until he'd stripped it bare,
but left me in his rush to check the meter,
to turn the stopcock on a copper tank,
count stairs and memorize that manhole's clunk,
the first hawked phlegm, the way a window pane
was answering the early Lime Street train;
and posted back his keys to nobody.

I've hung here naked since, by day barely
able to force a shadow to be thrown.
It's nights I come into my own:
a halo for the ceiling, corners for mice,
and through the glass a phantom of all this,
a twin star that is shedding kilowatts
in translation. Beyond these dark outskirts
my creator sleeps. I recall how his eyes
would whirr just like this night-time visitor
that might outlive me. Of all his ideas
I burn on, having been conceived in error.

ELECTRICITY

It comes as a shock to that first audience.
The street they walked in off just moments before
hangs pale on the wall. All the colour has gone,
and its faces and carriages have ground to a blur.

Remember, no one has thought of pianos
or credits. The performance will start off mid-scene,
once each hard bench is filled, when the first usher nods
and the lamp is turned up and the crank starts to turn

and their hairs stand on end to a shimmer of leaves
or the movement of clouds, and the way that the tense
has been thrown like a switch, where the land turns to dreams,
and where, sad to say, we have been living since.

TERMINI

We lived where buses turned back on themselves,
when drivers still referred to us as "scholars,"
winding on their final destination
and we would end up here: PIER HEAD.
Today, a spinning blade blows *surf 'n' turf*
from a steakhouse kitchen, luring those
with appetites sharpened by river air
after a windswept round trip on the ferry.
What else is there? The city has shrunk back
from the front, slowly, over the years
leaving this airy strand the buses bypass,
and now nobody's journey into town
ends with a top-deck, front-seat panorama.
I left the slashed seat and the listing bottle
to finish this journey on foot, in the rain,
the same route where the brothers Lumière
cranked the first nitrate from a moving train;
and stand now where we sagged the long school day
eating hot dogs, watching buses turn
back to the far estates with lower case names,
an audience staying put for the minor credits.

DEPOT

You wouldn't know a place like this existed.
It shows the street its modest, oily features
(a door I walked right past on my first day),
but opens into hangar-like proportions.
Here are the bays where dustcarts spend their evenings,
where grit summers, dreaming of Januaries,
and barriers mesh like deckchairs off-season.

I've dreamt of something like this sorting-house,
and walked its film-set streets, and tried its swings
some nights—the perfect playground, deserted—
but didn't know a place like this existed;
that crippled boys who stood outside our chemists
would form ranks like a terracotta army
in lives beyond thalidomide and weather.

Was this what lay behind the knowing winks
I caught between binmen, or am I dreaming
that road sweepers held doctorates in philosophy;
and knew, after the miles behind a big broom,
they would return to worlds not unlike this one,
find a spotless bench, and read their *Echo*
in the irony of strip lights over street lamps.

EAUX D'ARTIFICE

The moon we know from dreams or celluloid
is high tonight. A dried-up fountain bed
gawps back, a baroque radio telescope
the race has left behind, always on the up,
defying gravity. The park seems of an age
that tried, in other small ways, to oblige
the same imperative—this domed palm-house
that brought the sky down closer; these dark yews
clipped conically and pointed heavenwards;
and fountains that suspended arcs and cords
of water, one so powerful it could hold
the weight of terrified cats or "a Small Childe"
in its jets. The water only comes here now
to rest after the dream-days spent in cloud,
to swill round with the leaves and empty cans,
and then moves on. Its work is never done,
like man's, a thought that brings me back to earth:
soaked through with sweat, under her bone-light,
bouncing my signals back and forth all night,
the moon drowns out a point low in the south
that could be Mercury or the Eutelsat,
though these days she in turn has to compete
with our restless nightside. When I can't sleep
I walk these rhododendroned paths that keep
to strict ideas of sunset and sunrise,
and find my level on a bench, like this.

FROM

THE BOY FROM THE CHEMIST IS HERE TO SEE YOU

1998

Paperboy and Air Rifle · · · · · · · · · · · · · · · · · · · **127**

The Westbourne at Sloane Square · · · · · · · · · · · · **128**

Dormouse Stronghold · · · · · · · · · · · · · · · · · · · **129**

NEW POEMS

Cyan · **133**

Google Earth · **134**

Odometer · **136**

The Power · **137**

Moles · **138**

Quality Street · **139**

The Mind · **143**

FROM **TRAMP IN FLAMES** (2006)

The Front · **85**
The Lapse · **86**
Liverpool Disappears for a Billionth of a Second · · · · · · **88**
The Newsagent · **90**
Brutalist · **91**
As the Crow Flies · **93**
Civic · **94**
Duel · **101**
Tramp in Flames · **102**
Johnny Thunders Said · **103**
Requiem for a Friend · **104**
Filler · **115**
Philistines · **117**
Mongrel · **119**
Whitebeam · **120**
Winter Games · **121**
The Heron · **122**
A God · **123**
The Scarecrow Wears a Wire · · · · · · · · · · · · · · · · **125**
An Orrery of Hats · **126**

CONTENTS

FROM **THE BOY FROM THE CHEMIST IS HERE TO SEE YOU** (1998)

Eaux d'Artifice · 3
Depot · 4
Termini · 5
Electricity · 6
A Thousand Hours · 7
Laws of Gravity · 8
Era · 11
Aquarius · 12
Treacle · 13
Dependants · 15
Monopoly · 16
A Minute's Silence · 17
Without Potatoes · 20
Retrospective · 21
"Cream" · 22
Documentarist · 23

IN MEMORY OF MY PARENTS

Faber and Faber, Inc.
An affiliate of Farrar, Straus and Giroux
18 West 18th Street, New York 10011

Copyright © 2010 by Paul Farley
All rights reserved
Distributed in Canada by D&M Publishers, Inc.
Printed in the United States of America
First edition, 2010

Grateful acknowledgment is made to the following publications, in which some of these poems first appeared: *Areté, GQ Style, Grand Street, Granta, The Guardian, Harper's Magazine, London Review of Books, Metre, The North, The Observer* (London), *Poetry London, Poetry Review, The Printer's Devil, The Spectator, Thumbscrew, The Times Literary Supplement,* and *The Yellow Nib*. Some of these poems were first broadcast on BBC Radio 3 and Radio 4.

Library of Congress Cataloging-in-Publication Data
Farley, Paul, 1965–
    The Atlantic tunnel : selected poems / Paul Farley. — 1st ed.
      p. cm.
    ISBN: 978-0-86547-917-3 (alk. paper)
    I. Title.

PR6056.A675A93 2010
821'.914—dc22
                                          2009042215

Designed and composed by Quemadura

www.fsgbooks.com

10 9 8 7 6 5 4 3 2 1

THE ATLANTIC TUNNEL

PAUL FARLEY

SELECTED POEMS

FABER AND FABER, INC.

AN AFFILIATE OF

FARRAR, STRAUS AND GIROUX

NEW YORK

THE ATLANTIC TUNNEL

ALSO BY PAUL FARLEY

THE BOY FROM THE CHEMIST
IS HERE TO SEE YOU

THE ICE AGE

TRAMP IN FLAMES

DISTANT VOICES, STILL LIVES

FIELD RECORDINGS:
BBC POEMS 1998–2008